The Management of Ig

*To Lesley Aers
and Phillip Whitehead*

The Management of Ignorance

*A Political Theory of
the Curriculum*

FRED INGLIS

Basil Blackwell

First published 1985
Reprinted and first published in paperback 1987

Basil Blackwell Ltd
108 Cowley Road, Oxford OX4 1JF, UK

Basil Blackwell Inc.
432 Park Avenue South, Suite 1503
New York, NY 10016, USA

British Library Cataloguing in Publication Data

Inglis, Fred
   The management of ignorance: a political theory
   of the curriculum
   1. Education _____ Great Britain _____ Curricula
   I. Title
   375'.00941   LA 632
   ISBN 0-631-14348-3
   ISBN 0-631-15582-1 Pbk.

Library of Congress Cataloging in Publication Data

Inglis, Fred.
   The management of ignorance.
   Bibliography: p.
   Includes index.
   1. Curriculum planning.   2. Education—Great Britain—
   Curricula.   3. Education--Philosophy.   I. Title.
   LB1570.I554   1985   375'.001   85-9012
   ISBN 0-631-14348-3
   ISBN 0-631-15582-1 (pbk.)

Typeset by Dentset, St. Clements, Oxford.
Printed in Great Britain by Page Bros (Norwich) Ltd

Contents

How did it come?
From outside, so it seemed, an endless source,
Disorder inexhaustible, strange to us,
Incomprehensible. Yet sometimes now
We ask ourselves, we the old citizens:
'Could it have come from us? Was our peace peace?
Our goodness goodness? That old life was easy
And kind and comfortable; but evil is restless
And gives no rest to the cruel or the kind.
How could our town grow wicked in a moment?
What is the answer? Perhaps no more than this,
That once the good men swayed our lives, and those
Who copied them took a while the hue of goodness,
A passing loan; while now the bad are up,
And we, poor ordinary neutral stuff,
Not good nor bad, must ape them as we can,
In sullen rage or vile obsequiousness. . . .'

Edwin Muir, 'The Good Town', *Collected Poems* (Faber & Faber, 1960)

Acknowledgements

In this book, as in the earlier ones I have written, an implicit but, as I intend, compelling theme is the idea and reality of friendship. Beyond that great name, I have sought to describe those values and beliefs, the disagreements as well as the mysteries of connection which hold men and women in friendship all their lives and at a greater depth than they understand. Further still, I have wanted to sound chords which resound not only in the membership of friends, but also join us to strangers who feel sufficiently the same about things to be counted, in a much-abused but still noble term, comrades. In the litany of socialism, the bonds of kinship are used to welcome those strangers who have come to ask for membership. I would like to think there are still thousands of teachers, whatever their institution or the ages of their students, who would be more moved than amused at the dignified and antique address of 'sister' or 'brother'. It is to them that I have tried to speak.

Directly also. For the book is dedicated to my sister Lesley, simply the best English teacher I have ever known in schools, and to Phillip Whitehead, loyalest of friends, sharpest of critics, and most faithful of comrades. In so far as this book professes a political agenda, then perhaps the best membership of teachers may still hope to see him pick it up on behalf of a future government.

There are many other friends who will, I hope, respond gladly enough to what I have written, but to whom in any case I owe much – in the way of ideas, hospitality, argument, kindness. Almost all this book was written while I held a Visiting Fellowship at the Humanities Research Centre at the Australian National University, Canberra. The extraordinary combination of generosity and comfort, geniality and intellectual energy which the Centre offers, cannot be exaggerated or too highly praised, and my gratitude to all its members, especially Ian Donaldson, who so unerringly combines kindness with acuity, and to his colleague,

Graeme Clark, is here set down. In Canberra also I learned to be glad of the rough and raucous way Peter Widdowson and James Grieve had with my ideas, and to take readily from Peter Herbst's prodigal store of learning.

I have often thanked Basil Bernstein and Quentin Skinner. I do so again. William Empson once said of T.S. Eliot, 'I do not know how much of my own mind he has made', and so it is for me with them. As much in their manners as in their thoughts, their patience and magnanimity are lessons in the good life of scholars, and there are few like them. Lastly I am grateful to my daughters for their fluent and fighting way with the educational obduracy reported and theorized in these pages; if the book *does* work for good, it works for them. Jessica also gave precious help with proofs and index, as did David Collins.

Acknowledgements are due to Faber & Faber Ltd for their permission to quote the lines from 'The Good Town' by Edwin Muir and 'East Coker' and 'Dry Salvages' by T.S. Eliot, and to Routledge & Kegan Paul Ltd and Harper & Row Ltd for the quotation from Martin Heidegger.

Fred Inglis

1

The State of the Nation

There is a battle being fought for the nation's soul. It is not a very military sort of battle. Its site is much more the familiar scenery of urban wreckage, of blasted and despoiled waste ground, smashed windows and kicked-in doors, ruined and rusting car chassis and derelict cookers, than a proud, archaic battlefield of Middle-earth, with banners and trumpets and lances. Half the time its soldiers don't know who's leading them on, or where the enemy is, and whether they'll be paid at the end of the month. Many of them, it is true, have no idea what the battle is about, or how on earth they would hear about it if they had won.

But there is a battle, all the same. And this book is meant to be read at the front and by the guerrilla. It is not for the General Staff, nor for the awful journalists from other countries who have come to watch the fight, to cheer on one side, and to vilify the other. It is meant to be a help, and help in a battle can only come in the shape of reinforcements — weapons, troops, food — or in the shape of intelligence (a good word) — reconnaissance data, secret information, maps.

I write as a teacher and parent of the taught. The battle now being fought, like all battles, is about power and territory; as a matter of necessity, it follows that it is also about freedom and justice, and the structures each denotes of property and habitation. As a result of victory or defeat, people may say, 'we've won or lost our home'. A just war is fought in defence of your home.

The battle of Britain now being won and lost has been going on for much more than a hundred years, and won't be finished for a long time yet. It turns on such essences of home as shelter, safety, protection from sudden injury, care in illness, a seemly veneration for the old, the promise of happiness held out to young children, the possibility of love, understanding, continuity, a live identity and an honest role for every man and woman.

The armies of the night arraigned against these fundamental qualities of a good home and a good society are multitudinous, headlong, and dreadfully destructive. To say that they are led by the grim horsemen of capital and old corruption is, however, like saying that Wallenstein or even Catholicism won the Thirty Years' War. For people give themselves crazily to bad causes, or are swept up into great currents of change, dissolution and ruin by mere accident, and just now these dark, poisonous forces incarnate themselves as indifference, hatred, vindictiveness, malevolence, greed, murder, all the unkillable deadly agents disguised in the bland reiterations of public communication as unemployment, robbery with bodily harm, racism, claiming sectarian responsibility, enterprise, rationalization.

To redescribe our nation in a harsher language is not to collapse politics into morality; it is, however, to seek to undo the lethal work of demoralization. Street murders in Belfast, the seedy running-down of decent nursing in London or Birmingham, the silent, workless wharves of Glasgow and Newcastle, the smashed and empty tenements of Liverpool, these are all the acted and individual consequences of political structures which have been put together and mechanized by the deliberate decisions of men and women. This is the damage inevitable in civil war, and the casualties – the old and ill and unemployed and beaten up (by the lawless or by the law) and very small – are as usual mostly civilian and all of them doggedly uncomprehending. The armies come in, and no one can stop them; you can't tell whose side they're on or what the sides are; but then more of the factories along the waterfront fall silent, or another wing of the hospital becomes half-empty and unkempt, or straight rows of once-decent terraces are boarded up and bricked in and become filthy with refuse, or a redbrick-and-railings school shuts.

Within this common, familiar present the lines of a very long, antique history can only be seen if the actor steps back for a moment and becomes a spectator. The great paradox of the thought that broke Europe open at the end of the eighteenth century in the name of enlightenment is that its spokesmen, whether in philosophy (Hegel), art (Turner), poetry (Wordsworth) or music (Beethoven), while committing themselves to the energies of progress, everywhere insisted on the certainty of tragedy. But only the spectator can see and feel tragedy; to do so requires exemption from everyday life, a compassionate leave of a kind that everyday life as lived by most people never grants, because the demands that business go on as usual are altogether too imperious and pressing. The spectator watches the action; the actor merely performs it. And so, within the deep disturbances, the abrupt and absolute fractures of present British experience, its fierce, sporadic conflicts and resistance, all of which are so chronically and complacently generalized as 'crisis', there is constantly the generation and actuality of tragedy.

Not many people speak of things like that, of course. For our public political language has long been devised in order to manage that same crisis in as harmoniously inequitable a way as its different classes of speech-makers would allow. In what may be designated the labour culture, in which work itself is the most powerful resource of meaning (and in which meaning itself is an increasingly scarce resource), the modalities of public language have for the duration of this century been those of negotiation. In the earlier days of its crisis, that language took as its master-symbols in all classes what were then renamed the traditional English virtues of fair play, ability to compromise, tolerance, a sense of justice.[1] These were the rights and attributes of the 'free-born Englishman', inscribed in the very principles and structures within which Englishmen argued after those decidedly unEnglish occasions in which members of the famously unified national family had crushed one or two brother-skulls or broken a few parental windows. Fair play, tolerance, and the rest – all of them morally excellent and necessary qualities in any class-divided society hoping not to tear itself open along the fissures of its stratification – are cashed at the conference tables of public negotiation as amounts of percentage pay rises, of welfare services cut and restored, of numbers of people sacked or taken on.

But those tables have, inevitably, a chairman to whose quiet authority the negotiators must turn when, in the nature of things, agreement cannot be found, and someone has to be autocratic. Then this public figure must call on this authority and the master-symbols to which he (*sic*) is responsible, in order to reprove other negotiators for failing to speak for the Britain it is everyone's common interest to defend.

'We may even say, well I'm here and you don't speak for me.'
'Exactly', the figure replies, with an unruffled confidence in
his role, for now a different consciousness, a more profound
dramatisation, begins to take effect; 'You speak for yourself,
but I speak for Britain'. 'Where is that?', you may think to
ask, looking wonderingly around. On a good day from a high
place, you can see about fifty miles. But you know some
places, you remember others; you have memories, definitions
and a history.'[2]

That unruffled figure, with his many different and identical
faces, is at his work of national importance now, drawing up
different memories, definitions, and history for us all to negotiate
over and agree to. The redefinition of what he calls Britain (and I
call, as it happens, the unbelievably beautiful reaches of Teesdale;
as for you, you'll have your own places) is going busily ahead. The
reassuringly named home counties continue to surround the
capital of capital; in a briskly modernizing metaphor, the
London-Bristol ellipse has become the service zone to the
quadrilateral of banks, property, insurance, and state which
provides the force-field for this late, cruel stage of (in a phrase)
monopoly capitalism, with its leading edge in communications
technology and its centre of gravity in the weapons industry.
Beyond the ellipse, in a wide arc, there are the new landowners
(though plenty of them with the old names) and ranch or factory
farmers whose patriotic success in over-production has won such
benefits from the Common Agricultural Policy. And beyond *them*,
there is the other England, Scotland, Ireland and Wales whose
dead estuaries I began by describing and whose people have
suffered or colluded with the invasions, forced evictions and
emigration, the loss of power and territory of all colonies.
   These are the movements of the history of the new Britain; it has
reminded several people of the old Spain.[3] In its absolutist days, as
its capital and administrative resources proved unable to organize
more imperial expansions, and as its markets in South and North
America became mere dominated territory with little yield and a
killing cost in jurisdiction and military control, Spain went
coasting down into its long decline. The new piratical imperialists,
in the Netherlands and England, proved much more buoyant,
ruthless and adaptable. Grim old Spain, held in the rigidities of

church and state absolutism, lost the competition worldwide. The Spanish left their names, their architecture, their language and their social forms at every point of the compass; their ruling class, regrouped in a small enclave at the south of the Iberian peninsula, hung onto their money, and simply petrified, while the rest of the country went to pot by way of going back to the direst poverty.

It is a history, with its powerful and inevitable tragedies, which it would be easy to adapt to Britain at the present time (the Netherlands' loss of empire is instructive in a very different way). And indeed trying to write the present as tragic history is part of my intention. But I seek to do so with a decided eye on praxis, on what may be *done* about the response to this history on the part of that corner of the systems of production which produces knowledge and meaning. As I said, I write as a teacher and parent of the taught, and in the human and the natural sciences alike there is to my mind no formal distinction, but only a procedural one between teaching and inquiry (or, as they say, re-search), as well as there being no knowledge without meaning. (To allege there could be is surely nonsensical.)

Is such a claim merely (as they say again) a matter of semantics? Well, if semantics is the study of meaning, then that is all it is. But there is more to the study of meaning than there looks. Think of all that we mean when we say, 'that means a lot to me', as well as when we ask heatedly, 'what on earth do you mean?' At once it is clear that by the concept 'meaning', as by that of 'value', we designate a concentration of significance, a density of vital experience and of precious activity and materials which somehow focus and order parts of our life, and therefore of life itself.

Such a definition is not so much philosophy as tautology. I have said that we find meaning where something is significant; now something which signifies, means. So the weight of interrogation falls less on what meaning is, and more on that something. We all of us try to make sense of our lives – in the phrase we often use, when we say that we can see no meaning in something that has happened to us, then if the event was important, our failure to find some meaning for it will press upon the very centre of our lives.

In all this talk, versions of which can be found in the most unphilosophical and non-technical of conversations, the effort to define and create meaning may be said to be itself a main purpose of people's lives. Notoriously, that purpose has been harder and harder to understand, let alone fulfil, since Britain became more or less entirely secularized. But it is not perfectly essential to call in God if you are making a new religion. The defeated, no doubt, leave us their symbols, thoroughly perfected and disinfected by death, but there is no promise that the symbols themselves will answer to our beseeching. Making meanings, the province of the sorcerer, the magus, the monk and the shaman, is now the work not of necromancers, but of a quite unmysterious cultural bureaucracy. Nor do I intend any bright irony at their expense. The victories won over monks and magicians and their royal masters were clear victories for freedom and reason and truthfulness, and if it turns out that the dispersal and dissolution of old powers has left us with a lot of meaning to make for ourselves, then that blossoming labour is the simple price of freedom, itself a great meaning in Europe and the world, at least since the English civil war.

So the fact that the meaning-makers have a lot to do is an exhilarating fact, part of the excitement of which is that such a freedom has turned out to be quite unrationed, and therefore anybody has felt free (in a phrase) to make a meaning in terms which suit his or her historical convenience. Thus and thus, in quite recent British history, the new classes and new nations have set to invent themselves brand-new traditions and freshly made longevities from the bits and pieces history left about the place. It is a supportable generalization that present-day culture was more or less completely made up between about 1820 and 1860; certainly, the age-old and immutable traditions of, for instance, ancient British regiments, similarly ancient public schools newly emerged from the sadistic barbarism and rote-learning of a few years earlier, even the timeless tartan of the Scottish clans, were all the invention of new, self-made and self-making social formations looking for forms and expressions with which to stake their claim in Victorian Britain.[4]

By the same token and with much the same energy, the harder business of inventing a history and a symbolism for those determinedly excluded from such processes of self-determination was carried on by the English working class,[5] at first in underground rituals of membership, and then with a public splendour in the summer shows of power at the union galas, banner marches, and wakes weeks. Similarly, the longer struggle of British women, especially its bourgeois intellectual women, to make themselves a different history, politics, education and literature out of the same material as the men had organized for themselves, started towards the end of the century and was brought to its peak with the success of the suffrage movement.

Such work is the most familiar version of human creativity, and its business is unstoppable. Perhaps by now the justification for the military imagery with which I began will become clearer. For although the waste and expropriation of industrial change are every bit as severe and, if need be, as deadly as I described them, the larger battle, as is always said by the bluff spokesmen for the military these days, is for the hearts and minds of the people. And the present civil war over the meanings and values of our polity is as fierce and contested as any in the past. Its honours are less geographically precise than those of Edgehill, Naseby, Marstor Moor, or the scaffold, but they will be as significant, even if those names themselves should remind both the over-sanguine and the downright bloodthirsty that clear cut victories are much less decisive when you come to the post-war settlements.

The civil and civilian battle for domination over the territory of meaning is all the keener for meaning itself having become, as I remarked, in a world of depleted and overspent resources, exceedingly scarce.[6] Not only the death of Gods (who none the less turn out, as the examples of Warsaw and Tehran remarkably bear witness, to have the amazing powers of immortality their prophets always claimed for them), but the failure of many modern myths, myths of life and death, and love and truth themselves, which have drastically faltered and buckled at a time when their ideological load was too heavy, have left whole peoples with no satisfactory stories to give shape and purpose to the way of things.

For I shall take these large, overstuffed, necessary words like meaning and value to be usable and intelligible only in the arc of a narrative, and each narrative as part of 'the ensemble of stories we tell ourselves about ourselves'.[7] And indeed the story of the stories[8] is both the subject and object of my book. For it is not only the oldest religious tales which have had to undergo some crisis of implosion and renewal, but some very much more modern ones, including the story of modernity itself and how to attain it (modernization). In Britain, this is still a story revised and retold at every general election, and since it is so familiar to us, it will serve as a short text for practical criticism.

The modernization story may be said to date from the advent of capitalism in political economy, and from the advent of a theory of natural rights in political ideologies, both as coinciding in the rough, wide world with the half-century of revolution and insurrection in Europe from 1789 to 1848. In the story, the heroes are the new class which tears down the narrow prohibitions, the superstitious traditions which not only uphold, but *are* the old order, and free their own energies and gifts, especially those of enterprise, daring, freebooting, individual *élan*, in a world of free thought and trade, where natural justice ensures the nice adjustment of reward to merit, once the controls of an out-dated tyranny have been broken.

By the middle of the century, this story was institutionalized in a dozen forms of the culture's expression, from tales of the origins of the new department stores and imperial traders as they appeared on tea-caddies and jampots, to the many romances of a true love which threw off tyrannical fathers (and their out-of-date way of doing business) in the name of newly successful marriages crowning newly cascading fortunes. The modern success story took its personal, or private morality from the romantics, and its public, or economic morality from utilitarianism and the free marketeers. Karl Marx, in a genial aside, noted this ingenuous complementarity in the drafts for *Capital* that he wrote in 1856:

> The bourgeois viewpoint has never advanced beyond the antithesis between itself and the romantic viewpoint and the latter will accompany it as its legitimate antithesis up to its blessed end.[9]

Marx no doubt saw it all ironically, but the success story of the bourgeoisie, still recounted on regular television since the record–breaking *Forsyte Saga*, has moved great segments of the world irrevocably forward, and fixed some versions of individualism ineradicably in our national and moral vocabulary. The mighty doctrines of progress, of social advance brought about by the unfettered zeal and sheer hard work of many energetic men, of unprecedented prosperity and comfort following inevitably the headlong train of industrialization, of personal fulfilment and civil weal guaranteed by the natural workings of honest, upright yeomen and their faithful wives, these all have found their way into the frames of mind and structures of feeling not only of our present Britain, but, in weird translations, of our whole world.

It has a very strong appeal. The principles of individual rights allied to the Romantic celebration of feelings has something in it for boys and girls; the spiral of effort crowned by success driving on to new effort inscribes forceful motivation in the essence of individual identity, and in constantly postponing ultimate success, ensures (when it works) that aspiration continues to impel labour throughout a man's life; to follow up the sacramental nature of privacy encloses a special frame of life within which wives may be loved, mothers protected, and the life of the feelings cherished by its custodians.

Put in such general terms, it is a very familiar story, still going strong in the admonitions of not a few editorialists, headmasters *(sic)*, Mills and Boon novels, and even, when suitably got up in blow-dried hair, chocolate blusher and homely swimming pools, re-issued in sexy television bestsellers. But the story carries less and less plausibility, which is perhaps why it is so easy to summarize. Once upon a time, that was how people lived and what they believed; *they* couldn't see it as a story. Now there are too many contrary tales, about what happens to those who didn't get on, about the different values and virtues of a different class, which looked so much more human and decent when you'd left them for the room at the top, about the absence of fulfilment and the sheer misery which attended some of the successes, about the hideous emptiness of working to make useless objects or weapons of death. Ours being a liberal culture, and it being a premiss of such freedoms that every story has its opposite version, or negation, the success story, successful as it still is, has had to contend with more and more compelling narratives in which it is shown up as a lie. And so, as I said, interested parties have seized in their partial way upon the stories which suited them, and discomfited their enemies.

This is the struggle for meaning, and the meaning-minders are in particular difficulties now, pulled between the obvious falsehoods of the success story, and the powerful situation of those who want it told again in an up-to-date version. For whatever truth the success story held on behalf of a smallish number of the bourgeoisie between, let us say, 1848 and 1968 – dates offering themselves for their historical flourish – not only was it never true for most people, but it has come to look as though to tell it now as if it were true is to ensure bitter disappointment for many, certain conflict for all, and even, in some portion of the world, absolute destruction. Indeed, one reason why the story is so visible now *as* a story is because it has begun to die (in writing, nothing is easier than to raise the dead).

What is more, those I have called the meaning-minders are themselves hardly disinterested. The cultural bureaucracy, like all bureaucracies (as Weber pointed out once and for all[10]) is there as an impartial arm of the state to serve its clients anonymously and efficiently, whether or not it approves of their purposes and persons; but at the same time the bureaucacy creates its own fierce purposes and compelling irrationalities within its own milieu. A bureaucracy, like any organism, struggles for survival. The meaning-minders, within the divisions of labour of the advanced economies, are to be found in all the welfare bureaucracies as well as the cultural ones — which obviously enough include the official and most explicit story-tellers of the culture, such as television producers and their vast teams for story-making, novelists and journalists and teachers. Their stories are told to themselves, as well as the rest of us.

Teachers, as I intimated, are my hoped-for audience. But the vicious class divisions of Britain bite connections off everywhere, and the word 'teachers' generally connotes only those teaching in schools, and occasionally those teaching in that carefully design-ated sector, Further Education. Those in what we revere as Higher Education are invariably known as lecturers, and even the thin air breathed at these Himalayan levels is divided between colleges and polytechnics, whose heights are still a little lower than the summits touched by the pinnacles of the ivory towers of the universities. In spite of these unignorable and assiduously maintained distinc-tions, I shall speak of teaching as the common activity of all teachers, just as I shall invoke the domain of official knowledge as a single geography and history, rather than as a form of cultural capital[11], whose senior bankers are the university staffs.

The metaphor 'knowledge as capital' is the real subject of the book. Nationalizing knowledge, drastically altering the way in which it is portioned out and withheld, ensuring that its production was co-operative and its benefits equally shared, such a revolution in social relations would be as great as the equivalent revolution needed to change the control of capital itself. And the idea for such a change comes from the other, opposing story about the course of modernization, the story of socialism. That story also has become incredible in its simplest and original forms, not only because the classical version of speedy revolution brought about by an immiserated industrial proletariat has *nowhere* taken place, but also because where a revolutionary mixture, always peculiar to its society, of intelligentsia, patriots, peasants and workers *has* wrested power to itself, the great names of freedom and justice have so often been fouled and degraded by the purported necessities of the politics. Yet, like all great doctrines capable of sustaining men and women in oppression and hugely moving whole societies towards unenvisageable ends, socialism in its many versions (its stories) continues to survive dishonour and its self-generated and horrible vengefulness,[12] in order to offer one of the very few plausible narratives of the future which has a happy and not an apocalyptic end.

In Britain, just now, and indeed in most of Europe and all of North America, to speak commendingly of socialism empties most lecture rooms pretty quickly and demolishes most electoral support. In academic and intellectual circles, there is, as national economies prove intractable and indifferent to the theories which have worked fairly reliably since 1945 or so, an unsurprising and repellently self-congratulatory recrudescence of the kind of conservatism which sets out to justify the way things are, in order to hang onto the comforts of academic gentility without any accompanying duties. And in the larger polity of Britain, the word socialism only connotes the intermittent decency, incompetence, deep philistinism, honest effort and regardless time-serving which was the Labour Party in power between 1964 and 1970, 1974 and 1979.

So to address an educational and academic argument to the possibility and admirableness of an imaginable British socialism needs both nerve and, it seems, fatheadedness at the present juncture. Plenty of venerable spokesmen have intoned a grave valediction over the god that failed,[13] and it is certainly a telling objection simply to point at some of the more extrme zealots in socialist sects, and wait for laughs. None the less, I hold in a modest way two largish ambitions. In the first, I would like to address those in the teaching community who still want to recognize the feasibility and admirableness of the socialist story as well as wanting more or less urgently to retell it in a different form for a new generation. In such a venture, there is no need for the spreading abroad of the greasier kinds of supreme unction to which such story-telling may incline. Quite without attributing all the evils of the world to the old bitch gone in the teeth, capitalism herself, it is clearer than ever before what a beastly unjust as well as abominably dangerous place the world is, and further, that – also as never before – all history is world history, that every fraction of each economy and society interlocks with every other, and that the complex and absolute mutuality and interdependence of the world is complete and precarious.

In these circumstances, and sensibly stepping off the world stage onto the smaller, friendlier platforms of everyday necessity, it is perfectly possible to speak on these of goodwill and some appropriate knowledge of human mutuality, of the justice, loving-kindness, equal freedoms and duties, prevention of avoid-able want and resistance to cruelty, which are its material definitions. If an audience of those with such goodwill and knowledge is not to be found among teachers, where else is it? And having gathered itself together, for it to discuss the social structures and institutions which are the conditions of justice, freedom, equality, altruism, peacefulness and so forth, is in our time and country, with its deeply liberal and illiberal traditions, to discuss once more the practicality of a new socialism.

Any such debate, however, is grounded in a longer and larger one. For it is my second ambition to persuade those listening not only that the names of the virtues which in a quiet way they would stand by are the conditions and consequences of a decently socialist society, but also that their own best modes of thought are part of a long revision and recasting of the way in which Europeans (to go no further) do any thinking at all. That is to say, for over a century and a half many powerful minds have addressed themselves to correcting the distortions and to healing the wounds caused by the amazing triumphs of scientific thought-forms, and the depth and finality with which they have established themselves in Western culture. The dreadful monsters of modern weaponry are highly visible and crazy signs that the understanding of physical nature has vastly outstripped our capacity to understand human nature, and in the absence of a rational and morally adequate 'science of human affairs',[14] we are likely to destroy ourselves.

Such fearful adjurations before that hideous strength are very much of 1984. But the critique of a narrow scientism, of the view that man is a mind whose business is to know with certainty his surrounding natural environment as a set of objects open to his inspecting senses, a definition which includes other men also inspected as objects, has been going strong at least since the heroes of Romanticism launched it. Two heroes not always invoked as products of Romanticism may serve to fix my second ambition. The ambition is to reassure the teachers of goodwill, trying as gallantly as possible to criticize the depredations of their tiny corner of a bad dark world by the faint light of more human standards, that what they are doing, in the most actual, practical way, is to push forward a social and political theory of nearly two centuries in the making. Trying to match scientific knowledge of an *object* with self-awareness as a *subject* is roughly the same thing as trying to adjust scientific knowledge to fit a reasonable scheme of human interests. The two heroes are Hegel and Marx (our rural English versions could be William Blake and William Morris).

Hegel set off to criticize the monumental achievement of his predecessor Kant, and of the method of thought set out and advocated by Descartes, which identified epistemology, or the study which determines the grounds for saying that we *know* something (pretty well) for certain, as *the* subject of philosophy, and crowned philosophy queen of the sciences. In his great and baffling work, *The Phenomenology of Spirit*, which Hegel finished in 1808, he attacked the whole notion that knowledge and our claims about it stand in some immediate, direct relation to both our system of concepts and our unproblematic sense-experience. Hegel irrevocably relativized the whole inquiry, first by showing that all ideas, including ideas about reality and its unchangingness, are radically subject to historical change, and that, secondly as well as consequently, the subject who claims to know anything is himself historically and partially situated, and where he happens to be standing affects and inflects anything he thinks he knows. Accordingly, if we are to assess the validity of what people say they know, we have to evaluate *their* whole relation to their knowledge, and not just what looks like the simple knowledge itself.

Hegel's is the name we can pick out at the beginning of a movement now designated Romanticism which hugely disturbed the confident advance of thinkers and creators towards what they saw as progress and enlightenment, even while it exhilarated them with its powerful additions to the theories of human nature and society. In innumerable ways, Hegel's contemporaries individualized (and therefore made relative) the structures of experience, turned attention to the dark, passionate, irrational and unpredictable thoroughfares of the human heart, celebrated change and growth as new values in themselves, and drenched the European imagination in the sense of its own historicality, so that today even those millions of adults and children who share a general social amnesia troop helplessly past historical monuments and buildings in some token response to the changes of 1800.

These changes released the energy of those who wanted to criticize and resist the self-confident advance of scientific rationalism across the whole front of society. But as the nineteenth century proceeded, it became clear to many thinkers, and Marx was the greatest among them, that to take Hegel's critique of knowledge seriously meant also that the critic criticize the whole of the social conditions which produced knowledge. 'Turning Hegel on his head', as Marx himself put it, meant engaging with the totality of knower-plus-knowledge in his historical location, certainly, but rejecting Hegel's essentially conservative idea that full self-understanding, the unities of subject and object, knowledge and self-knowledge, can only come about retrospectively, and after the appropriate social conditions have been accomplished. Marx put away scornfully the idea, itself known as idealism, that ordinary finite men and women arrive at the good society by their successful identification with the absolute and infinite spirit of reason.

Marx made, for our genteelly thoughtful and educative purposes, two drastic innovations. First, he situated those finite men and women not in the uncircumscribed galaxies of inner reason, but in the finitude of their material, largely economically material lives. He at once theorized and demonstrated that only by patient, scrupulous attention to the material facts of life can we understand how the social institutions arise which make people as they are, and which shape the relations which define how they think and feel. Second, he sought to give this kind of knowledge prior purchase on these structures of society so that those in possession of it could *use* it, not as in Hegel's method for the recapitulative understanding of how they got to be where they were (though such historical understanding remains for Marx the logical first step towards praxis), but rather as an instrument for the transform-ation of society and social relations which are not adequate to the knowledge we have of them. Knowledge of material circumstances leads, in Marx's argument, to a self-knowledge that insists that our criticism of our present always asymmetrical ignorance (some of which is highly convenient to a few powerful figures) must lead to actions which, repairing that deliberate ignorance, make it possible to repair the want and cruelty it causes. For Marx, the dialectical play of thought over the methods of inquiry produces a knowledge capable, if properly understood and used, of unmask-ing the hateful irrationalities of actual, bourgeois society, and of guiding its transformation into the good life.[15]

Marx supremely gives those whose business knowledge is, the teachers, a powerfully liberating and inevitably subversive picture of that knowledge. This is not to profess any sanctimony on behalf of Marxism; as observed, too much foulness, lying and murder has gone on in Marxism's name for a comfortably middle-aged English academic, or some slightly younger denim Danny of the ILEA, still to be plumping for the slogans of 1917. It is to say, however, that no teacher should by now be unaware that knowledge is highly relative, that it may be highly critical and even, with the most liberal permissiveness, sharply subversive for both better and worse, and that the nursery scientist's view that facts are facts, and that theories are determined by observation and falsification, at least misses out on the whole realm of a different order of knowledge. Marx's name can be used to identify this different order of knowledge – order in the sense that ways of seeing and experiencing, objects of thought and the very things of the world themselves may be brought within its frames and made intelligible.

Later theories have given this version of the interpenetration of knowledge, inquiry, experience and values the title 'critical theory', and I mention this only to give my summary a ready handle, and to repeat that any teacher conscious of his or her responsibility to the changeability and uncertainty of knowledge (and the curriculum), and hoping, however mildly, for a better world in the future for the children to live in, should be able to take heart by standing on a few of these premises, many of them first assembled by Marx. (Beginners, as I noted, will find them paraphrased in honest and elementary English in William Morris's talks and lectures to working-class people.[16]

1   Knowledge is a product (and if so, it is more like a work of art than a manufactured object).
2   It can only be produced by the application to experience of theories.
3   Experience and theories about experience are dialectically related (that is to say, there is constant and reciprocal traffic between them).
4   This movement between theory and experience produces *reflexive* (or reflective) knowledge, i.e. it is endlessly subject to correction, as the theory is subject to history.
5   Such theory is aimed at producing enlightenment in the agents who hold them, i.e. at enabling those agents to determine what their true interests are.[17]
6   Such theory is liberating; it frees human beings from self-imposed self-frustration, and makes change for the better possible.
7   Such theory – critical theory – is reflexive, possesses its own valid epistemology and cognitive processes, and above all, is the essential, inevitable motion of *all* rational, self-conscious beings who are bound to strive (perhaps incoherently) for ever greater freedom, fulfilment, and self-critical awareness.
8   These three goals (or *telos*), freedom, fulfilment, and self-critical awareness, are the epistemes (or given grounds) of the epistemology which vindicates the knowledge produced by critical theory.

This necessarily technical summary leads to a conclusion any more or less awake teacher will want to endorse, that 'reflection' is an entirely valid kind of knowledge (and who on earth is the philosopher to tell us that it isn't), and that knowledge for educational purposes should always be, in a key word, 'relevant' to the best human project, as it conduces to the good society and worthy lives.

This potted history of ideas and small excursion into philosophizing is intended to restore to teachers at any level some sense of the necessarily intellectual form and content of what they do, and also of that engagement with knowledge, whether in helping 10-year-olds in their first decoding of fossils on the way to an idea of evolution or in aiding an HND student in his grasp on telephone electronics, as being powerfully and inescapably historical, and, in the most direct and most individual way, political and economic. While that 'economic' is no encouragement to the view that education is an adjunct to the gross national product, it is true for socialist and non-socialist teachers alike that they cannot get away without a commitment to standards and costs of living.

This is a reminder the point of which is worth sticking quite deep into teachers' sensibilites. We live, as remarked,[18] in a negotiation culture. Within such a culture, there is a public forum in which interest groups protest their desserts in an endless debate over the allocation of resources. Naturally, each group is obliged to break into wails of self-pity (sometimes justified, no doubt, but that hardly matters in the convention) when governments announce the year's rations. Only if they can represent themselves as badly done to, and always as meriting more generous treatment, will they be given a respectful hearing at the *next* debate. And so on. Such procedures institutionalize the structures of self-pity as framing dominant public feeling and serve to legitimate such mild political action as strikes, or measures against strikes.

It is therefore as difficult a task to persuade teachers as it would be any comparable and substantial interest group that theirs really is a voice to figure largely in that debate on national resources which issues in the many measures of our standards of living. 'Not us', they cry, 'no one listens to us. Now once upon a time . . . ' And in those good old days, teachers really were teachers, well-loved, well-hated, stern, gentle, telling you what, not asking what you want, sticking to the 3 Rs, and not getting mixed up in all this difficult stuff where there's no right answer. It's surprising how often these myth-heroes rise as giants from the folklore of teachers as well as parents; their great purpose is always to take the measure of a foreshortened present against an epic past. Beside these towering heroes, we can do nothing.

And yet teachers as never before are powerful, audible, visible, respected, *educated*. Such a claim cannot be put down either by the ghosts of popular novels or by the chorus of self-pity. Compared with the dismal barbarisms of the old elementary schools[19] and the arrogant instruction of the so much lamented grammar schools,[20] contemporary teachers are models of cultivation, conscientiousness, judiciousness and a worthy attention to the natures and rights of others. Set against the standing of the dark-suited professions – doctors, lawyers, architects and the like – then school teachers stand closer to academics than ever before (however much the academics shrink shamefully away), and for the same thing. By the exceedingly mixed tokens of, say, degree status, autonomy over training schemes, professional associations and research, their funding and public standing, proportion of public expenditure spent on education, access to public communications (television and newspaper), by all these indices, school teachers and tertiary teachers are indeed a vigorous, self-confident and well-heeded estate of the nation.

This being so, then above all at a time of such lowering loss of nerve on the part of all those whose public role it is to cherish the best values of the political culture and to be guardians of as good a life as may be lived in Britain at the end of the twentieth century, teachers may be expected to fight for the light in the civil war over meanings and values as reported here. The vocation of teachers is to knowledge and its cognates, the good, the true, and the beautiful. Their fight ranges over the terrain of what that offical knowledge is – over what is known, who shall know it, and what may be done with it for a living. They stand, therefore, at the intersection of values and production. Consequently, their practice is dramatically silhouetted quite near the heart of the action in which different people claim to 'speak for Britain'. 'Where is that?' we wonder once again . . . Well, let us agree that one place Britain may be found is in the stories we tell ourselves about ourselves, but particularly in those which are believed and believable. That rich tapestry, in the immortal phrase, is the nation's curriculum; within its variously coloured weave, every picture tells a story, and the meanings of the stories, as Hegel and Marx advised us, are always changing, according to who is in charge.

The stories have to change, as the nation's world-position, its rulers, and therefore its identity change. To speak at least for a corner of the British heart, through the vicious clamour of other hateful British stories about such delicious topics as getting on, doing well, making fortunes, killing other nationalities, booting out blacks, trampling on the weak, and standing on that populist form of transport, your own two feet, is to speak up for the humanly admirable purposes to which what we as a people know may be put in a future which certainly looks sombre, but it is not at all certain to be deadly. There is much laid down in the veins of British culture which may ignite the lights of the future; to mine that energy is the work of teachers. It is an innocent datum of this book that in this single, modest moral barony much may be done to advance a decent version of a transfigured and domesticated socialism. The nation's curriculum, the forms and contents of its official systems of knowledge, is the fount and realm of the stories which make any such future imaginable.

2

Grammar and Narrative

The forces ranged against such a project loom darkly and portentously; indeed it is their military commitment to kill it off. But in the present confusion of things, there is, and will be, no simple alignment of those defending or advancing a warm-heartedly benign and socialist view of culture and the curriculum, and those resisting them according to the principles of whatever the opposite may be called. In which case, history having so many labyrinthine corridors, is it not ignorance rather than innocence to protest for some reborn version of socialism? Wouldn't it be more prudent to redraw the map of knowledge according to some very much more provisional and non-doctrinal world picture?

Non-doctrinal prudence still carries solid political weight, even in a polity which, as Britain's has, has lived for three decades on an overdraft of such prudentiality that it has left itself bankrupt and dishonoured, combining utter timidity and insane militarism, professing civic virtues, while practising urban ruin. But the vast changes in the world order, and the craven myopia of the country in refusing to see them, now force on the attention of us all the immediacy of choices about how we live which cannot be covered by prudentiality and caution, doctrinal or not. The kind of life the children of the present day – those, let us say, now in school and therefore in classrooms from infant reception through to the A-level examination hall – will be able to lead as members of happy families of owner-occupying, tax-paying, vote-casting, TV-watching, cold-war-waging citizens in the year 2010 is being settled by what we do now. Central clauses in that settlement are written in the contents and forms of the school, college and university curriculum.

This is a truth, after all, pretty well acknowledged, at least as a conventional piety or source of hope, by anyone who speaks earnestly in public to graduation ceremonies or bunches of school-leavers; it is spoken for by any parent cornering his or her child's teachers in order to get a forecast for O-level grades. It is certainly acknowledged by those who pay the heavy cheques to the mighty piles of venerable stone disposed about the south of England for the guardianship of standards of excellence at the Headmasters' Conference. Such cheques are paid for the deliverance of knowledge certificates, which in turn admit bearers to precisely differentiated levels of income. This handful of A-level grades may be expected to be cashable for membership of that profession.

Independent-school fees prefigure a very stark equation between knowledge and the future. In a larger and less simple set of relations, quantities are set upon gross domestic product as ensured by numbers of children who can spell and compute to the base ten, upon the realities of democracy as upheld by citizens whose autonomy and rationality is kept in trim by doses of liberal principle, upon the planned-for quotas of creativity, technical innovation, enterprise and initiative, or honest obedience and docility. Notwithstanding all the arguments about education as organization or as manpower planning, as milieu or as relations-of-production, the domestically intelligible and directly popular view of education as what you are taught and therefore learn, what (more subtly) you are allowed to be taught and what you are up to learning, remains the heart of the matter, as it is in all senses the heart of culture.

This is now well recognized. The recognition follows upon the shock of political change: accelerating economic decline, the dislocation of values grounded in images of perpetual prosperity, the dispersal of a nation's identity as it lost power, the centrifugal tendency towards a disunited kingdom,[1] all these readily purchased, off-the-peg explanations of social uncertainty carry through deep into the forms and content of what on earth that nation knows, and thinks it needs to know. So, in the past ten to fifteen years it has become a truism to say that the curriculum as formally approved by the public educational system of any society is a product of the history of that society, and that as a history changes, so does a curriculum. Consequently there has been, in and out of school, a new level of consciousness about the meaning and function of a curriculum, and the dispute about the often conflicting interests a curriculum may be written to serve becomes, as I say, fiercer. In Britain, even in Westminster, prime ministers and their secretaries of state have at last spoken with party unison and inter-party enmity about curricular content and educational standards, the decline of both, and the import of both for a national economy.

In all educational institutions, teachers have engaged extensively not only in the practical discussion of new contents and their relevance to children's and student's needs and wants, but also, and necessarily, with the tension implicit in such matters which is entailed by claims about the maintenance of high standards and the inherent difficulty of certain kinds of study. Indeed, the often deep-seated changes in certain curricular areas (and the no less significant resistance to change) over the past quarter-century may be understood as a conscious and determined process of cultural reinterpretation, the agents of which – the producers and reproduc-ers of social value, meaning and symbol – have directly addressed themselves to questions of national and personal identity as these dissolved under the impact of the new world economic order.

This is a large and round way of naming the lines of everyday teaching experience. For the present fractures in the political economy (to say nothing of the theories which seek to direct it), the facts of unemployment, of youthful dissidence (riots), of old racial and class hatreds and new poverty, all more crudely visible than for many years, require unprecedentedly thoroughgoing and imaginative responses from deeply tired schoolteachers and distinctly timorous university lecturers, who are trying to build a believable world-picture into a curriculum. Furthermore, the present attenuations wrought upon the popular political vocabu-lary force those responses towards the disingenuously stark categories of the caricature left or right, and make entirely intransigent the definition of the moral and political meanings which may, in a difficult country, support a reasonable theory of the human interests, and an educative curriculum capable of expressing it. And yet it is not unduly pessimistic to claim that without our science of human affairs – or as one might say, a speakable, sane and affirmative political vocabulary, speakable moreover by a whole national community – then the headlong destructiveness of the world can only accelerate.

To raise such questions with the official forms of the curriculum in mind looks at first sight like megalomaniac bathos. And yet a curriculum is no less than the knowledge system of a society, and therefore not only an ontology, but also the metaphysics and ideology which that society has agreed to recognize as legitimate and truthful; it sets the canons of truthfulness. In the industrialized nations on either side of the Iron Curtain, the curriculum, widely forgotten and even more widely misunderstood as it is bound to be, is the reference point and acknowledged definition of what knowledge, culture, belief, morality, really *are*. Parents refer naturally to it all the time, even (perhaps most of all) when they never learned any of it themselves; their children at their most obdurate faithfully accept the school curriculum as official, at worst so that they can celebrate the unofficial as a ritual of defiance.[2] And clearly, the society itself maintains, reinterprets and revises the varieties of its curricular experience as a way of reproducing itself in the next generation. The curriculum is a message to and about the future.

It is in these many grand meanings that the curriculum, from the reception class in the infants' school to the newest doctoral thesis, is both public and political. To understand its message to the future is to see something of central importance about our whole view of how we wish the next generation – our own children – to live well in an exceedingly threatening world.

But to use the pronoun 'we' is to simplify matters impossibly, even though it gets that genial, unruffled spokesperson of the real Britain away from the cameras. The pronoun smoothes over the deep corrugations and ruptures caused precisely by struggle over how that authoritative and editorial 'we' is going to be used. The curriculum, it is not melodramatic to declare, really is the battleground for an intellectual civil war, and the battle for cultural authority is a wayward, intermittently fierce, always protracted and fervent one. Its different guerrillas include parents, pupils, teachers, bureaucrats, left, right, centre, nationalities, and the compelling mercenaries of the market forces. To join that struggle over the meaning and essence of the conversation of culture and the structures of educated discourses is to enlist under certain colours, largely reddish ones, and to claim that the dispute must be settled in the names of a decent theory of real interests, a valid sense of individual identity located in a believable moral polity, and a sufficient account of how to live well in (and not to blow to bits) the frightening new world now trundling towards us over the hill.

I have twice spoken of a theory of real interests; it is a phrase which portends much, and what it has much portended and then brought to frightful realization in assorted politics since Hitler came to power in 1933 and Stalin began the treason trials three years later has been mostly lethal. Other people's theories of your real interests were then and are still very likely to be hardly recognizable as such, and to promise such very long-distance satisfactions in return for such abrupt and present discomforts that many people lose interest at once, and go back to dreaming the dreams of the television advertisement, which even if it never comes true, is at least nicer than the alternatives. Yet it is surely uncontentious to say that the world can hardly go on as it is, what with famine and plague and war, and that even if it could it wouldn't, because men and womem, in the name of a preferred scheme of real interests, would intervene to stop it, and turn it in other directions.

Whatever the dangers of a theory of interests, everybody has one, and in devising new curricula, purporting to answer the needs and wants, the interests and purposes, of individuals, classes and a nation, such a theory is always and easily in sight. For the moment, however, I shall stay away from the severer implications of the word 'theory', and propose that, along with a number of family terms which for this context includes model, metaphor (and metonymy), picture, hermeneutic (which means a theory of interpretation), fiction, even hypothesis, we go back to speaking of all categorial frameworks and structures of ideas as constituting a story, a consequential narrative. I have already claimed that all political beliefs connote or make explicit a story about the world, and the two most popular in the West[3] remain the liberal and socialist stories of modernization. Having asserted the essential connections between political world-views and the forms and contents of knowledge, perhaps it makes sense to claim now that every subject tells a story.

This intellectual handhold – 'every subject tells a story about the world' – is first of all useful in a tautological kind of way if we agree to associate the loose group of cognates which have been listed. Model, metaphor, categorial framework, hypothesis, as well as story itself, may all be said to classify the linguistic figure (the hope) by which human minds seek to characterize the many dimensions of experience in as compressed and economic way as possible. This is to speak with a marked partiality. The classical view of science itself, together with one history of the advance of mind, is of a process whereby nature is rendered, in a pure naturalism, by a system of perfectly transparent symbols whose referential value translates without remainder. Mathematics is the ultimate scheme of such aspiration, and the subject has been famously successful in bringing within its transparencies and exactitude much that was once intransigent or unintelligible. But over the same time, such a story has been criticized for a reductionism not merely unfaithful to the facts of natural life, but also regardless of the necessarily manifold and validly ambiguous nature of language itself. By this token, metaphor is *the* type of thought,[4] and imagination the faculty which, in devising new metaphors, enables new versions of nature to be seen in such terms, and therefore new theories to become thinkable. This view takes to heart the reality of magic words and spell-binding. It insists that when we devise and apply metaphors to the world, then we see the world as those metaphors organize our seeing for us. A standing joke from the school dining-room makes this clear. Small boys routinely try to put other small boys off their meal by re-describing the school lunch as something else, disgustingly inedible – 'dead man's leg' (meat loaf), 'elephant's foot' (spam fritter), 'bogey pie' (cornish pasty). If they are successful in putting someone off their lunch, then what they have done is to persuade the victim to *see* their lunch *as* the disgusting object; they have indeed spellbound them. Such a view makes metaphor into the defining mode of apprehension of the world. That is, we may (as babies, for example) conceptualize some at least of what we see without language intervening; when, however, we name what we see, language becomes the lens through which we can see at all. Once we go beyond the very simple naming of objects in the material world, by which we teach children their earliest vocabulary, the manifold and multivalent nature both of objects and the cultural seeing of those objects can only be rendered by the transposition of qualities which we generalize as metaphor, but the many details and gradations of which are listed in the classic rhetoric books discovered and vastly extended after the Renaissance.[5]

Perhaps this elementary account of the relations between percept, concept and metaphor has much too nominalist a look about it for the professional, whether philosopher or cognitive psychologist. But what I am trying to represent is a rough-and-ready scheme of mind in which metaphor, as an essential feature of language (a feature without which there could hardly *be* language), meets the imagination, the human faculty by which the vision and re-vision of mere events is turned into experience of an intelligible, meaning-bearing sort. The case is that the structures of our metaphors not only frame our seeing and understanding of the world, but constitute that world; they are its ground and being.

The case, however, does not stop there. When we speak of the structure of a metaphor, we imply the power it possesses to inform and reform our articulation of the world. But the word metaphor typically suggests the formation: noun (and adjective); more rarely does it suggest: subject plus predicate. If we take a tip from literary criticism, however, we may treat whole poems as metaphors, and, by extension, a single poetic drama (initially, at Wilson Knight's suggestion, Shakespearian drama) and eventually a novel as 'extended metaphors'.[6] Such usage may seem too technical and local an occasion to justify the production of a straight line from metaphor to narratives of all kinds. But without going further into a tricky argument, perhaps it will do here to say that, as metaphors, especially those with an indicative predicate, attribute an association of qualities to a world-out-there, which, inasmuch as they are felicitous and economic, enable us to comprehend (which means, etymologically, to en-fold) that world more practically, scientifically, aesthetically, according to what our present purposes are, then a metaphor is an incipient narrative.

At any rate, then, I am risking the loose association of metaphor with narrative, as well as with theory, model, paradigm,[7] hermeneutic and so forth, in order to emphasize the theory-laden character of knowledge, even in its most primitive forms. So in order to be able to make such innocent remarks as 'I know that for a fact' or, as a teacher might say of a history essay, 'don't go in for theory; just give me as many of the facts of the matter as you can', we have to have a doubtless underived epistemology (that is, a theory of what the grounds are for claiming to know anything at all), a theory of interests (or, as one might say, a system which identifies *those* facts as those we need, out of the chaos of undifferentiated and inane materials and events which might be on show) and, lastly, a sort of *plot*, as a narrative has a plot, in the actions, characters, structure and sequence of which the facts may take on outline, significance and meaning.

It is at this intersection of many different -ologies (levels of knowledge as well as of signification) – ontology, epistemology, ideology – that theory generates facts and situates them in a story – a story which, as I say, implies a scheme of human interests, a history, and a *telos* or purposive onward movement. The different levels may be systematically distinguished[8] by the philosopher's stone; they need to be if, in the most commonplace inquiries of the primary-school classroom, we are not to make misleading errors in assuming commensurability, and radically confuse, say, classes of subjects, forms of data, or relevant criteria of evidence. Learning to think rationally, the ideal language of which process is universally appealed to,[9] if not observed in practice, requires all of us to make these distinctions and this totality. They harmlessly and fatally resound behind all the claims so unthinkingly made, 'that's a fact'.

But in claiming that every fact implies a story, I want to go beyond arguments about epistemology, and well beyond mere definitions of what knowledge is, or indeed what rationality is. These are substantial questions, and we shall have to return to them, but their substance is contained within the far larger, rounder ambit of the human story, and the innumerable versions of this story which knowledge authorizes (*sic*), confirms as true, organizes and vindicates. By this token, the facts are part of a story whose meaning is to give meaning, all knowledge is then acquired and pursued not for its own sake, as they used to say to freshmen convocations, but in order to 'edify'[10] the human life to hand, to give it meanings new and old, to educate in its passage from birth to copulation and death. These brass facts are gathered up into the larger story of how to live, and made as interesting as possible. The proposed demotion of knowledge 'for its own sake' from its central place in the curriculum of cant is only disconcerting to jobbing philosophers of a realist persuasion. Nobody, after all, seriously concerned either with edification or with old life itself intends to demote truth, let alone beauty and goodness, from being the heart of all matter. The enemies of truth are at and within the gates, and it is the homely and traditional claim of this modest proposal that the point of education (the meaning of edification) is that the educated girl or boy, man or woman, tells the truth and tries to be good. Shifting knowledge for its own sake from the centre of the intellectual and educational prizes is no more than recognizing the obvious feature of everyday assumption, that knowledge is intimately related to power, is a form of what has been called 'cultural capital',[11] which is to say the more you have of it and the more shrewdly you invest it, the more it will pay off, and that the disembodiment of its claims to truth until they reach a state of sakelessness is an old lie told by those innocently or disingenuously suited by the present distribution of rewards to those in possession of knowledge for its own sake.[12]

It is important not to be misunderstood at this stage. For I am about to go on and summarize the essence of the stories of the subjects: a synopsis of the intellectual gospels. Every subject tells a story about its own worth, its extrinsic and intrinsic justification,[13] its deservedly or unmeritedly low place in the hierarchy of the national curriculum, fights a gallant or a cowardly fight in the competition of subjects[14] and, above all, struggles to vindicate a view of human interests in which its own practitioners have a heroic place in the history of human emancipation, self-awareness and fulfilment. But to imply an amused, all-knowing and ironic distance from these stories is to fall into the self-congratulation of at least one school of history men, whose radical or deutero-marxist exemption from the little local difficulties of historicity enables them to spot the non-historical cooking of the books by everyone else. These demons of the times arraign everybody else for implying legitimations of their subjects that merely apologize for the subject's partiality, while at the same time defending an intellectual protectorate that safely marks in and out a terrain nobody else could possibly want or feel menaced by. On this account, such subjects and their defining structures interlock with all others to insulate their priorities from interference, to ensure the reproduction of subject-membership in assimilable and non-disruptive numbers, and to interrogate their preferred material in ways which never put in question their own dominant paradigms of thoughts and criteria of authority.

This critique derives ultimately from Marx's *The German Ideology*,[15] but more latterly it has been devastatingly reformulated in a home-grown version applied to all academic disciplines in the human sciences as practised by the British universities. In so far as they define the conduct of all subjects in secondary schools, both by their control of A-level syllabuses and university admissions, as well as by their formation of the students who become the teachers, the intellectual practices of British universities are indeed the ground and being of British education. Perry Anderson's celebrated onslaught[16] convincingly indemnifies the arc of the university curriculum marked by the useful heading (it comes from the French) 'the human sciences', which includes literary criticism, history, philosophy and aesthetics, as well as what are commonly called the social sciences in Britain. Of course this list, omitting both the creative arts and the physical sciences, is highly selective, but his charges of philistine mindlessness and self-seeking silence on major issues of social status, relevance and the generation of theories capable of putting in question the culture and society which support them are exhilaratingly plausible.

He was followed, in less heady prose as well as a far less brilliant and accomplished summary, by critics of the school curriculum,[17] reproaching it justly enough for favouring the language, characterizing thought-forms, and preferred subject-groupings of the professional middle classes and their children, and for devising time-filling and humanely time-killing activities for working-class children, which had neither content, status, nor purchasing power. The process, these critics argued, was as self-delusive among teachers as it was illusory for children, for whereas the teachers protested that they sought to bring children up to their individual and creative potential, what they really did was impose deeply conventional and anaesthetic frames of thought and being. These stifled creativity, foreclosed collaboration, and encouraged only a banal and docile readiness from junior school upwards to accept official categories of time, work and discipline, and then to retain the energy to subvert these when all forms of official patience and reward expire, as they do with the unemployables: the West Indians and the children of very poor, white and utterly unskilled, often single-parent families.[18]

Now there is no doubt that these analyses stick: that, in Marx's and Engels' tautology, 'in every epoch the ruling ideas are the ideas of the ruling class',[19] and that those ruling ideas are most audible and visible in the official version of knowledge organized as the curriculum at all age-levels. To say so is to follow the theory of ideology that systems of ideas provide a systematic masking of the

real relations of power and subordination, which are the spontaneous and inevitable consequence of capitalist production.
These ideas bring about a condition of false consciousness in those
who believe them, such that their more or less willing victims
accept the ideas, even though they work against their own best
interests – hence 'false'.

This potted version of a never very subtle thesis, which was
originally dreamed up to explain why on earth the working class
failed to deliver the proletarian revolution, will perhaps serve to
identify the 'masking' or 'fix' theory of ideology, according to
which knowledge systems are vigorously legitimated by those they
suit best in terms that pretend to show how they are also good for
everyone else. Thus the British bourgeoisie builds an educational
ideology, decent enough in its own terms, according to which each
child is a uniquely precious individual (the pleonasm is typical)
whose essential creativity and rich potential for selfhood may be
best brought out by the careful devising of educational conditions
which combine proper libertarianism with the inculcation of a
severe respect for hard work, personal effort, self-discipline
(especially as public examinations draw near) and the intrinsic
integrity of the forms of knowledge.[20]

That such a view may be viciously self-seeking is cruelly
apparent not only in the results of national selection for higher
education (and therefore higher salaries), but also in the most
mundane details of teaching the rich and poor subjects, or
teaching in the rich and poor schools. All the same, the bourgeois
ideology is not merely self-seeking. Its provenance lies somewhere
within the best doctrines of Romanticism, whose unprecedented
emphasis on the responsibility of the self towards its own deepest
feelings and its capacity for pure, spontaneous and passionate life
is its most serious and lasting bequest to the chance modern
society may have both for understanding itself, and turning that
understanding towards new versions of the good life.

There is therefore another version of ideology which sees it at
first as straightforwardly a structure of values. Values may be
thought of as never having meaning by themselves, but like
language itself only having meaning within a system of differences,
each inflection of which is articulated with another.[21] These values
are, straightly, values, not the property or product of any given
social class. However, as classes come to dominance in changing

historical conditions, so they bring to partial, peculiar embodiment those values which, fully embodied and lived, would conduce to the realization of the project for human freedom. It is this historically distorted version of real human values which constitutes ideology, whether that word designates the fix or hypocritical animation of ideology, or whether it more sympathetically indicates the always unsuccessful and local attempt to live up to noble ideals.[22]

Ideology, therefore, is a concept which, as I use it here, strains apart in the directions of two opposed meanings. In the first, it is an advertising instrument on the part of the powerful, intended to persuade the less powerful to accept a misleading story to their own detriment and the continuance in power of the story-teller. In the second, it is the interpretative structure of values which (to put things very roughly indeed) the agent brings up to the meaningless flow of events past and through him, and attempts to fit over the events by way, as we say and I have already said, of making sense of life and lives, and turning them into intelligible experience.

Either way, ideologies tell a story: are at the centre, as Clifford Geertz puts it, of the ensemble of texts which compose a culture, 'stories we tell ouselves about ourselves'.[23]

On this arguable definition, educated language forms a totality of discourses within which each subject draws upon the ideological field of the culture in order, on the one hand, to legitimate and advance its own standing and membership, and, on the other, to realize some recognizable version of its own ideal speech-forms and exchanges. The stories that subjects may tell are therefore complicated, and different groups of subject-members may certainly tell sharply conflicting versions of the subject story.

So, 'once upon a time . . .' there was the subject biology, physical education, home economics, English, physics, French, history. In each case, the story has its heroes, who determined the subject in the face of uncomprehending and obscurantist opposition; its villains, who tried to keep an alien version going in the name of a different elite; its arbitrary snobberies or anti-Enlightenment cast of mind or mere self-protection. The story includes a view of its past as surpassed, but mythologized, its oppressions contrasted with present liberties won by its heroes, and a strong account of its contribution to the post-enlightenment trigonometry of human self-awareness, self-fulfilment and freedom. That is to say, the story nominates those human faculties which the subject uniquely prompts and cherishes (the intrinsic justification) as well as those social roles and necessities which it no less singularly fills and meets (the extrinsic justification). Like all good liberal novels, its heroes are individuals battling to free themselves from the dead weight of their parents' generation, and to find space for their own daring initiative within which entirely new freedoms, expressions and ideas will find embodiment.[24] Its history has beginning, middle and an end which begins in the present, and which, while not at all complete, provides ample scope for present self-congratulation. The largely unwritten novel of each subject includes, as one would expect, a canon of sacred texts which precede it, periods of exile and sudden revelation (peripetaeia), just as Aristotle said it should; less obviously, it implies a method of personal development and redemption, which is coterminous with the method of the subject itself.

Consider, of our short list, biology, new crowned queen of the life sciences, served always by her lesser sisters in the muses of science, zoology and chemistry, but assured of her own pride of place by her undoubted and undaunted contribution to the human project in terms of improved life-expectations, freedom from arbitrary epidemic, and therefore its triumphant warding-off of the last enemy. Unforgettably, Clive James has noticed that the history of the life sciences as represented in television is caught in a repetitive tableau on which are inscribed the everyday stories of solitary men with big black beards being thoroughly misunderstood by largish groups of other men with long white ones. Well, that is one popular version of the hero and his success story in the West.[25]

If we turn to the narrative of biology as told in a standard sixth-form and undergraduate textbook,[26] we find a happily pure version of the story of a subject. In the pages dealing with the great release of ideas in the early 1950s, which so dazzlingly applied the latest X-ray crystallography together with the earliest conceptual innovations of particle physics to molecular biology, the author recounts the interplay of collaboration and rivalry between the great prizewinners – Hans Krebs at Oxford and his work on citric acid structures, Linus Pauling at the California Institute of Technology, Fred Sanger at Cambridge – at the same time as he specifies both method and discovery. The geography is an essential part of the tale – Oxford, Cambridge, Harvard, Princeton, Los Altos, Santa Barbara, more occasionally Zurich and Moscow (it is a strikingly anglophone, not to say patriotic story). In each case, but often not until later in the texts, credit is given for the human and medical benefits of the discovery – for instance, Sanger's devising of a taxonomy for the amino-acids in insulin, the hormone notoriously secreted by the pancreas having the most obvious benefits for the control of blood-sugar irregularities in sufferers from diabetes.

The most glamorous heroes of the book are the Cambridge scientists, Francis Crick and James Watson, no doubt partly because of the drama of their discovery and their successful theorizing of the famous double-helical structure of the deoxyribonucleic acid (DNA), the vital molecular chain which carries the genetic messages of an organism, but also because the stops and starts, passions and divisions of their successful inquiry have all the ingredients of a popular movie about scientists. Watson himself biographized their research as a sort of novel[27] with an entertaining lack of disinterestedness, and surely part of their fame must be due to the smoothness with which their plot and its characters fitted the cultural-ideological space left open for the public acknowledgement of science.

In the sober, clear, confident march of the textbook's prose, however, what is as important as the drama, competition, and collaborative advance across the frontiers of knowledge is the homogeneity of metaphor, which rolled up these problems in the cellular structures of protein in a single, beautifully economic image. Krebs, Sanger, Pauling, Crick and Watson were all trying to adjust their X-ray photographs to the model of the helix, single, double or triple. They are caught in the magic icon of the scientist, gazing at the baffling and impenetrable phenomena until, in an intuitive flash, their meaning is released in a single, elegant and economic model.

The elegance and the economy are essential qualities in the story science tells itself and us about itself. Naturally, there are those who blow the gaff on this smoothly regulated and calmly successful practice. Thomas Kuhn[28] sociologized the placidly powerful conventionalities of paradigmatic science and how they work to exclude eccentricity or subversive inquiry until such time as the new science forces itself upon the scene and changes the paradigm. Then in no time at all, the new science establishes its conventions, and the old plot with its heroes, discoveries, human benefits, order, economy, elegance, calm and rational and intelligible *progress*, is rewritten to suit the new language, its tropes and forms. After the revolution, the new order. Roberts is the entirely believable and excellent ideologue of post-1950s biology. His is a good read.

Biology may stand here as a type of the natural sciences, and the tale they each tell of themselves. As I have suggested, the ideological strain of any such tale is between the fix which subject-members hope to put upon the world, especially their subordinates, in order to confirm and if possible strengthen their position in it, and their genuine aspiration to devise ideal speech-situations for their subject which will ensure the perfect harmony of truth and freedom, of the conflict of ideas and the eradication of personal interests.[29] The ideological strain creaks audibly in the story philosophy itself tells, a subject which has (extraordinarily) in Britain kept entirely aloof from all but higher education — it simply isn't taught in schools — and which has a highly self-congratulatory account of the ideal speech-situation.

Its history is of course a long one. In Britain, the official curriculum has worked steadily to present the subject as the public relations agent of epistemology, and the securing of science's unselfconscious and non-theoretic achievements as its most important work. It is hard, of course, to avoid falling into parody[30] in trying to sketch the outlines of philosophy's hero. Such a hero, mocked on stage by Tom Stoppard and in the pages of her novels by Iris Murdoch, goes to David Hume for a theory of human nature, to Kant for a rather gaunt, chilly morality, to Russell for scepticism and scientific realism, and to John Austin and A.J. Ayer for the repudiation of metaphysics, especially from France and Germany, as well as for the social, non-spiritual locating of self and mind in the many contexts of everyday language. The biography of this hero as he matures in the story of his subject is subject to a complete rainbow of political and economic metamorphoses, of course, but even allowing for his faint contamination these days in the murky languages of both Heidegger and Marx, he remains a liberal empirical figure, preferring the philosophy of science and modal logic to ethics or politics, and in his style and cast of mind, rationalist, empirical, sceptical, urbane, authoritative, social democratic, atheistical, tolerantly opposed to grand theory. It is also plausible to claim that his intellectual standards and the professional criteria of his peer-group are the highest in the academies and are apt to paralyse members of other subjects into a helpless deference. At all events, philosophy's self-justifications in its story are the most nakedly intrinsic of all: philosophy bestows upon its children the clarity of mind, the lucidity of argument, the sceptical provisionality of posture, the resourcefulnes of rationality, the certainty of the complexity and infinitude of things without which not just liberal, but *any* culture will lapse into barbarism. These are marvellously abstract values, and indeed to achieve junior appointment in philosophy is to be apprenticed to a senior, dead philosopher, and serve your indentures filing his universalizations and keeping his archive up to date. The story of philosophy as presently told, if we exclude assorted mad prophets reeling in from the transatlantic wilderness (Richard Rorty) or the dug-outs nearer home of the Marxist guerrilla (the editors of *Radical Philosophy*),[31] is a strictly academic one and being so, has to advertise less stridently in the educational market place. In the house of fiction, its room is a clean well-lighted place, small, neat, white, and well-appointed.

The stories of poorer, newcomer subjects, with no rooms at Oxford or Cambridge, and too much to do on too little money in comprehensive schools, are more badly written, much more prone to self-pity and the intellectually snobbish dismissal of others, nervous, awkward, and with a very doubtful family history. Indeed, they spend much of their time trying to find or invent that history, in order to license themselves as respectable in the present, and beneficent in the future.

Take a self-designatedly homely instance, that of home economics. The genesis of the subject lies, no doubt, in the decade before the First World War and after the 1902 Education Act, which established the new, national Board of Education and its Permanent Secretary, Robert Morant; indeed, in the *Regulations for Secondary Schools*, issued under his signature in 1904, we find a now-famous regulation setting out for the first time in Britain a simple codification of time to be spent on instruction in different subjects – 'not less than 4½ hours per week must be allotted to English, Geography, and History ... not less than 7½ hours to Science and Mathematics ... ' and 'with due provision for

Manual Work and Physical Exercises, and, in a girl's school, for Housewifery'.[32] With that to hand, school teachers can remind themselves that they have come a very long way since then, but contributors to *Naked Ape*, as well as those less self-righteous and more doggedly social-conscience-stricken about not making girls do only girlish things, can acknowledge the significance of the 'manual work and physical exercises' for boys, as well as the housewifery for girls.

By a prime historical token, both items are an early sign of a time in which a nation realized that it was broken in half. The violent unsettlements and huge reconstruction involved in the unplanned or, in the phrase, free-market industrialization of Britain had famously torn an unmendable rupture in the taken-for-granted pieties and graces of the agrarian order.[33] Within eighty years, the urban poorest no longer knew how to bake bread or make butter or brew beer, even if they could have found the ingredients. Cheap fish, especially shellfish, had vanished, and reappeared on inaccessible porcelain slabs as expensive fish – oysters, shrimps, clams. Steak and sirloin had gone with it, to be replaced by what Richard Hoggart, writing of the dispossessed but still gamely gourmandizing Leeds poor in the 1930s, noted[34] as the cheap and 'tasty' cuts – offal, chitterlings, faggots, black (blood) puddings, trotters – 'those portions of the pig' as Dickens immortally put it in *Great Expectations*, 'of which the pig, when living, had least reason to be proud'. Whatever brave efforts Hoggart's Hunslet family made with its kidneys and Bath chaps, no one can doubt that by then the class stratifications of the English cuisine had gone deep. The very poor, who are reported by Mayhew and Rowntree[35] as living on bread and scrape and the meat extracts which came on the market to give that debilitating diet some flavour, had lost not only the knowledge needed to prepare and the money to buy the porter, claret, port and punch, the saddle of mutton, sage dumpling, chops and water-pastry pies eaten at such comparatively humble tables as Nicholas Nickleby's and (in *Bleak House*) Mr Guppy's, they no longer lived in a culture in which, in the strictest as well as the philosophical sense, the materials were there for such a repast.

It is always easy to utter maledictions over the decline of the times. Things have never been what they so surely were when he or she, or you or I were girls or boys; the country's short trip down to the dogs began for each generation as its youth began to fade. So to write a careful history of the British kitchen and its decline[36] would have to take account of complicated continuities which run strongly against the dread culture-killers of industrial capitalism – the processes of mass-production which ensure the standardization of parts, the concentration of capital, the Taylorizing of labour, the ruthless organizing and occupying of markets. But such a history, it is my insistent, repeated and *structural* claim, would come up against the incomparable changes wrought upon nineteenth-century experience by the amazing creativity and destructiveness of the world's first urban society. Somehow, between the vast upheavals of the Reform Acts, the Charter and the Chartist marches, the end of Ned Ludd and Captain Swing, the emergence of free trade unions, the bookish signposts of the political landscapes like William Lovett's *Life and Struggles in Pursuit of Bread, Knowledge, and Freedom,* or the many years of Cobbett's *Political Register,*[37] and the staid and stately prose of Robert Morant's *Regulation* in 1902, there came into being the apparatus of the modern state bureaucracy, at once protector and oppressor of the people.

This is the institution, vast, sprawling and incoherent as it often was, which was devised and committed by the governing classes to be sure, but encouraged and worked out by working people of all kinds, in order to repair the hideous depredations of the new political economy. And like its monstrous siblings, the institutions of capital and production themselves, the state sought to build a new order capable of holding down the new disorder. Inevitably it did so in terms borrowed from the culture which lay smashed and in ruins around the hitherto unseen machinery.

All over Britain, the business was in play to make such a new world out of these old fragments. Brand-new private-public schools were built with an architecture, an escutcheon, and sparkling-fresh traditions which declared their allegiance to the victors of the tribal Wars of the Roses. Equally neonate regiments were set up to police the working class, the Irish, the Africans and the Indians, which dreamed up battle honours and badges linking them to the vanished mercenaries and militias of a century before. Even nations rediscovered a sartorial atavism, and Scottish businessmen and agricultural industrialists put on the kilt and the dancing brogue craftily designed for them in Leeds,[38] and claimed they smelled of purple heather and less picturesque thistles.

Four countries and their different classes made up a new set of stories with which to connect themselves to the past, and to explain their present states of beatitude or misery, failure or success.[39] For such fictions to be plausible, it naturally had to be the case that some of them could be given a sufficient modicum of historical truth. But a very little went and goes a long way, and although the effort to practise historical truthfulness is no doubt essential for the perpetuation of virtue, such truth-telling must take its place in the given structures of narrative, and these are not so much legendary as natural, which is to say that without them there could hardly be either stories or histories at all.

These assertions are less of a detour from our smaller history of knowledge and its praxiology than they look. For it is a simple, platitudinous premiss of this book that all our key British narratives were hugely rewritten, reinterpreted and revised during the second half of the nineteenth century.[40] These narratives had to reach back to the imagined order before what is accurately called the industrial revolution changed the world (and like all revolutions, it was very long) and retrieve enough from that past to make the present seem intelligibly continuous with it. Morant's *Regulation* was inevitably part of that enormous and unco-ordinated marking out. Housewifery, our example, sought to put right the colossal rupture in continuity which left young girls unable to do what, according to the old narratives, they should be able to do: thrifty darning, simple seamstress and cutting-out work, laundering, bottling, preserving, baking. The old contexts for such work had gone, of course, those of dairy or kitchen in a large agricultural household of the kind we see Tess of the D'Urbervilles working on at Crick's farm, Marlott; the new kind is all too palpable in the awful inept poverty of her own family's life, especially after her father's death. The school curriculum was devised by the servants of the state out of the inevitable ingredients of their class formation to teach girls how to manage the tiny economics of a poor urban household and, no less pressingly, to obtain the skills necessary to domestic servants. The relations of agricultural production, which had been the proper context of (as we say) home economics and domestic science, had gone; the new terms of the small, sufficient consumer household had not yet been settled. The fragments of old custom were real, but insufficient;

the materials of the new curriculum were earnestly and decently reformatory, but lived only in schools. Out of the two, a school subject was made.

There was much, of course, to be done. The nastiness as well as the thrills of industrial and proletarian life since 1840 had released horrors unthought of on the grimmest farm – cholera, diptheria, typhus and meningitis joined the macabre and epidemic dance of unavoidable and deathly illness and deformation led by smallpox, rickets and tuberculosis. Custom and culture could do little about these demons; the new science, especially of hygiene and dietetics, could do and did much, and the liberal reformers rightly added that to the subject.

And so housewifery (cooking and needlework) changed into domestic science, and that in turn became home economics. On the way, the assorted inadequacies of the girls and the experience they brought with them had led other teachers to want to add elementary training in parlour and teatime manners, in the correct setting of places at table and entertaining of guests, and by the present day, when one has worked off all the irony and wryness one may upon the scoured formica and antiseptic tidiness of the home economics flat, its picture and its implied narrative of the good life, its genteel and decent regard for hearth and guests and hospitality is not so little but that, in social conditions which do so much to restore barbarism and brutality, we could readily do without it.

It is in some such form that I shall write of all subjects – whether disciplines, sciences, themes or topics – and their histories. Indeed subjects *are* their histories, on this purview, however much we acknowledge as we must that all knowledge has its realist form and content, and is truly a mirror of nature,[41] however distorting.

To understand each part of a curriculum, and to do so in order to change it on behalf of the future, we can only turn to its history, and that history recounted as a story it tells us of itself and about ourselves. Such a story, as I suggested, is a theory with which to find out what experience means, and how to wring knowledge out of it. Securing such knowledge is the work of a lifetime, and state education, together with its Victorian antecedents, is only one, though now a vast and powerful one, of its productive institutions.

3

Theory and Experience

Theory is vastly bigger than the province of intellectuals or even of universities, just as curriculum is a term which may take in all the price of experience, and certainly goes far beyond its present confinement to what is more or less officially taught to primary and secondary schoolchildren. Everybody has a set of theories, compounded maybe of fact and value, history and myth, observation and folklore, superstition and convention, but these theories are none the less intended to explain the world and, as I said, discover and confirm its meanings. Most of all, those who refuse all theory, who speak of themselves as plain, practical people, and virtuous in virtue of having no theory, are in the grip of theories which manacle them and keep them immobile, because they have no way of thinking about them and therefore of taking them off. They aren't theory-free; they are stupid theorists.

This stricture is no less fair if we define theory tightly, as a testable hypothesis for the explanation of phenomena. If theory is more widely taken, as a symbolic representation of the real world for the purpose of understanding it, and further taken that models, metaphors, fictions, systems of principles, and narratives are all versions of theory, then, quite without being committed either to relativism or naturalism, it is clear that using language is an action which cannot take place without theorizing, and that by definition we are all theorists.

None of this does anything to clarify the different contributions of imagination and reason in the making of theory. And certainly such a view of theory says nothing about the status of the theories made. If we define relativism[1] in a very reach-me-down way as the view that the truth is something which we make up (collectively or individually) more or less as we please, and realism as the view that whatever we make up less or more as we please, it certainly is *not* the truth, then to insist that cognition-plus-language formulates theory gives no particular opportunity to either persuasion, but only claims that thought entails theorizing.

It is surely the case, however, that the cultural rhetoric out of which theory is spoken in anglophone societies veers almost insanely between the view that knowledge is a realist product (as in the natural sciences) and that knowledge is wholly subjective, the only truth capable of making you free being the truth about things which is true and serviceable for you alone (because you, in the jargon, 'constructed' it for yourself). This baleful paying-on-both-sides of relativism and realism corresponds to deep divisions in the cognitive and emotional formation of all classes in the society, and understanding our knowledge means understanding them.

The first move in this enterprise has already been to revalue the idea of theory itself; but the second, which is more drastic and more ambitious, is to give far denser, more material (and materialist), as well as historical substance to the contrary term, experience itself. Anything – but largely the mere passing of old time – may be credited to the column marked 'experience' in the historical ledger. In our society as perhaps in any other, rewards, seniority, wisdom, power are accorded to those in whom the category 'experience' is thought to be stored and recognized. But:

Had they deceived us
Or deceived themselves, the quiet-voiced elders,
Bequeathing us merely a receipt for deceit?
The serenity only a deliberate hebetude,
The wisdom only the knowledge of dead secrets
Useless in the darkness into which they peered
Or from which they turned their eyes. There is it seems to us
At best, only a limited value
In the knowledge derived from experience.
The knowledge imposes a pattern, and falsifies,
For the pattern is new in every moment
And every moment is a new and shocking
Valuation of all we have been.[2]

The interrogation was hardly heeded. Experience remains the champion educational category, along, perhaps, with intuition. Both are valued precisely because they sanctify the radically individualized and relativized view of life and its meanings – 'true for me' 'true for you'. The force of the primacy given to 'experience' comes out routinely when schoolteachers ask their children to write from 'their own' experience, or curriculum builders demand that children be given curricular material which begins from that same indubitable realm which is also their own property.

In the cases both of experience and intuition what is staked has a very high value: it is the personally possessed and unchallengeable standing and meaning of these concepts as vindicators of free identity, of domains of personality, which escape all coercion and are the object of no social structures. You can't, conventional wisdom teaches, be deprived of your experience, and it is the fact of its inevitable accumulation, together with its uninterruptedly direct acquisition as *your own*, unmediated by anything between you and it, which is held to give it its resonant validity among our values. By the same token, even if somebody might be shown to be mistaken in their intuitions, agreement on such a score would be a consequence of changing your own mind for yourself: 'no one can make it up for you'. Once more, the significance of an intuition, like that of experience, is its standing as a personal possession which confirms the possessor in his or her deepest sense of self.

There is plenty of truth in these beliefs, as well as a clear justification in the value which accrues to the concept when it is understood in this way. Criticism and revision, however unpopular, are timely on three grounds, none the less. The first and most obviously important is that, along with the truth of the beliefs, there is also serious falsehood; the second is that the emphasis on the possession and incontestability of experience has the consequence of further individualizing people's view of themselves and of life, of accelerating down the long slide from the genuine strengths of Romanticism to the consumer narcissism within which the employed and well-off three-quarters of the population devise an adequate picture of who they are. To cherish the personality of experience prevents your seeing your connections with others. 'Only connect', E.M. Forster's famous dictum, has a wise old owlishness about it which obscures the truth that connection in the many senses of common humanity and deep mutual interdependence is the ground of life. That being so, experience isn't just ours, but social and historical; it comes at us organized and shaped by all the experience others have had before us, as do our intuitions. An intuition cannot simply be felt along the heart, picked up and earthed there as though it were a stray electrical impulse. It means something, and it can only do so as it assumes shape within a conceptual framework capable of so shaping it. As I suggested, theory and experience are as mutually necessary as (and are in part synonymous with) concept and percept.

This antinomian insistence on the necessity of theories, paradigms and narratives in order to make sense of experience does not mean, of course, that each category is unanalysable. It is more a matter of starting from the premiss that such terms create the room for individual men and women to act as free agents by means of their choices and decisions, and bring these into some rough accord with their intentions and purposes, all of which deliberate movement is summarized under the heading 'voluntarism'. The strong counterweight to this easy-going assumption is that all such voluntary activity can *only* take place within and would be inconceivable without a complex network of antecedent structures. 'Experience' indeed is the name we give to the lessons learned in the often harsh encounter between agency and structure. It is not the transcendental talisman that life is worth something, as liberals and Romantics suppose; nor is it a term consigned by the determinate laws of a history without subjects[3] to the rubbish bin of politics.

Rather, as Edward Thompson tells us, while telling off the Marxists for jettisoning the notion,

> What we have found out (in my view) lies within a missing term: 'human experience.' This is, exactly, the term which Althusser and his followers wish to blackguard out of the club of thought under the name of 'empiricism.' Men and women also return as subjects, within this term – not as autonomous subjects, 'free individuals', but as persons experiencing their determinate productive situations and relationships, as needs and interests and as antagonisms, and then 'handling' this experience with their *consciousness* and their *culture* (two other terms excluded by theoretical practice) in the most complex (yes, 'relatively autonomous') ways, and then (often but not always through the ensuing

structures of class) acting upon their determinate situation in their turn.[4]

Thompson's rich rendering of what experience may mean need not delay us at the philosophical level. My purpose in this chapter so far has been to rescue the idea of experience as conventionally deployed by most teachers (and I cannot insist too often that by 'teachers' I designate all those who teach, including the men and women listed as lecturers or even professors) from the sacred, inaccessible groves of personal life and individual perception, and to restore it to the profane avenues, mean streets and main roads of history.

To say so, however, does not take us very far in charting the relations of experience to theory, and of both to the larger, no less comprehensive, but slippery concept, knowledge. Experience has its structures; these precede the individual's ordinance of his life; similarly, knowledge and *my* knowledge have their non-individual structures, and here too we come up against a system of categories whose familiarity and ease of handling seem to assure their accuracy of fit with a reality it is the business of language and other symbols to mirror faithfully. Thus, just as experience is happily supposed to be directly acquired and possessed by me, so knowledge is comfortably divided into the complementary domains of subjective and objective. The latter domain is ruled over by the natural sciences, whose precise methods of observation, framed by hypothesis and leading not to verification, but to the single absolute of falsification (that is, if my hypothesis is falsifiable, it cannot prefigure a general law; a working experiment is *always* liable to falsification), give them a jurisdiction, completeness and instrumentality whose prime materials are quantities and classes – which is to say, numbers and facts.[5]

This has been the victorious story of how to acquire knowledge and discover the truth since scientific method really began in the seventeenth century.[6] The colossal triumphs of science over nature and by means of technology have settled it in its place as the overpoweringly dominant model of inquiry in the curriculum of the industrial nations – which is to say, *all* nations of the world as they aspire to become or remain sufficiently self-determining and well-off.

Within the compulsion of this system of concepts, the standing of facts, of empirical obervation, of computation, of routine and method uninflected by changes of individuals practising that method ('value-freedom') for the reproducibility of phenomena, of reason itself as given structure and direction by its methodical framework, all these securities settle the natural sciences in their present position in the curriculum, and deliver their parallel dividends in terms of prestige, resources, cash and privilege in the society. The victory has been so complete that it is hard now to stand back a little way, to return science itself to the everyday battle of men and women to make sense of their experience, and to devise theories to select portions of life-in-earnest which will yield that kind of sense. In the past twenty years, the effort to show how even clinical and objective science has had its merely social distortions was initiated by Thomas Kuhn's famously subversive essay, and John Ziman's books[7] have continued that good work. At the same time, some of the most daring and original of mathematical theorems, notably Gödel's, have proved the limits of proof itself, and shaken the once secure and incontestably impersonal nature of numbers.[8]

In spite of this sapping of the underground of sciences, however, science defined as the successful wringing of objective knowledge from natural reality, and scientific method as the only true and reliable guide in inquiry still rule the national and international curriculum. For a long time, the human sciences struggled to gain the authority of the natural sciences by borrowing their methods, and history, psychology, sociology each conscripted their members into the ranks of the hunters and gatherers of numbers. There were, as will emerge from the next chapter, both good and bad reasons for this, but either way the tribute money and rates of interest were paid to the natural sciences.

There was always, from the inception of scientific method, another theory of knowledge and knowing,[9] one which, in specific opposition to the natural scientists, stressed the personal, intuitive, non-mensurable and non-provable actualities of knowledge. This other form of knowledge is the product of our human inter-subjectivity, with its forms of discourse and discursiveness, its unreasoned wrangles and chanciness, its gradual and experiential testing of circumstances until the results can be thought of as knowable; above all, such seeking to know goes on its humanly critical, self-reflexive, purposeful and intentional way about the world not in the name of knowledge for its own sake, but on urgent, voluntary errands, during which the knowledge is required to answer moral questions. Obviously, on one side, such knowledge is not rigidly distinct from the knowledge gained by the natural sciences ('hard v. soft sciences'); obviously, on the other, such knowledge carried a sometimes sinking fund of folklore, superstition, commonsense but nonsense, invalid saws and proverbs, mystification and jargon. Indeed it is exactly the business of the second science, in its various disciplinary, symbolic and productive forms, to chasten the folklore as well as to remind natural science that it, too, has its ordinary human ballast, to say nothing of its human crew, as liable as non-scientists to envy, greed, sloth, hatred and mendacity.

By this stage, without collapsing the knowledge yielded by physicalist method into the knowledge created by the reflexive (or human) sciences, it seems reasonable to point to strong affinities between both, and both as emerging from (being, in a rough sense, made out of) the stuff of a common history and customary ways of life. And indeed, while this book advances a tolerantly naturalist doctrine of knowledge (which is to say, it argues for a close enough correspondence between our symbol systems, including ordinary language, and a natural reality at once 'out there' and inside each of us, here), the use of such phrases as those which refer to knowledge being 'made out of something' and as being 'created' bring out, as a philosophic beginning, the significance of naming knowledge as some kind of social product. If it is such a product – and as chapter 8 insists, the production of knowledge, and then of 'work' as distinct from knowledge, is a main point of what is well called the education *system* – then knowledge, whether gained by the individual or by the society, is more a product like a work of art than a product Taylorized for the assembly line.[10]

The analogy is with the process of inquiry in, say, a painting, whereby the unenvisageable end – the finished picture whose finish can only be known when arrived at (and plenty of painters could never bring themselves to a finish, or put the picture away unfinished, because they couldn't find the end they were looking for) – constitutes a *discovery* when it is done. The artist knows something he didn't know before (and the discovery – the answer to his unspoken question – would probably have to remain tacit).

The knowledge, which is there somewhere in the symbol *and* the materials, the marks of paint and the grain of the canvas, may be of how to achieve a certain effect with the paint, or it may be that the world from which he took his picture really is as the picture is. In Cezanne's case, for example, Provence is in fact composed of those harsh, divided planes of umber stone. Either way, his way of working is a way of knowing, and what he has made, he knows.

A curriculum, however, is more than a map of knowledge; the two nouns are not interchangeable. I have spoken with deliberate looseness here of 'forms of knowledge' as if there were only the two, those as conventionally assigned to the natural and to the human sciences, 'Sciences' and 'Arts'. But in the larger divisions of the curriculum, the purported attributes of either scheme of knowledge, either in its methods of production or in the products themselves, are gathered into realms of meaning[11] which, according to the divisions of intellectual labour in the society, define key forms of consciousness, of social relationship, and ultimately of power itself.

A curriculum is no doubt, although only to begin with, the official register of a society's knowledge. But it is also dynamic. The word 'culture' is asked to bear very many meanings these days, and it will hardly emerge from this book any less heavy-laden, but if we take some such non-contentious definition (always hard to come by) of culture as the making (or production) and remaking of a society's values, meanings and symbols, together with the transformation of these as they circulate through different groups and different times, then the force of the adjective 'dynamic' may come through a little. For in the context in which I have presented the civil and incivil struggle for meanings and values, culture cannot merely repeat itself, any more than history can. A curriculum is embedded in a culture, and that culture reproduces and transforms itself such that to speak of its knowledge without asking what purposes and intentions that knowledge serves, or what questions the knowledge constituted answers to, is to speak meaninglessly. A curriculum is not just a matter of what someone is supposed to know, but also what they are supposed to do with it; it is, therefore, an *intentional* structure, at least in its origins, while at the same time its rates of change, its discarding processes, have their own erratic rhythms, and many even of its most prominent knowledge blocks may no longer be adequate to present purposes, and have strictly residual and traditional meaning and significance.

But there again, 'residual' and 'traditional' are not swear-words for the devoutly iconoclastic liberal to pounce upon and hold up to the bright enlightenment of derision. In the name of both an imaginable and a liveable continuity, any curriculum will house traditional materials and make space for residual activities whose most important meaning is just that: that they recognize the necessity of connection with a visible and audible past for its own sake, and the sake of a present which is perpetually becoming a past.

Such an argument[12] is, in all senses of the adjective, conservative. But the carefully polemical socialism of this book requires that conservatism to be taken seriously, in part as the voice of the enemy, an enemy who has been winning the day and doing the ruling for so long he *has* to be taken seriously. In part, however much socialism commits itself to a new start, you can't start from nowhere, least of all in a country whose condition of old age, decline, decay, traditionalism, immobility, and all the rest, are what you have to work with. Innovation theory as presently spoken is, then, a peculiarly inapplicable game, fun in its own way, but perfectly inconsequential.

So tradition and its cognates, custom, ceremony, habituality, accord, authority, ritual, worth, even value itself, are formal elements of being without which any social order would hardly be thinkable, and from which the new version of the good life, which socialism so variously claims to make possible, must make its selection. The battle restarts when the content of these forms becomes contended. For the argument of this chapter has been that the theories and principles of the hard and soft sciences, though importantly different in actual practice, alike emerge from the vivid actuality of human interests,[13] as these shape and are shaped by the immediacy of both nature in the raw and culture as cooked up by men. The argument has further been that our knowledge, although organized and allocated according to these interests and their categories, can only be understood and *used* in relation to exceedingly contingent and historically relative purposes, intentions, misconceptions and versions of the self. And we may furthermore claim that a curriculum just *is* this network of purposes, and far more than a map of knowledge, however much the cartographer of the curriculum must start from that.[14]

In other words, by implying a view of what to do with knowledge, the curriculum, like the culture, implies a picture of how to live and who to be; even in liberal society, it adumbrates the passages of the good life, in private and in public (and how the two are divided), and it proposes a structure of the self in relation to this praxis. Quite without any too large a dose of irony at its expense, since its strictly political and civic gains, however unevenly allocated, have been incontestably magnificent, liberalism may be indemnified as not knowing what to do about the good life. For if we pause for a definition of liberalism, it is its main, negative premiss that you must not tell other people how to live or what to believe, except in so far as they must learn not to infringe the liberty of others in such a way that the free development of each is at the individual's unfettered choice, and within a clear space he or she can call their own. Hence the primacy given by liberalism to the act of choice, the action which most defines the doctrine, and hence also the central place assigned to the individual as at once the realm (or domain) and the fount (or endlessly self-renewing origin) of value and meaning.[15] Liberalism, accordingly, has difficulties with the good life, since every individual chooses and creates the terms of that life personally. What tends to happen is that the immortal and invisible social structures, to which liberalism is bound by its premisses to deny determinate force, take over and shape visions of the good life willy-nilly. The honest liberal must, then, believe (the dishonest one need only pretend) that he freely chose the Habitat kitchens and Maples sitting rooms, the Volvo estate car and the Provençal holiday villa, together with the conscience-stricken opinions and *Guardian* morality, and not that they were given by the systems and relations of production, privilege and wealth in (as the phrase goes) late consumer capitalism.

This way of life, or, as we with suicidal accuracy say, this life-style, derives directly enough from the curriculum, as from the culture. The values it carries lead to the department store. But perhaps that line will be more fully drawn in at a later stage. For now, it will be clearer to list in two columns the terms which, betokening as they do the values, meanings, practices and principles which are conventionally, even popularly, held to organize and typify the soft and hard sciences, help to explain in this simplified form how social identity (of individuals and classes), subject or discipline membership, and the divisions of labour themselves, take the essence and substance they do.

SOFT KNOWLEDGE	HARD KNOWLEDGE
subjective	objective
evaluative	factual
intuitive	calculable
personal	public
imaginative	rational
emotional	cognitive
warm	cool
of the heart	of the head
artistic	scientific
indisputable	provable
feminine	masculine
moral	political

It is important not to be misunderstood. The prior argument has at least suggested the mistakes inherent in such a dichotomy; more to the immediate point, these are very broad designations of meaning, value and so forth which can only operate in the form of disembodied lists. As soon as one gets down to detail, plenty of people might be ready to acknowledge the imaginative quotient in physics, the cognitive core of philosophy, the moral necessity of politics. All the same, the roughness and readiness of everyday thought and action is what people live with; what they mean by science and the scientist is expected to look sufficiently like the right-hand column in its white-coated or laboratory actuality, just as the mere fact that the ratio of women to men in British university humanities departments[16] is 4.5:1 may serve to vindicate the claim that the left-hand column is widely believed to describe womanly knowing.

Either way, perhaps such a pair of lists will do to foreshadow the power of structures in everyday life to shape all our thoughts, and therefore to shape our very selves. Such structures may be ontic, which is to say they may be made out of all we think is the stuff of ultimate reality; they may be social, which is to say they are alterable as long as you don't forget how very permanent social institutions have a habit of being; they may be epistemological, in which case they are the deep orderers of all we think knowledge truly is. In all cases, however, they will be historical, and because this chapter is so much one of Hegel's numberless progeny, it is relevant to invoke his name again as the recalcitrant theorist of the curriculum and its culture as only discussable from the restless and precarious planes of history, old and new.

History is a cue for a new song, or at least for a descant on the tune of a personal knowledge. This is because the lessons one learns, in the doughty old phrase, from experience, become one's personal knowledge, but that knowledge looks out for confirmation from the same process in others, and in finding it, becomes less personal. Somewhere in these progresses, people have habitually distinguished between the learned, ineffectual clown, a joke figure all the way from *Love's Labours Lost* to Mr Casaubon in *Middlemarch*, and the man whose educatedness has been won from his successful insistence on finding the books that could, in turn, be made to order and make sense of his life.

That encounter – between known experience and an unknown book – is the heart of education, the moment at which you become the book. Such absorption is more than just being, as we say, lost in the story. It comes, presumably, from some deep recognition that what is said in the book comprehends (in the sense of en-folds) a movement of our own, but out of our own life towards some enclosure of the mind and heart which will satisfy them. In childhood, a single story can do this for us: we occupy the world of Swallows and Amazons or of the Chalet School[17] with a completeness and complicity which fulfil the promise of happiness such stories hold out. In adult life, the same absorption and the recognition it is token of may bring with it an excitement that is like terror, the consequence of seeing both the order and disorder made possible by a new understanding of a continuing life, one's own, one's wife's, one's children's, one's people's. Chaos threatens, because to relinquish old explanations and intellectual frameworks is to endanger identity; if you make a new past to replace present history, you might find no room for the person you think you were. Another order beckons at the same time with its invitation to a world made different, more beautiful perhaps, more intelligible perhaps, and one in which you and she and they will have greater power and freedom and wisdom, because you all know more.

A curriculum is not a moment, nor even a sequence of moments such as the one I have described. But unless a curriculum ensures such moments, then the individual, the class or the nation will alike remain ill-educated. Such a failure, whose results in terms of ruined lives and ways of life lie all about us, is not narrowly a matter of knowing too little. Neither is it a matter of self-congratulation on the part of those who are generally regarded as being well-educated at the expense of those who are not. The ignorance and stupidity which are the inevitable markers of an uneducated people are flagrantly visible amongst our oligarchies, as they are amongst the official custodians of education, in and out of universitites. One way of identifying what is wrong is to say that there is a rupture torn between knowledge and thought, so that we do not know how to use the knowledge we have in order to make the world a better place. Or as we might say instead, we cannot think with what we know in order to identify the ignorance which cripples us.

It is a premiss of this book that the social order of the developed capitalist nations is on the hinge of an epoch, that its forms and relations of production (in a phrase) are impelled towards great and submarine changes, one awful sign of which is the present busy preparation for nuclear war.[18] What this epochal movement may mean for the everyday business of learning and earning a living (or being paid to do nothing) is, certainly, my theme, but it would be an act of vertiginous megalomania to dive into an argument to find the right relation of thought to knowledge, and of both to action (let alone belief). Such have been the subject-matters of the greatest philosophers of this century: Dewey, Heidegger, Wittgenstein;[19] Merleau-Ponty, Lukacs, Adorno, Collingwood. It makes more modest sense to sit in the company of one or two men who had to make a curriculum to fit their lives (and vice versa); who battled to think in ways which the received books could not match; and whose determination to find ways of thought which would truly and truthfully order what they knew and what they wanted to know drove them to make an education for themselves well away from the main roads of the subjects whose bland powers of assimilation posthumously reclaimed them.

It is important that such reports come in the form of autobiography. Autobiography comes, as we might say, naturally, as the form in which to think out singular problems – it is sharply to the point to add that it is supremely the natural form for men and women whose education drastically failed to fit their needs and wants and interests, because their class or their race had no allotted identity in the present schemes of official education. Martin Heidegger set himself the task as a philosopher, one of the greatest as well as one of the wildest of the century, of posing the deepest metaphysical questions – about being and time, identity and presence – and proposing the modes of their answers, in a much homelier, speakable, but also corrugated and more physical idiom than that of usual philosophy. We might say, he tried to think and feel right through his body.

Such an enterprise was bound at times to lead to crankiness. But it is exactly this attempt to cancel conformities of mind, being and physique which I am hunting for as one of several versions of the story-guide, How to Get Educated. Heidegger wrote:

> From the perspective of Hegel and Husserl – and not only from their perspective – the matter of philosophy is subjectivity. It is not the matter as such that is controversial for the call, but rather its presentation by which the matter itself becomes present. Hegel's speculative dialectic is the movement in which the matter as such comes to itself, comes to its own presence (*Präsenz*). Husserl's method is supposed to bring the matter of philosophy to its ultimately originary givenness, that means to its own presence (*Präsenz*).[20]

Unfamiliar readers of Heidegger have to allow some room for the queerness[21] of a vocabulary trying to break up the relations imposed by everyday terms upon everyday things. He is trying to change the rules and conventions of the discourse, to give us not only something different to think about, but also a different way of doing the thinking (Kant and Hegel did no less, of course). Reading such philosophy is a business not only of attending to the argument, but also of living its special strenuousness, physically as it were, and hence the importance of intellectual autobiographies, as I hope to show. Heidegger, therefore, is not easy to quote from briefly, because he is trying to render what it is like to think and feel these thoughts. He goes on:

But what remains unthought in the matter of philosophy as well as in its method? Speculative dialectic is a mode in which the matter of philosophy comes to appear of itself and for itself, and thus becomes present (*Gegenwart*). Such appearance necessarily occurs in some light. Only by virtue of light, i.e., through brightness, can what shines show itself, that is, radiate. But brightness in its turn rests upon something open, something free, which might illuminate it here and there, now and then. Brightness plays in the open and wars there with darkness. Wherever a present being encounters another present being or even only lingers near it – but also where, as with Hegel, one being mirrors itself in another speculatively – there openness already rules, the free region is in play. Only this openness grants to the movement of speculative thinking the passage through what it thinks.

We call this openness that grants a possible letting-appear and show 'opening'. In the history of language the German word *Lichtung* is a translation derived from the French *clairière*. It is formed in accordance with the older words *Waldung* (foresting) and *Feldung* (fielding).

The forest clearing (or opening) is experienced in contrast to dense forest, called *Dickung* in our older language. The substantive *Lichtung* goes back to the verb *Lichten*. The adjective *licht* is the same word as 'open'. To open something means to make it light, free and open, e.g., to make the forest free of trees at one place. The free space thus originating is the clearing. What is light in the sense of being free and open has nothing in common with the adjective 'light' which means 'bright', neither linguistically nor factually. This is to be observed for the difference between openness and light. Still, it is possible that a factual relation between the two exists. Light can stream into the clearing, into its openness, and let brightness play with darkness in it. But light never first creates openness. Rather, light presupposes openness. However, the clearing, the open region, is not only free for brightness and darkness but also for resonance and echo, for sound and the diminishing of sound. The clearing is the open region for everything that becomes present and absent.[22]

Heidegger was the child of a carpenter, and was brought up in the Black Forest. Thinking through such images as this of the clearing characterizes a thinker not simply in search of good analogies to illustrate an argument, but in search and research for identities in experience which embody less an argument than a way of living in the world. His philosophy, now called existentialism, belongs here not because I want Heidegger to win the day against an imaginary philosophic opponent, but because he so strenuously introduces the way each of us really thinks, feels, moves and *is*, when we address ourselves with the proper seriousness and commitment to questions which demand ultimate answers – questions, in Tolstoy's phrase, of 'the mightily important . . . men's relation to God, to the universe, to all that is infinite and unending'. It is these questions, and whatever answers we make shift with, which come up bluntly and obstructively when the forms of our official education and its curriculum do not fit the way an individual wants to think about his or her experience. Since it is another presupposition of this book that our present forms of thought drastically do not match our present experience, the important points for immediate study are those at which we find somebody sorting the disjuncture between what he wanted to think and how he was taught. Such a man, then, if he was determined and intelligent enough, built himself a structure of ideas and a method capable of handling the experience and joining the split between material and idea, or between what was past, or passing, and to come.

Such people, if we start in the academies, typically do not fit the received frames of subjects and disciplines. The great Oxford philosopher of between the wars, R.G. Collingwood, spent his life – and as he says, his thought *was* his life – wrestling his way out of what he found to be a deep unsatisfactoriness of prevalent evasiveness about ultimate questions, towards an adequate method for grounding what he called 'a science of human affairs'. The need for such a science was obvious to anybody who had seen as he had, from the laughably-named Intelligence section of the Admiralty, the pointless destruction of eight million young men and women in a few hundred square miles of France, Italy and Turkey, caused exactly by the presence of nescience, and who had gone on as a junior official at the Foreign Office to watch the triumphs of idiocy at the Versailles peace settlements of 1919.

Collingwood wanted to found an inclusive discipline which would make possible a structural investigation into the relationship between theory and practice. It may sound an impossibly large-minded and abstract way to put it, but I insist that some such purpose is at the heart of all education. That it is indeed general as a human enterprise is the message of this short excursus on autobiography.

For Collingwood summarized his life's thought in *An Autobiography*,[23] when, in a four-month convalescence after a sadly early stroke at the age of 49, he wrote a compressed, genial and brilliant revision of his ideas, in case he had no time left to write more. The form of an autobiography was pressingly apposite at such a moment: his own mortality must have been his uppermost thought in writing, and at the same time his isolation among his peers, his refusal of their way of talking, made some such polemical statement of his method and its necessary shaping of his morality and metaphysics, spontaneous, vivid, indeed 'auto-matic'.

Collingwood made his curriculum from the moral luck[24] and momentum of a life happy and successful, at least until its abrupt foreshortening and his last three years of fatal illness. His father was Ruskin's secretary and an accomplished painter; the early education provided for this dazzlingly precocious child was made up out of his own curiosity and his father's considerable efforts to teach him. When he later came to discard the routine tours of the text which passed for the history of ideas, and the pious refusal to answer urgent questions about how to live on the part of realist philosophy, he found in the paintings stacked against his father's walls a model of a method. The paintings were answers to questions which the painter put to himself, or which his experience (life, if you like) put to the painter. Some of the answers were unsatisfactory, or seemed to be becoming so, and therefore the painter left them unfinished. Some 'worked', and therefore were finished.

Collingwood thought again. He was an immensely gifted man — philospher, historian, painter, pianist, archaeologist, administrator, ocean-going yachtsman.[25] While on archaeological digs for Roman remains in his native Cumbria and Northumberland, he reasoned that on a dig nobody was 'just digging'. He himself had questions to put, first, to the patch of turf; next, to the bits and pieces he dug up; finally, to the ground plan he discovered. At each stage, Collingwood concluded, he was following a 'logic of question-and-answer', and each question sought to recover the intentions and purposes to which the artefact in front of him constituted the answer of those long-dead historical figures whose life, in terms of these objects to hand, the archaeologist sought to recover. But the method (the re-search) didn't stop there. The archaeologist, and the historian or philosopher – the reader of Plato or Shakespeare (or the Dead Sea Scrolls or the ciphers of an enemy military or the scrawled anonymities of a banned trade union in the 1830s) – was working to recover past thoughts and actions from their 'traces' in order to achieve a historical knowledge which would be 'the re-enactment of a past thought encapsulated in a context of present thoughts which, by contradicting it, confine it to a plane different from theirs'.[26]

The point is not merely to make the past live again in your present life, and the present lives of others, for it will do that anyway. It is to find a way of turning that past into practical knowledge, which you can use to lay hold of the present. That present, as his stirring last chapter tells us, will, as it passes, be represented by the gangsters, liars and hypocrites who are running it as if they were acting in the clear light of truth and reason, unless better men and women capture for themselves the historical knowledge that will give the lie to the falsehoods which disguise the cruelty and callousness of the time.

Collingwood ends his great, brief book with these words: 'I know that all my life I have been engaged unawares in a political struggle, fighting against these things in the dark. Henceforth I shall fight in the daylight.' An autobiography is the obvious place for a thinker to fight for his life, and Collingwood's is the best first advertisement for such a fight. Let his be the first account of what it is to make our own life and experience, and that includes as full a knowledge as may be won of all the other lives and experiences which are contained by our own, into our curriculum.

Collingwood is no doubt a bookish example with which to begin. Well, education comes from books all right. But he is exemplary in entirely accessible ways, which do not turn on his reading Kant at the age of 8 or becoming a great philosopher. He does all that, in the name of our education, we all should strive to do, what a teacher or a parent intends to show his or her children they should do. He makes his life as told in the autobiography into a work of art. The work of art then provides at once a way of thinking about his life and of fully representing it. Our education, as told in our autobiography, becomes a narrative – inevitably a work in a sort of fiction ('true' enough, but given an always retrospective structure), with characters taken from many parts of one's life, some of them fictional anyway. Think how a child makes its changing, constantly edited autobiography out of Mum, Dad, Dr Who, the Famous Five, the dog, an invisible friend, Dennis the Menace, the gang, the school caretaker, the Trumpton fire-brigade. In the best autobiographies, as in the best works of art, the central consciousness and the central attention are on how to make a life you can be proud of out of the fragments of history which you can win some command over. This is the lived question and its answer, the dramatization and an inward finding and realization of values through this extrinsic and historical medium.

Everyone has a history. That is why History with a capital H is made so much of in these pages. For the subject History purports to tell people's own stories, and the story of the people. But then each of us has to decide whether that story as told about us is true; whether our story can ever be told at all.

In another great *Autobiography*, the Scottish poet Edwin Muir writes:

> It is clear that no autobiography can begin with a man's birth, that we extend far beyond any boundary line which we can set for ourselves in the past or the future, and that the life of every man is an endlessly repeated performance of the life of man. It is clear for the same reason that no autobiography can confine itself to conscious life, and that sleep, in which we pass a third of our existence, is a mode of experience, and our dreams a part of reality. In themselves our conscious lives may not be particularly interesting. But what we are not and can never be, our fable, seems to me inconceivably interesting. I should like to write that fable, but I cannot even live it; and all I could do if I related the outward course of my life would be to show how I have deviated from it; though even that is impossible, since I do not know the fable or anybody who knows it. One or two stages in it I can recognize: the age of innocence and the Fall and all the dramatic consequences

which issue from the Fall. But these lie behind experience, not on its surface; they are not historical events; they are stages in the fable.[27]

Muir arranges the story of his life in three blocks. In the first, utterly formative stage, he is a child on his parents' rented smallholding in the Orkneys, and what this gave to him, as the quotation implies, was direct experience of the pure, innocent life in the Garden of Eden. 'That world', Muir recalls, 'was a perfectly solid world, for the days did not undermine it but merely rounded it, or rather repeated it as if there were only one day endlessly rising and setting.' In this Eden, held within the boundless freedom of his parents' free kingdom, Muir comes closest to living the fable of his and all men's and women's lives. The space of that great happiness almost fills and is congruent with the huge blue heaven of the fable assigned not merely to childhood, but to the human potentiality for freedom and fulfilment. From that early life, Muir takes the pure and mighty emblems of a traditional rural order, ideally unimpaired by brutality, poverty, degradation – stone and water, tree and leaf, roof and hearth – and uses these throughout the splendid picturesqueness of his poetry to prefigure the unnameable fable which every person seeks to embody, but can only find in a contingent history of wizened and misshapen outlines.

In the second stage of his life, after the age of 13 or so, when the family were driven out of their living in the Orkneys, Muir experiences not only the Fall, but the descent into Hell. Like thousands of families before them in the history of industrial capitalism, poverty drove them from the land to the more horrible privations of the city: dirt, disease, friendlessness, homelessness. His parents die. Two brothers die. Muir himself is ill and undernourished, making an education out of his tiny clerkly wage, the socialism then spreading with such justified-looking heat and fleetness through Glasgow and all the other cities of the industrial north, and the books read in a grim office or grimmer, bleaker bedroom, which registered this widespread, dreadful plight. Yet he confesses in the *Autobiography*, he could find no form nor metaphor for these lonely and pitiless years. They are a time he wishes simply he could cancel from his life, and there is nothing he can do to find in them a necessary meaning or to situate them in the narrative of his life such that he can perhaps make a virtue of their necessity.[28]

He cannot take subsequent condolence from T.S. Eliot:

We had the experience but missed the meaning.
And approach to the meaning restores the experience
In a different form . . .

Those years had no meaning, and he can give them no form. So the venture of the *Autobiography* fails in its purpose across the 'Glasgow' section. The best he can do is to recognize the stony barrenness in as truthful and bare a way as possible.

Restoration is achieved in the 'Prague' section, for here Muir brings together his successful emergence from his long, twilit depression by means of psychoanalysis, the happiness of his marriage to Willa Muir, his growing mastery as a poet, his love of a noble city, and his pioneering work with Willa in translating Kafka into English for the first time: Kafka whose deadpan and stoical rendering of insane state bureaucracies gave Muir a way of placing the hideous no-meaning of modern politics against the fable of an ideal city and its morally excellent polity, and therefore of understanding how Prague and the Czechs were again betrayed in the vicious history of 1948.

It is the claim of this chapter that everybody compiles an autobiography as they go, whether they write it down or not, and that it is the readiest, most common and most intelligible way in which to tie a knot between those large, counterposed abstractions, history and biography, thought and learning, knowledge and experience. This is most obviously true if we end by turning to the autobiographies of those who, recognizing that their experience was indeed, in Eliot's phrase, 'not the experience of one life only But of many generations', none the less could only tell their own story as they saw it (in the common phrase) and hope that others could recognize their lives there too.

These are the kind of men and women whose history had never been written down, either because they couldn't write, or because they'd been told the story was worthless. We hear them now, in the writings of those women who speak up for a view of the world, and of intellectual life within the world, which has been more or less ruthlessly excluded by the men who make and wield the power of that world. It is striking that, according to the divisions of labour and of value that I listed earlier, so many of these women have found their own voice by way of doing the different voices of university courses in English literature. Autobiography and novels were the natural forms for this class to take up, and a shelf of books under the admirable Virago imprint – including, say, Storm Jameson's *Journey from the North*, Vera Brittain's *The Testament of Youth*, and Naomi Mitchison's *You May Well Ask*[29] would, in the sound image, bear witness to the way in which these strong-willed brave women bent themselves and their books until they grew more or less together. And by the same token, the same is true of such an autobiography as Ezekiel Mphahlele's *Down Second Avenue*,[30] where the deprived, intelligent, solitary black South African reads and writes his way to the freedom of exile in an American univeristy.

These are, so to speak, the autochthonous, or born from the earth beginnings of writers on behalf of a speechless class. The voice is piercingly audible in the moving series of English working-class autobiographies which came out of the Reform, Chartist and trade union movements of the years 1830–70. Samuel Bamford, perhaps the most famous of these, friend of the agitator Hunt, reporter of Peterloo from under the scabbards of the cavalry, author of *Passages in the Life of a Radical* (1844) says of his own efforts:

> We had not any of our own rank with whom to advise for the better – nor many of other days who had gone through the ordeal of experience; and whose judgement might have directed our self-devotion.

That is to say, as (in E.P. Thompson's title) the making of the English working class was accomplished between 1790 and 1830, its leaders had to write a new history, create the forms of unprecedented political organization, and invent class traditions from a bookless and largely speechless past and present. This is how and why experience becomes theorized into knowledge, how in this case history becomes institutionalized, how it creates and holds a membership and thereby establishes a community of learning.

All Bamford himself could do was write an autobiography, and hope that it made sense. His narrative brings out clearly how hard membership was to come by for men used to the close, known community of friends who had grown up together in one place, who had then to organize associations of complete strangers in the fearful, bustling anonymity of the new industrial cities.[31] Similarly, Alexander Somerville, in his *The Autobiography of a Working Man*[32] had no theory of class or expectation to draw upon when he describes the poverty that drove him to become a soldier, nor could he name the nature of the system which set out to destroy him, when he and a group of other young soldiers published an anonymous letter advising both the Chartists and their foes in the established order that they as soldiers would not interfere with the demonstrations as long as they were peaceable. The army framed Somerville on a trumpery charge to do with a riding offence in his cavalry regiment, and he was sentenced to two hundred lashes.

It was, literally, a killing sentence, although he was cut down after half had been carried out, in case he died. The point here is that the whole frightful incident is very minutely described, the details of his being tied up, the wiping of blood and flesh from the thongs of the lash, all without any reflection on what it meant or who was responsible for such hideous cruelty and injustice. There being no theory, nor even a known community of listeners, Somerville wisely leaves the facts of the matter for the composition of later historians.

Autobiography therefore is the first foundation of identity. As personal identity[33] grows, and, let us say, becomes educated, it discovers extrinsic or even objective instruments and media of thought which permit it to reflect upon itself. The stories of art and of history are the first and last of these, as I have said. At the same time, these reflecting agents gather their own identity, so that reflection is (obviously) reciprocal. It is in these ways that objects of study become subjects, and we in our divisions of educational labour and value become subject to those identities even when, perhaps most of all when, we are students like so many who dislike, reject and do not comprehend the subject themselves.

4

Identity in Selves and Subjects

It is plain that in writing of education and the curriculum, which is its subject and object, we have to have some pictures of those who undergo that education. If it is true, as I claim, that the curriculum not merely implies, but actually teaches some versions of how to live a good life, then it follows that it, in turn, has subjects who are logically capable of living those variously good lives. There is, in other words, a necessary connection predicated and sought between what a society teaches its children and how it wishes those children to be: truth becomes truistic.

All the same, the formal connections between knowledge and learning, culture and action, are worth insisting upon at a time when many teachers will make a butcher's severance in the curriculum between who people are and what they can do. The blunt axeman of the staffroom can be counted on to dismiss considerations of the self in the philistine name of making sure that students get the skills which they may be able to turn to a living. His more sensitive colleague in pastoral care may shrink a little at his outspoken instrumentality, but she will largely connive at the distinction by treating the troublesome child from the fourth year as an individual whose selfhood and identity are not to be violated by any gross irruption from a more powerful being (the correct principle of liberalism), but more importantly an individual whose self is not a function of what he or she knows and can do, whose identity is uninflected by knowledge or learning. Either teacher might agree that a pupil may gain satisfaction from their instrumental skills — being able to reassemble an internal combustion engine, say — or may gain what is called self-confidence from some official act of teacherly recognition — the publication in a magazine of a piece of writing, perhaps. But the notion of identity, largely an unproblematic one in ordinary reference, is kept distinct from a repertory of skills and competences, and in the curriculum itself, the domain of instrumental skills – the practical, needful world – is kept distinct from the expressive life of a person, whose self and its values finds its voice and images in the strictly impractical world of symbolism.

There are deep confusions and incoherences here, and while it may be not only human but necessary to abide with muddle, or to keep apart both in the soul and in the society mutually incoherent frames of mind, the uses to which such master symbols of the society as 'identity', 'self', 'individuality', 'person', 'role' and 'character' are put in relation to the curriculum are often so radically self-deceiving that the results wound just those people such symbols are called upon to help, to liberate indeed, and enter into their own country. Our picture of who these human beings really are (let alone who we as teachers really are) is compounded of versions of all these concepts of individuality (including individuality itself), and it is only by sorting out a little of their entanglement in the first place that we can go on to say something about what knowledge and its modalitites can do to you, what difference it makes to you if you are learned or ignorant, as well as what it can do *for* you.

Identity is often seen to be in a critical state: 'crisis of identity' is the off-the-peg diagnosis of many a breakdown in the novel and in the psychiatric ward. But behind the diagnosis, whether sympathetic or offhand, is the large cultural assumption that the discovery, choice and affirmation of one's identity is a – if not *the* – key to a successful life. To generalize rather flatly in everyday language, that identity is thought of as something in me which, existing now, is identical with that something in a future me.[1] It is that something which is the test of survival after some drastic event has supervened – a severe accident, say, or going to prison for years – and which, being identical with a present something in me, *is* who and what I am, even if I were to have had a very different life.

Without launching into any very technical analysis, perhaps it will do to run quickly through the terms we habitually use to designate the agents of our individuality, in order to suggest the complexity and historical changefulness of this figure, together with the extreme difficulty of attaching much substance to this identity which is so truly you or me. As far as this chapter goes, it will be better to plump for a less solid picture of identity made up of our 'mental continuity and connectedness' (Parfit's motto[2]), in which what really matters in these terms is the holding of relations between an experience and our memory of that experience, between an action now and the intention to perform some later dependent action, between embodiments of present characteristic and later embodiment of developments of that characteristic, all this as well as these relations themselves being held in a continuous overlapping chain of many such relations.

Such a view doesn't make identity as a concept quite as loose and arbitrary as at first sight appears. Each of the many relations which compose the chain of continuity has its strong historical presence in our view of what we can be, and each, it had better be said, is assigned a particular path among the many routes of the curriculum, to be trained and cultivated accordingly. Thus, the concept of character[3] rests upon the givenness of the characters concerned. They simply are their powers and dispositions, largely in attachment to the adjective 'strong'. A strong character is someone who exhibits those characteristics in all circumstances; he is predictable and reliable, rather than subject to change or self-effacing. The term shades into indulgent derogation when we speak of someone 'being a character'; this someone exhibits, it is implied, an almost wilful insistence upon living out his characteristics. None the less, this usage also brings out the fixity and certainty of character; the nature of a character, even one with deplorable characteristics like Prince Hal or Falstaff or Grandfather Smallweed or Harold Skimpole, forms the structure of his experiences, rather than is formed by them.

Such characteristics are not of course individual; identity is hardly a word to use here. The distinct character which Arthur Lowe made of Captain Mainwaring in the television series, *Dad's Army*, turned upon the precise rendering of very general traits – a calm, complacent stupidity; a clipped, unselfconscious rudeness; a splendid and pompous incompetence – all externally exhibited, and wonderfully funny in virtue of their predictability as well as their awfulness. A character gives you little sense of what it is like to be himself; he can shed little light on himself, as witness that strong character Soldier George in *Bleak House*, who confesses to being as puzzled by and resigned to himself as his iron-willed mother is. What the character is, is powerfully present: as miser, as crook, as good tough guy, as leader, as lover.

We can gingerly venture the view that character at the present time is less preferred than 'person' or individual. The strong character looked for by the grammar-school headmaster as his head of prefects has faded a little in historical importance (though the pastoral counsellor will still speak as to the delinquent's character in the juvenile court). The head boy and head girl of character have been superannuated in a polity whose class definitions, though still so pervasive, are become abruptly soluble, and whose dominant meanings have been attached to freedom of choice and 'radical personalization',[4] which reject the fixity of the character. Indeed, one way to study the meaning and effects of a theory of (strong) character is to study what happens when one kind of character is overtaken by a social order that has no use for such characteristics: the daring and cunning adventurer when the war is over, the rugged frontiersman in the new business world, the *grande dame* after the revolution. If these people cannot change their characters, they will be destroyed.

In the present forms of our social change, as the modes of production shift acceleratingly away from manufacturing and extraction from nature towards service and consumption, the person takes precedence over the character, although the character retains strong residual life. The person, however, is defined by his or her personal responsibility for action. What she does is less important than that she is recognized as author of the action. To withdraw recognition of that responsibility, or to attempt to delimit it, is to fail to treat her as a person. This comes out clearly in the treatment of individuals or institutions as persons at law. The refusal of full rights or the plea of diminished responsibility (in the differing cases of children, or defectives, or aliens, or anyone else not counted under different judicatures as fully present) reflects and identifies the standing of a person as an issue of human or other *rights*, the exercise of which is both accorded to and assumed by that person as a function of his or her autonomy. Hamlet, for example, is caught on the historical twistpoint at which tribal obligations of revenge for his father's murder, utterly attested by his father's ghost, are contested by quite new demands of answerability to evidence and judgement in the court of law and not of ancient pieties. In this new legal and religious light (the advent of the legal doctrine in its Renaissance forms coincided with Luther's account of the individual's attainment to personal salvation), all men and, very gradually, all women came to stand equal at the bar of judgement. That is what it is to be a person, whether the person be a king's son or a court jester, and in judging persons in the light of their legal and moral responsibility, judgement increasingly turns not upon action (which, as Hamlet's case once more testifies, can go horribly wrong), but upon intention. What did you really mean to do? is the crucial question, and in attending to intentions and motives (a central aspect of legal proof, as the detective story underlines), the focus of moral attention wobbles and dissolves again, because the legally liable person is no longer directly answerable in terms of his role and its duties, but in terms of his personal duty and his moral adequacy. Morality is separated both from jurisprudence and prudence itself. So the person is interrogated for his motives and, beyond this, for who he or she really is, such that this was the choice made, and these the principles or lack of them that explain and justify that choice.

A legal person, then, is defined by his or her rights, and these are made visible by their property (the 'displaced person', as refugees were known after 1945, were stateless and without rights). But as individual human beings in the long transition of Europe and the New World from absolutism to a market and property capitalism came to acquire their rights in virtue of their personal powers, so they became selves. The quality of an individual self is determined by his qualities, as Amelie Rorty puts it: 'they are his capital, to invest well or foolishly'.[5] Their stories are then told in dozens of novels as their achievement in accumulating property and wealth, generally in a contest where victory has been won over those who tried to insist on power as appropriate not to powers, but to lineage and dynasty. The snob is the most easily derided figure in the nineteenth-century novel. Those vibrant selves, Jane Eyre and Heathcliff, make mincemeat of him.

The self, however, is rapacious. As Romanticism let loose a doctrine of self as defined by the irresistible beauties of spontaneity, the old civic virtues could no longer hold it. The self sought passionately for itself in the fulfilment of its own true interests, interests defined as knowable by their 'truth to oneself'. For a self to fail in truth to itself or to be negated is to lose an essential integrity (or, precisely, the integratedness of that same self). Of course, if fulfilment of the self is defined as the possession of inaccessibly distributed goods, there is an unfair fight on for the good life. This is very obvious in education: no use a university degree fulfilling you, if you can't get in or don't do as you're told — the point broken off by the film *Educating Rita*.

The self is in as deep trouble with its metaphysics as with its politics. In so far as the self is fulfilled by the unfettered exploration of its interests and passions, and in so far as it confirms itself by the acquisition of a rich store of possessed experiences with which it is at one, who is it who is organizing these intentions and this mobility of action? Where is its centre, if it is not to be a bundle of caprices? The difficulty is illustrated by Erving Goffmann's famous and subtle book, *The Presentation of Self in Everyday Life*,[6] which dissects the mechanism by which we variously show up and show off in the different roles society provides for us to occupy: customer, client, parent, daughter, plaintiff, lover, citizen, voter, mortgage-owner, and so on. The trouble is that nobody knows who is doing the presenting. The self seems to have no centre.

At this point, we call up the last and still the most rhetorically potent of our moral-educational symbolic figures, the individuals. He and she have appeared before in these pages, of course, and their present significance is largely taken from their alleged conceptual capacity to contain characters, persons and selves in a single nominative. That they cannot do what they claim to do is a discovery only gradually being made, and its consequence for the meanings of the curriculum and of education, indeed for the continuity of the social order, is of as large a significance for us all as anything we have to worry about. However, the largeness of that shadow looms over chapter 10 rather than this one, where what we are looking for is what is real about this individual who is so much appealed to, as both value and fount of values.

For a start, individuals[7] are their own entities, rational, self-sufficient, counterposed to the determinate force of Society with a capital S. The individual, like the person, has rights and duties, not given by law, but by the individual conscience; Kant is its honorary arbitrator, but even he, if the liberal individual were to meet and understand him, would be viewed with one auspicious and one dropping eye, because the imperative of duty which Kant universalizes may be overridden by the free demands which the individual makes of life (a way of putting it which gets round the charge of selfishness).

In trying to free itself from universal imperatives (in the other cant, 'laws are made to be broken'), the individual starts on the search to find absolute uniqueness or originality. His individuality is then a function of his difference from others, his serenely sufficient capacity to live free of others. D.H. Lawrence's hero and heroine in *Women in Love* aspire to this condition, helped on, as Lawrence readily admits, by a small private income, and Lawrence is perhaps the most fervent and profound explorer of the country to which a commitment to one's own flaring and vivid singularity will take you. Dedication to that singular vitality is the criterion for seeing others; and by this intolerable light all the rest of social life – as in Lawrence and as so often in Henry James – is shown up in its socially conformist, hypocritical, lying and self-betraying impurity.

The only answer, then is, to go into exile, and Lawrence, never afraid of following the logic of his beliefs, did just that. But exile is a lonely place, and the individual who, like Ibsen's doll-wife Nora in *The Doll's House*, strikes out for the fiords as the locus of individuality will find it a cold going. The individual is then at the mercy of her own choice, in a world of mad individuals living the consequences of *their* choices, with no means of acknowledging their complicated mutual interdependence nor the necessity of altruism.[8] The individual, seen as *the* realm of meaning, can have no scale for situtating itself in a history, nor a means of restitution for the gross structural inequalities which prevent the realization of individuality for all those individuals on the wrong side of opportunity.

The queasy condition of all these key points of appeal is of direct significance to the subject-matter of the curriculum, whether we take it large or small. The curriculum at large is another name for the officially sanctioned and world-political picture which we produce, circulate and reproduce in our society; it *is* our politics. And when the question of the curriculum is, as they say, an academic one, then its theories or its unexaminedly ready reckoning-up of what a person, a self, or an individual are, are at the heart of its praxis, in the natural as in the human sciences. For natural science is investigated and developed *for* someone; it cannot be purposeless, any more than any human activity can be purposeless. Its proponents cannot work without a theory of interests, and those interests can only be human. The point is even sharper and more penetrative in the human sciences; the very subject of the subjects is the human being,[9] and so are the student and the teacher. Their view of what that subject-matter really is — whether individual, character, or mere porter of the forces of historical evolution — is product and producer of the conduct of inquiry, and no one can escape this as a condition of teaching and studying, whether their fellow-students are in the reception class of the infant school or the reading room of the British Museum.

Furthermore, either form of the sciences has gone forward since the Enlightenment[10] on the view that science is both the doctrine and vehicle of progress, and that the vast project of human emancipation will be brought about under the clear light of its new system of human reason. Even now, when faith in progress has been so badly damaged at Auschwitz, Gulag, Hiroshima, and in uncountable smaller torture-chambers, that project of emancipation is still appealed to in the schools and universities of the rich countries of the world as guaranteeing personal development in the terms of scientific rationalism and educated subjectivity.

There is therefore a direct reflection from our preferred name and notion of a human subject onto the methods of inquiry by which we turn experience into knowledge, and both into values. It is worth extending the implied criticism of the dead-end reached by too enthusiastic a pursuit of selfhood and individuality, by saying that now that progress is faltering as a master-symbol in a world poisoned by its own effluent, bleeding from its own weapons, and deformed by its simultaneous gluttony and starvation, we would do well to return the individual to his and her lived and social history. In classrooms and seminar rooms, of course, there is still much necessary play to make with persons, selves and individuals, if we are to understand anybody else at all, but a useful corrective to the studiously anti-social connotations of 'radical personalization' is to stress again the proper significance of character as a locus of intellectual being, to turn sharply away from a narcissistic preoccupation with the state of self, and strongly towards the development of character traits which might make for a better world. It is so obvious that a more provident and humane economics[11] would make more for a benign world would encourage structures of behaviour in which the character traits of naked piracy became at least mildly recessive.

The connections between character and learning are never

direct, and paradise cannot be introduced by the curriculum. None the less, if the official institutions of education do not think about virtue and reason, and how one may engender the other, no one else will. The sociology of knowledge may be paraphrased as the study of the structural conditions within which knowledge works for or against the good life, just as sociology at large is the study of the social structures of being. Now the structures of knowledge may doubtless be antecedently the product of the way our concepts work upon our percepts in the name of understanding. But necessarily conservative arguments[12] about the logical form and grounds of knowledge still leave an awful lot of room for sociological impositions, and it is these that are too often represented as natural ontology, when what they really are is an unnatural ideology, locally self-serving and self-righteous.

Social structuration produces agency, which in turn produces structures.[13] To put it less propositionally, we make and are made by formal arrangements and dispositions which occupy the frames of our social identity, issue in actions which are our own, though involuntarily mediated by those structures, which same actions constitute subsequent structures for the future actions of ourselves and others.

The most immediate way to study social structure is to find the boundaries of classes of people and things: to understand the principles of classification. In a celebrated book,[14] Mary Douglas, starting from the implicit premiss that all human beings fear the unclassifiable as a danger to identity, studies a series of examples of strongly classified taxonomies, violations of which may in some societies lead to very severe punishment, as in the list of Jewish food prohibitions and permissions given in *Leviticus*. In an endearing example, she cites the case of family friends who, while converting an old and backward house, had made a bathroom out of a ground-floor corridor, to which there were two doors. One door was kept locked, and the other became the official bathroom door, but the bathroom itself was still 'polluted' by impure elements which belonged to the back-of-the-house corridor it had recently been: a gardening mac on the unused door, a pair of heavy wellingtons, assorted garden implements, old shoes and gloves, and so forth. The room was perfectly big enough to take all the clutter, but Douglas recalls that, though herself 'naturally tolerant of disorder', she felt uncomfortable with the bits and pieces which didn't belong there, and the locked door, which might suddenly open upon the privacy – the sanctity, even – of a bathroom. These are tokens familiar to us all. A dirty plate, knife and fork are in place beside the sink, out of place on the bedroom dresser; the unmade bed prevents the bed-sitter becoming a sociable sitting room. Whether simple rules of this kind derive from innate instincts to order (which obviously some people lack) or are culturally learned doesn't matter here. The point is that principles of classification are the same thing as principles of order (dirt is only matter in the wrong place) and may be detected at work wherever society opens or closes its forms and structures.

This can be quite a literal as well as an experiential matter. When shops, factories or schools close for the day, you find the line drawn between work and leisure for the classes of people involved. Where doors are only opened on request or at a summons (private houses, office doors, prisons), you find the regulation of access according to the criteria of privacy or power. So with telephones: the more calls you have to make on the way to speak to somebody, the more powerful they are. The fewer people allowed into a particular place (the bedroom, the shrine, the morgue, the study), the clearer the message about the sanctity of its space. Where combinations of substances or identities are forbidden (girls and boys, white and black, ceremonial and casual), there too are the personality-creating classifications of a society. And where these classifications are flouted, as when men grow long hair or women wear men's clothes, there you find a struggle for different forms of classification, and a reconstruction, sometimes trivial, sometimes important, of the sources, forms, and control of power itself.

Once upon a time, a London East-End working-class Jew brought up a Catholic, having edged his way into the mixed classifications of the still superciliously regarded and 'so-called' (in the Olde English put-down) social sciences of about 1950, found Durkheim as his way of sorting these impossible contradictions, and of recognizing the fact (in his own words) that 'out there it's all ambiguous'. Basil Bernstein, in two volumes of his collected works,[15] has devoted himself to an anthropology of British education along the planes, as he puts it, of its 'classification and framing'. Classification refers simply to the principles by which knowledge is organized into subjects, areas, disciplines, and so forth, just as elsewhere in sociology and anthropology it refers to ways in which openness and closure are socially effected. Framing is Bernstein's instrument with which to analyse the ordering and organizing process of teaching itself, as opposed to what is taught. A teacher frames his classified knowledge by his timing and sequencing of his material, above all by the degrees of freedom allowed to students to interrupt these sequences, displace and reorder them, or the extent to which students may glimpse and move towards quite new and untimetabled fields of study. In either case, classification and framing are strongly coded where the insulation of social relations is heavy and impermeable, where process and order are thought of as difficult to alter, inevitable in their momentum, and immune to idiosyncratic preference. The textbooks, notably in maths and science, of the 1950s, were strongly framed and classified in this way: arithmetic, geometry, algebra; Euclid, Pythagoras, trigonometry; multiplication to the base 10, long multiplication, logarithms. O-level children went solidly through these sequences in the order required by Messrs Hall and Knight and their rivals without any comprehension of how it all worked, but some sufficient address at cranking the mathematical handles and turning out answers which nearly corresponded with the answers at the back of the book.

Bernstein introduces a third articulation of what he calls educational knowledge codes, and this is the ordering system which controls evaluation – or more crudely, examining. The strong evaluation system is inscribed in the three-hour examination paper, with its terse commands and its imperious variations in typeface ('Candidates must . . . four questions only . . . go on to part III . . . write clearly on ONE side of the paper'; 'Failure to comply will result in execution'), which, however unfailingly comic, indicate great confidence in what the examiner–evaluator thinks of the realizable knowledge of the course. Now to 'realize knowledge' means just that: to make the knowledge 'real' in a public form – to answer questions publicly, accessibly and approvably. An essay question or linguistic exercise or scientific experiment is intended straightforwardly to give practice in the subject and to reveal whether the student can do what the teacher wants her to do. Strength of coding is always easiest to see in the evaluation system: just read the examination papers.

Bernstein wrote the first of his papers on curriculum analysis in

1970. Its occasion was the sudden quickening of interest in integrated studies, that is, studies in which classification and framing were radically weakened in the name of the universal dovetailedness of knowledge, and of important advances in learning psychology which, with Piaget's name to hand, asked for pupils to organize the pace and scope of their learning for themselves. Bernstein is often misunderstood as positively recommending the desirability of integrated studies, but his concern is much more to show what is involved, and to connect the upheavals in curriculum development with seismic displacements in all the classification systems of society. In an exceptionally subtle and symmetrical analysis, he identifies the surface forms of integrated study as congruent with those of Durkheim's mechanistic society, in which the principles of solidarity are mutual and equal; but he then points out that this is only made possible by the making of explicit, statable premises and arrangements of the kind necessary in Durkheim's other, organicist society, in which solidarity rests on an interdependence born of the many divisions of labour. The mechanistic society does not need to make things explicit; simple and limited divisions of labour make for implicit systems of order and verbal redundance. Complex divisions of labour, in which the relations of production cause marked differences between producers (not just between, say, engineers and designers, but as between electronic and mechanical engineers), require highly elaborated and verbally explicit systems of order. Paradoxically, integrated studies are of this order.

So far, indeed, from advocating integrated studies, Bernstein points out that a frequent failure in making principles of order explicit and intelligible, or the no less frequent tendency of teachers to devise order merely from a trivial or arbitrary topic ('the breakfast table' on the primary-school display table, or, vaguer yet, but respectable-sounding 'prehistoric man', the 30-million-year jump from dinosaurs, stalwarts of the junior school, to flint axes, all made in a couple of models) leads to bewilderment and disorder in the individual. The child can't make sense of a mess. The deciphering of knowledge from inquiry has no clear procedure. Value is dissolved.

It is at such moments that Bernstein fixes for us the social structures which make or unmake individuals, as persons or as characters. For there is nothing much to comfort those who want to start 7-year-olds off with a rock-tight timetable divided into history, geography, maths, English. Such teachers are endorsing the high insulations of the 'collection code', the consequences of which are hardly less arbitrary than its opposite. By its directives, pupils in England collect their bagful of O levels, a collection whose contents are dictated by no more educational purposes than that those are the subjects which are available in their school, those the ones they seem on a pretty random estimate from trial examination to be sufficiently good at, and those which university boards of examination define as available at O level in these versions.

Beyond O level, the same topography deepens like a coastal shelf. The separation occurs between the academic A level and the technical Higher National Diploma, a division which advertises the worldwide privileging of mental over manual accomplishment. A levels are managed by universities, who are embarrassingly unselfconscious about the mixture of historical chance, redolent snobbery and ideological self-seekingness which is the real structure of their subjects. There are supposed to be 'natural' groupings of A levels — maths, physics, chemistry, for instance, or history, English, French — admission to which is largely won by doing well enough in O level, but membership of and identity in which becomes more and more compelling. It is now that the value-systems I listed in the last chapter lour strong and permanent in their pressure — fact against value, objective against subjective, science against arts — while those who have been successful in getting as far as A level learn to be proper members of their segment of the divisions of labour.

At university, the marks of Cain are those of success. Membership is confirmed by confinement to the language of the discipline, and anomalies are watchfully controlled. In an ingenously flagrant exemplification of Mary Douglas's thesis, certain subjects are even designated 'pure' — pure maths, pure science — as opposed to the social inferiority of 'applied', with its overtones of labour and of manual effort, as in 'applied engineering'. And all through English-speaking universities, in Australasia as well as those of Western Europe, mixed categories, either of a collection kind (Russian and mathematics) or of an integrated and inter-disciplinary sort (cultural history and mass communications) are either hunted down, or exiled to junior institutions like polytechnics and colleges of advanced or higher education. Within these strongly classified institutions, individuals who have been gradually marked out for success by way of A levels and university entrance learn the structures that confirm their membership of a subject and their place within the divisions of labour and of value.

They learn by heart what characterizes a subject as *there* in its own right. It is first a way of marking off educational (or school) knowledge from non-educational, non-school knowledge. This is the most battled-for boundary of all — between what they tell you at school and the customs of the country. In one narrative, the strong classifications of educational knowledge deny to a man or a woman what each thought they knew, hard and real, out of their customary life. As we shall see, such a battle was once fought most callously over language itself — 'You're not going to talk like that here'. But in the other, educational story, knowledge must be somehow objectified, made to stand still in the library or the laboratory, and thereby rendered immune to the variations of transient passions and separate wilfulness. For any science to be a science, it must simplify and rigidify experience to make it studiable.[16]

There are, however, accidents and unevenness in the development of any subject, and the accumulation of its properties and empire are fortuitious and piratical. If a subject may be said to become such by its attachment to certain regular experiences, by its view of what constitutes its special system of concepts, by its chosen techniques, its tradition of authority and its past masters, by its list of great achievements in its field, it is not hard to see how the characterizing features of such a landscape, its main roads and landmarks, may quickly seem at least disputable and at worse capricious. And the same goes for the so-called realms of meaning and forms of knowledge. The conceptual division between practical and aesthetic thinking took place sometime in the eighteenth century; there was nothing necessary about it. Although it is obviously true that physics typically deals with a different set of materials to psychology, and even though some schools of psychologists have tried to treat their material human beings as though only physical things could be said about them, neither subject-matter excludes the other in an ultimate way. Neither set of methods expels the other's. Indeed, one of Hegel's greatest contributions was to notice how sets of ideas, once liberating, supple and open, become hardened and constricting after a certain length of time, and explanatory models of action obstruct and disable thought until it can find innovative models and metaphors.[17] that carry it past the dead end into new intellectual possibilities. This was obviously the point reached when physics began in the 1920s to collect the data inexplicable on the old terms, and the break was only made when Heisenberg used Janneau's maths to bring into order the eccentricities now known as quanta.

Subjects, it seems, have an aetiology. They are liable to arthritis and hardening of the arteries. The brilliance, insouciance and daring of John Austin's analytic philosophy and Ayer's scepticism in Oxford of 1945, which did so much for the very closely finessed understanding of everyday language, trickled away into social triviality.[18] Mathematics, always an exacting and exiguous subject, was suddenly released into disorientingly new dissolutions of its own premises by the last work of Turing, and then by Barnach and Ziman, as well as Gödel in the 1960s. For once, most unusually and beneficially, what intellectuals thought changed what happened in school classrooms. In a rare case, the line from the genius to the 10-year-old was quite direct.

These and many others are occasions for speaking of the decay and resurrection of fields of study. Some of these histories are intoxicating; but whatever the subject-matter, our immediate concern is to notice the way in which those who are successful in their education are more and more deeply socialized into their intellectual difference from others. Understandably, the longer you have been doing a study, and the more it has contributed to your advance (teaching is the best-known, most thronged avenue of social promotion), the more you believe the story it tells you about itself. Who in teaching has not been confided in as to the preposterousness of upstart new disciplines? – 'not really subjects at all' as the bluff and bluffing voice has it. To revert to Bernstein, the pervasive classification and the mechanistic framing of traditional subjects at degree levels of education deepens loyalty to a subject (and hostility to others) as well as membership of its intellectual community (compatible, naturally, with the English educational class system: higher, further, secondary, primary) in order to make the very self (*sic*), its criteria of authenticity and sincerity,[19] into a soldier of its subject-regiment or its constituent-audience – physics, biology, French, drama, junior children.

These fidelities are visible in the most commonplace social life of the staffroom; they are even enviable there. The divisions of labour ensure that the biology department takes its instant coffee in the lab, the PE hide their inferiority complex with the horsebox and the steel-yard next to the gym, the English department sneers politely at the alleged thickheadedness of the geographers, the mathematicians walk alone. And it won't do to say that these things only impinge on that small minority of children who do A levels and take a degree. The symbolic violence, which Pierre Bourdieu speaks of[20] as being done to the masses (as socialists used to say), who do not comprehend the ultimate porousness of the curriculum and the swampy, saline and enveloping grounds which undermine the foundations of all knowledge, is violence done in the name of the integrity of the discipline, which cannot be polluted by the stuff which would make it intelligible. The one thing children feelingly understand about what they do not understand is that they are not good enough.

5

Access and Prestige

It is this that the national curriculum of any country does with great efficacy: it makes clear to its students who is any good and who is not. And here it is important to put down the myth that four-fifths of the school population are unmarked by school anyway, so whatever we do makes no difference. The strong legend of teacher powerlessness is not only rebutted by everyday experience – look at how clearly people remember their school-days, even if they hated them, and reflect a little on how intensely and clearly all children take in the experiences of early years, and lastly notice how absorbed one's own children are by their school life (how popular *Grange Hill* is): it is, after all, where they live. And if we need the backing of formal research, there is Jerome Bruner's summary[1] of a mass of cross-cultural inquiry into the effects of schooling which shows, so far as such conclusions can be shown, that children who have been to school the world over are more like one another in their handling of abstract concepts and their consciousness of different points of view than children in their own countries who have never been to school at all. From the age of five on, children live and learn the essential divisions and structures of their society as these order the immediacies of time and space . They learn the difference between work and leisure till time and times are done: schoolday and weekend, termtime and holiday, lessons and play: they learn that lunchtime is, within polite limits, if not theirs, then not the teachers' either, but those weird social officers, the dinner-ladies'. They learn that Friday afternoon is a special time because it's nearly, but not quite, the weekend, and the teachers are allowed to feel exhausted and entitled to the easier time marked by 'story', 'activity' or games.

Thus and thus are children and students initiated into the individual-making structures of curriculum and life as we live it. It is often overlooked just how fundamental and unnatural such arrangements are: we turn to what they signify as the necessary meanings of the bureaucratized state in relation to production in chapter 8. For now, however, there is the more intractable question of what kind of individual the society does want its curriculum to help make children and students into, and then, more complex and elusive still, how it will organize the curriculum in order to produce these in more or less recognizable versions and in the required numbers.

In the first question, we are returned to the protracted struggle for personal and social meanings from whose historical battle-ground we started out in the first chapter. This time we shall need to be more precise. Capitalist economies (to go no futher) are undergoing a drastic redistribution of their productive centres of gravity. The four waves of communication revolution which have been at once the dynamo and the common condition of capitalism since it took off in the nineteenth century – railways, motor cars, aircraft, electric and electronic communication – are widening outwards in a series of irregular and colliding circles, leaving some economies at once stagnant and stormswept. Britain is the case in point. The modes and relations of production in the nineteenth century required (we may say, following Bernstein[2]) a durable and relatively inflexible proletarian workforce, commanded by an entrepreneurial class in which the successful traits of resolution, ruthlessness, personal authority and strength of will were likely to be the character formation the system looked for and sought to mould. By the present late stage of British monopoly capitalism, with its investment entirely overseas and its home markets dominated by imports, the booming of its finance sector and the collapse of its manufacturing one, a very different human creature is needed in order to maintain the social order on the road of tranquil and relative decline. In its workforce, what is looked for is docility, certainly, but also flexibility, readiness to move, change and retrain, as well as to adapt quickly to new keyboard technology. In its managerial and professional classes, what is needed is a science of management, which is to say, of persuading people nicely (as opposed to the nineteenth century method of telling them nastily) to do what you want, including take the sack, and a controlling style which as far as possible works through the personalized procedures of negotiation. These are the control systems of liberal political economy, the product less of successful resistance by trade unions and more of the needs of new conglomerates for whom finite capital, resources, and above all finite markets with dangerously unstable international currencies demand the delicate balancing act and mutual collaboration which world communications now make possible.

It seems a far cry from the Bank of England to A level, or from the world economy to a 16-year-old's ambition to be a hairdresser. But there is choice as well as the determination of circumstance in these processes; the school wants to see its pupils in employment, so it recommends jobs where there are jobs, in the service industry: there is less riveting for Rosie the riveter to do now than there would have been on the Tyne or Wear in 1948. It is a platitude to say that investment patterns determine available employment: which A levels would *you* pick in Port Talbot?

More invisibly, however, the new forms of the instrumental curriculum, shaping the ideal manager, sales representative, software operator, word processor attendant, fast-food servant, or amiable unemployable, run up against the powerful and entrenched forms of the academic curriculum. And this is no bad thing. As we have noted, the curriculum carries a picture both of what to do for a living and how to live a good life. Being instrumental about things should not mean that people will offer themselves as instruments for anything whatever, so long as they're paid. Inasmuch as curricular forms and the requirements of manpower are at odds, then at least education has its small autonomy and is not merely a processing house for the systems of production. What is the meaning, purchase and leverage of that resistant autonomy we shall hope to estimate. But the combination of the academic curriculum, with its many internal battles between revisionists and traditionalists, and the strong pressure from very recent subjects such as business studies or computer science, make curricular discussion sound at first like babel; it is only where we understand how efficient it is at doing what's wanted, and this in spite of universal complaint (and everyone has always complained about school), that argument over the curriculum sounds less like the tower of unnumberable tongues, and more like the Stock Exchange.

Within the strictly academic battle of the books, the immediate competition is between the old and the new. Now any such battle has its vigorously ideological squadrons in it, as well as more crudely repellent weapons like money, numbers and resources, and 'ideology' is a word much and rightly invoked in arguments about the curriculum. It has two versions, but in both versions I will claim[3] that there are three planes of ideological admonition. The first version of ideology derives not from the earliest usage in the *Encyclopédie*,[4] where the word meant straightly the history of ideas, but from the first influential use in Marx's and Engels' notebooks, written in 1847 and ultimately published as *The German Ideology*,[5] and their celebrated formula, 'The ruling ideas of any epoch are the ideas of the ruling class'. Marx and Engels propound the brutal, but convincing view that since the bourgeoisie was the historically necessary, but drastically unemancipated arm of victorious capitalism, the self-justifications of that bourgeoisie would have a comparably ambitious reach as well as an inevitably sanctimonious and inadequate grasp. That is, the bourgeoisie would devise legitimations claiming the conditions and the quality of their own fulfilment and emancipation as being the conditions of liberation for all men and women; their apparently startling success in persuading those in the proletariat whose interests were so patently *not* served by the happy triumph of the bourgeoisie was stigmatized by Marx as the victory of 'false consciousness'.

This is the Marxist doctrine of ideology; it may be labelled the fix theory of ideology.[6] In a safer, more everyday version, ideology is the loose designation for the structure of values and beliefs with which we take or dare the assorted strains of the universe. The strain theory and the fix theory are alike in that each sees ideology as the inevitably distorting lens through which individuals and classes must look at the world from their historically relative position, although Marxism has a notoriously optimistic programme about the regrinding of the Marxist lens until what it will finally permit is a vision of the world as it really is. Furthermore, the analysis of ideology preferred here nominates three levels of its operation: a first, metaphysical level, of what Collingwood calls 'absolute presuppositions', which is to say the given premises of a thought-system which you have to hold if you are to think within it at all – the God-created nature of the universe for Christians, for example, and the motions of economically driven change for Marxists. The second level connects these data and assumptions in an explanatory form with the actualities of history, such that

Marxism can represent striking workers or insurgent guerrillas as determinate actions in a class struggle born of the collision between contrary motions of the systems of production, and Christianity may present an actual, but miraculous cure or the saintly courage of a single figure as the revelation necessary in the circumstances of divine providence. The third and final level, which sustains the practical and everyday workability of an ideology is that of the precepts which join data to explanations by telling believers what they should do about it. Ideologies typically admonish their supporters about how to turn belief into action: Marxists must work for the revolution, Christians for redemption, both carry a clear picture of the need for self-sacrifice.[7] But the prominence of Marxizing inquiries into ideology is due to their need to explain the failure of Marxism itself to make more headway in the West, and the potent explanation is the power of ideology itself.

It is for this reason that education and the curriculum have drawn the close attention of theorists of ideology. These are indeed 'the ruling ideas' which have ruled successfully. If people believe them so comprehensively, they must have unusual penetration and staying power in order to overcome the weight of obviousness which surely shows that the real interests of the masses lie with taking things into their own hands. This is the basic position from which Western analysis has proceeded, and the analysts, looking for help in the Marxist tradition, found Antonio Gramsci, the Communist leader of the Fiat workers in Turin in the early 1920s, their best guide.

This book is not a Gramscian handbook.[8] Gramsci is merely the occasion for mentioning his rather catch-all, but much-quoted concept 'hegemony', by which he meant the all-pervading and saturating power of cultural control, a power whose omnipresence caused people to think of as natural and unalterable the circumstancs which made for their own subordination and oppression. Such hegemony, it is claimed, is won by the curriculum and reproduced by education generally.

The lesson for radical critics of education within education is then logically taken to be, change the curriculum, for by changing that you will be able to change what is done to popular thought, its frames of mind and its mentation. The straight way into such a change is to start by exposing the present self-interestedness, arbitrariness, hypocrisy and lies within a given discipline or subject area. There is no need to be radically unctuous in this adventure – always an infectious, but also noisome tendency in curricular criticism. *Any* field of study (or realm of meaning) will be distorted by mischance and misdeed, and will be tautologically ruled by its rulers. To criticize content is to try to alter the historical location of a subject, to free it from its boundedness in a position in which it holds students down, narrows and constricts them, makes them less able, rather than more to live up to their times and to imagine boldly and well in them. Education, like any art, is a way of learning to think well of the future: the artist, as John Berger puts it,[9] gives us reason for thinking the best possible thoughts.

This is why the battle of the books is always between the new and old, a battle of generations,[10] though there is never any saying who in either generation will pick which side. Nor (again) is there any hidden sanctimony in that remark. Bernstein observes placidly that 'in a period of heightened social change, it seems likely that continuity can only be maintained at the expense of a false yesterday or a mythical tomorrow'.[11] Discuss, as the exam papers say. It seems just as likely that both are always the expenses of continuty; the efforts of keeping faith with a sufficiently plausible yesterday or a not too dizzily apocalyptic future is what initially determines enlistment in the colours of old or new.

See how they run in a particular subject, English. It is a complicated subject, moreover, because in schools, obviously, it is the medium of instruction, hence the rallying cry, 'Every teacher is a teacher of English',[12] and it is also nominated by many employers as a qualification for large numbers of clerical occupations in terms of strictly instrumental competence – which is always held to be declining in standard ('the youngsters we get, can't write, can't spell, can't speak properly, – now in my day . . .'). At the same time, for historical reasons as well as because of the nature of the subject, which is after all the native language itself, a vanguard of teachers themselves turned English into the vehicle of progressivism, the legitimate occasion for the develop- ment of personal creativity. The latter energy derived from theories of teaching, which in England took great heart from the doctrines of Wordsworth and then of Romanticism and liberalism by way of John Stuart Mill, Matthew Arnold and T.H. Green, about the educability of all children, about the power of what came to be called high culture to transform and redeem those who had known only poverty and humiliation, and about the universal capacity to create.

At the same time, in the universities (which meant Oxford, Cambridge and London) some of these same strong stirrings came together to challenge the dominance of the ancient tongues Latin and Greek in the name of a now distinctive and immensely distinguished native literature. The classics, known at Oxford as *'litterae humaniores'*, had been long studied in two forms: the one, by hard learning of declension, conjugation, voice and mood, followed by grammar and etymology; the other a direct engagement with the texts, with Thucydides and Tacitus, Aristotle and Plato, Catullus and Martial, not historically, but as though these were living and contemporary masters with whom one debated and from whom one learned the history, morality and aesthetics of the day. If English was to match them, it had to have respectability in its antiquity, formality in its study of language, and immediacy in its moral substance.

The argument broke up in different directions. Oxford's English course plumped for scholarship and antiquity – students had to study the linguistic origins of English in Anglo-Saxon and Norman-French, and the official literature stopped, until the 1960s, at 1832, a fine symbolic date for conservatives. The Cambridge English course made Anglo-Saxon optional, and out of the chance assortments of interests present at its early years, prescribed as the content of its curriculum the historical, classical, and genteel medley which made up culture in its roughly anthropological sense (it called one group of exam papers 'life, literature and thought'). Its architects attached to this framework a highly selective version of the development of English literature to which nevertheless the student was invited to make his or her personal response. The formal results of the discipline were to be the taste and judgement which the procedures of what was called practical criticism, or the very close reading of the words on the page for their tone, meaning and organization, would inculcate. This latter was, as it turned out, the crucial innovation. For, in Bernstein's terms, once you as a student are able to interrogate the pacing, sequence and significance of what is taught, the authority bases of the classroom are dissolved.

The date as well as the membership of the formation of Cambridge English was crucial. Discussions were active in 1917; Oxford's had been settled before the war. By the time the war was over, a new generation of teachers and students had arrived who were committed to discovering a method and object of study which would provide for the ideals and the determination of the best remnants of the ruling class in 1919 to make a land fit for heroes to live in. Well, most of the heroes were dead: the essentials of power and property in bloody old England were unchanged. Yet without sentimentality, perhaps it can be claimed that the forms of Cambridge English were in part provided by and for the idealistic men and women who came to university in order to discover a way of living well and on behalf of others unavailable in a moral philosophy empty of anything to believe in, and for whom no cultural authority existed in a society whose intelligent members could only despise a ruling class of such hideous incompetence and callousness as were to be seen at work in Flanders.

The immediate relevance of this compressed history is to show just how complicated the formation of an educational subject area is and with what variously ideological voices it may speak. As devised by the venerable universities betwen 1900 and 1920, English was compounded of grammar, etymology, what was then the canon of honoured literature (Shakespeare to Dickens), and a running fight between modernists and traditionalists about the worth of the new writing – T.S. Eliot, Yeats, D.H. Lawrence: an American, an Irishman and a sexually arousing coalminer's son. At this distance we can see the terms of the disputes pretty clearly, made raw and painful as they were by the terror and haemorrhage of the war. The struggle for continuity *and* for a new, decent start, the confusions of restoration and retribution, made teaching stand in much more direct relation to life than usual. It is not just dead old history that is being told, however, it is the origins of the same arguments in the present. Continuity and connectedness in the subject as in the self are the criteria of identity, and they exact a fierce loyalty.

Consider, therefore, the terms of membership in present-day English. The traditionalists take their stand in the admirable name of a necessary continuity, a 'storehouse of recorded value', on a canon of literature which, although only settled upon by the ideological upheavals of the 1920s, indeed *because* only so recently agreed, should be left to see us through the bewildering and patternless proliferations of the new technetronic culture. For them (putting it crassly), first films and now television are inadequate for academic study because they are mass produced and mass watched also; the cultivation of delicacy and wisdom, which is the life of culture, demands the deliberate pondering of what is written by the best who read it, and literary culture on this definition is the canon. The canon excludes enormous amounts of writing, certainly — of what is classified on the library shelves as philosophy, theology, most history, all working-class writing until it has been promoted into an individualist category, most American literature but not all (Henry James is admitted, but not Hemingway), crime writing, thrillers, translations, or anything which might be discomposingly political.

Put like that, the arbitrariness is plain to see; but it is my ecumenical point that any curriculum is similarly arbitrary. The traditionalists, battling in the name of continuity and a coherent social memory to value a past which tells a worthy story, pick on *The Prelude, Jane Eyre* and *Middlemarch*, because those stories provide such a past. Yet that past and its story only fit a particular historical biography, the tale of someone for whom the great surge of Romanticism gave a proper belief in the truthfulness and ardour of their deepest passions, but only as validated and judged by the strength of a mature, scrupulously self-conscious conscience, whose intelligence was bent on balancing the life-significant claims of sincerity against duty, choice against wholeness.

This is to moralize literature with an ideological vengeance, and a vengeance that falls on infidels alone. For the severities of membership allow the arbitrariness of the canon to go out of focus; in the battle of the books, the standard of the canon is defended against the tatterdemalion vandals who come on with a new, wild and hoarser cry about different, bloodier worlds and more sudden climaxes. And after my best efforts at fairmindedness, in this short analysis of ideological preference, I shall come out cleanly on the side of the hooded hordes. For the great and unironic strength of the canon as set up in the forums of English in its first phase is exactly its historical responsiveness to the image of the brave, sensitive, freely choosing and responsible soul. But once this soul takes on the body and clothes of the respectable and petty-bourgeois English lecturer and teacher, its merely time- and self-serving imagination strikes you like a bad smell.

Even at its best, the traditionalist view has been broken open by the facts of cultural prodigality and the obliterating deluge of its electronics. The modernist English teacher, following the precepts of his great most recent forebears – of T.S. Eliot and Yeats and Lawrence among the writers of the canon, of F.R. Leavis, Denys Thompson and Donald Davie among its theorists – follows language and, in Leavis's fine phrase, 'the inevitable creativeness of ordinary everyday life' wherever they lead him. His own responses and his students then take him to some academically insalubrious places: to the innumerable fictions of that everyday life in exceedingly non-canonical literature, to more of the same in films (since, as is the way of things, a handful of different films are now edging into the very canon of the traditionalists built to keep them out), and to the whole unstoppable rout of television. This, the modernist says, is where the imaginative life of the present is really being lived, and if you try to interpret it with the forms and manners of the old canon, one of two things will happen. In one action, the old canon will break up, and you'll have to acknowledge that, wonderful novel as *Middlemarch* is, its incontestable, settled moralizing goes with a settled order and doesn't easily transplant to disorientingly different frames of feeling. In the other, those teachers whose final commitment is to the strictly pedagogic fiction of the moral Romantic and the passionate puritan withdraw from the undoubtedly awful mess which is modern culture into that smallish number of enclaves hidden in a few schools and universities where the tones, forms and manners of that fiction and its structure of feeling still hold. Those places being where they are – cells of rigorous and principled intellectuality in socially exclusive places – the University of Bristol, say, North London Collegiate School for girls, Rugby or Westminster schools for boys – then such teachers may still touch for moral good a small fragment of the power elite. But their ideological self-justificaiton no longer holds on a larger world. Their enemy the modernist, seeking to make sense of an English curriculum in inner London schools or to build a cultural studies course at a polytechnic, has to try out every new strange language to see if it will hold down the mad disorder of things: hence, structuralism, neo-Marxism, semiology, socio-linguistics, post-Freudianism, hermeneutics.

The political inflection of most of these, whether borrowed from Paris or Bologna, Yale or Chicago, is the key to this fragment of ideological analysis. For the latter pages have not been an idiotic tale told merely to English teachers; they have been an essay in the politics of knowledge. Now by politics is meant no more than is usually meant, the struggle for and control of distribution in power, privilege, rewards and resources. In England (the emphasis is deliberate: the other three countries stand at the wrong end of the axis of power), English, our example to hand, is defined by its history in universities as a way of thinking about literature with fairly clever members of a particular social class, a fairly senior fraction of the clerical and servicing bourgeoisie, many of the recruits from which become producers and distributors in the cultural industries. If your formation and your experience take you that way, you'll stress continuity and tradition and end up with vehement ideological justifications as a soldier of reaction. If you go the other way, you'll plump for identification with the common experience of unprecedented amounts of new fiction and its dramas and for membership of a wide linguistic community, and end up as spokesman for the children rather than their rector, and as their archivist rather than their guardian.

The English story and its ideological meanings are amply corroborated in the European languages most usually studied in schools, French and German. Both languages are longer lived in universities than the native tongue, and both for obvious reasons retain satisfyingly heavy emphasis on the difficulties of an inflexible correctness in grammar and vocabulary. One much-noted consequence of this was that until fairly recently – the 1960s, say – all their attention went on writing the language, and very little on speaking it, which is what people do rather more. In addition, both languages, and their poor sibling, Spanish, share with English a stern definition of the tongue as defined by its novels, plays and poems, plus a few of an elusive genre known as 'essays', largely known to be such by a lack of any substantive content (Montaigne, Chateaubriand), specially promoted biographies (a few non-theological ones), and a selection of collected letters, either those famously by poets (Keats, Rilke) or more of the substanceless, aesthetic and 'personal' kind (Gautier, Walpole). Philosophy, history, let alone art and music are excluded from as queer a looking canon as could be imagined, the more as German literature so classified is extremely thin, and German scholars have to make too much of Goethe, a very scattered genius, and preposterously more of the puny achievement in *Novelle* writing, while all the time the great giants of German philosophy from Kant and Hegel via Marx to Nietzsche and Schopenhauer go disregarded. If instead, as is surely reasonable, students of a whole culture and its language were, with German, to take in philosophy, music and a little science, and with French, to take in art with a little politics, then to read either subject at A level, let alone learning to speak rather than write it at O level, would already have made for rather more understanding of and admiration for our sisters in the Community than is to be found in the columns of rancid xenophobia which fill the press.

These are topics, I repeat, in the politics of knowledge, and in this as in any other kind of politics, they are focused by the concept of power. But power is not a merely coercive force, though the concept most certainly and centrally includes coercion.[13] Power is also whatever it is that gets things done, and metaphors for its effectuality may as well recall electricity as machine guns. Power, that is, is not merely brutish and not merely in the hands of other people. In spite of what is a neurotically self-exonerating propensity to self-pity among them as among any other of the official authority figures of the society, teachers have real power of their own, and that power is unevenly, but circumspectly distributed not only according to seniority and what is defined as responsibility, but also according to subject membership and loyalty.

This is true from the infant school chronologically upwards to higher and further education, and is intricately, but cartographically linked to the hierarchy of knowledge in the society at large. Such truths may be propositionally put, for the benefit of method in curriculum theory.

1   Power in the curriculum is hierarchically ordered in direct and systemic relation to the parallel power of comparable areas of knowledge and inquiry in the society.

1.1   This systemic ordering, however, is refracted by the interposition of universities between schools and the economy, and the university's curriculum hierarchies are reproduced by its own class fraction which mediates and resists the wider economy.

1.2   The relative power of subject-areas increases and consolidates with the age of the student.

1.3   Power in the curriculum is only over resources; no subject-area has power over the content (or existence) of another subject-area. Eliminative power is strictly political.

1.4   Political power of this sort is assigned to members of high-prestige areas.

2   Prestige in the curriculum is determined by resource allocation in the parent economy in torque with culturally situated definitions of conceptual difficulty as determined by the dominant class.

2.1   Prestige loss or gain fluctuates as the dominant class revalues or devalues the significance of longevity or innovation, but only as these are invisibly loaded by the mode of production (which is not fixed).

3   Crises of power and prestige, such as are now being undergone, are signs of important shifts in the mode of production.

Thus all disputes of power in schools or anywhere else are regulated at first and ruthlessly by the supremacy of mental ways of knowing and inquiring over manual ones. This distinction has its slipperiness, if the quickness of the hand, or anyway its importance to physical comfort, is allowed to deceive the category and is backed up by heavy theory. This is the case with medical and veterinary surgery and with dentistry, an interesting anomaly not noted for conceptual difficulty or even for demanding very marked locomotor co-ordination, but assertively on the right side of the divide.

The theoretic understanding of power in the curriculum, according to the short list of propositions, needs to work in a number of dimensions, which are best suggested by example rather than by the sort of generalizable propositions which lead quickly into jargon.[14] Broadly, therefore, we can say that those subject-areas are most powerful which command the largest amounts of timetable, staff numbers and salary allocation: in universities, science and medicine; in secondary schools, science and English; in primary schools, numeracy and literacy. In the competition for time, space and money, these areas win easily, with science, leaning heavily on its alleged material necessities – laboratories, safety conditions, ostensive methods of teaching with very low teacher-pupil ratios, expensive apparatus and so forth – assuming and getting the share due to a lion with a big mouth and a roar to go with it.

But power is built up across a wider geography than is measured by numbers, money, time and space within a school. The case of reading in primary schools illustrates this. The model for understanding its rise to power is much more like that expounded for classic imperialism[15] than by the everyday story of a country subject. First the explorers, then the missionaries, then the settlers, then the soldiers. Then, when everything on the ground is safe, along come the agents of not-very-great-risk capital. So the researchers, eager for colonizing all early educational life after the vast achievements of Piaget, opened up the ground of reading – how on earth children do wring meaning out of black runes on white paper? With a few areas staked out – look and say, colour coding, early teaching alphabet, phonic method – the zealot missionaries came into schools, hot-eyed and fervent, to convert the new world to the new method, and the settlers, hoping for a new life with new degrees making possible their bright new standing, and underwritten by a special trading station at the university, brought their agronomy with them and broke up the old customs for the promised increases in productivity. Lastly, the colonial police patrolled the classrooms making sure that no new laws were broken, no old primitive ways revived by recalcitrant natives (whether parents or teachers). And so the first of the three 'Rs' was replaced by a fully administered literacy, bureaucratized by the publishing industry in a dozen well-capitalized schemes.

Telling the history this way throws into relief once more the politics of knowledge. It also brings out its anthropology. Very little of what is asserted to justify power and prestige or even method in the curriculum is justifiable. Teaching reading has certainly altered the relations of production, but it can't be said convincingly to be a better way to teach. The great prestige of research and even of phoney expertise conceal the old human hugger-mugger of hand-to-mouth practice, folklore and super-stition, honest effort and individual intelligence.

Such obfuscation works everywhere. Sometimes it works shamelessly, as when the University Grants Commission in Britain, enjoined by the Minister in 1981 to cut the budget and itself dominated (of course) by Oxbridge scientists, indefensibly privileged pure science at the expense of everything else, especially applied or technological science (mental over manual again). Usually it works so much in the grain of everyday life at school that we hardly notice. Thus when the powerful subjects in secondary school move in on sixth-form resources, which, naturally, are higher per head than the resources made available to the children who don't understand and leave early and uncomprehending, they need to hold their numbers as high as they can compatible with good exam results, while for the sake of prestige they make themselve sound difficult.

An intricate and long-lived ceremony of difficulty-incantation has gathered over the year in reinforcement and signification of these last meanings of power and prestige. It is discoverable at work on any parents' evening: 'No, I don't think your child can quite manage O-level biology, how about CSE?' 'It's not been a good year, they all did badly in the mocks', 'He's not really a bookish boy, but very good with his hands', 'She's really artistic so you can't expect her to be good at maths as well', 'No, she's got a real feel for languages, so why not drop general science?' Without in the least wishing to deny the reality in childen of great gifts suddenly declaring themselves, of the varieties of intelligence, of the facts of difference between being a good painter and being good with animals, of, indeed, being a boy as opposed to a girl, it is by this folklore and these quite unexamined premises that power and prestige in the curriculum subtend the arc of privilege and reward in the society.

There is a well-known curricular verb which all teachers instinctively conjugate at parents' evenings. It goes like this:

I am clever and bourgeois: I shall do nuclear physics or Russian at Cambridge.
I am clever and working class: I shall do electronics and Telecom will pay for me at polytechnic.
You are middling middle class: you shall do geography and estate agency by correspondence.
You are middling and poor: you shall do home economics and a catering course at the tech.

She is dim, and very well off: she shall go to finishing school and train to be a receptionist at the Dorchester.
He is dim, black and effortful: he shall do car maintenance.

These are the conjugations which get as far as the examination hall. In a worthy effort to fill time without killing it, and to acknowledge the entire lack of fit between the official forms of educated life and the customary forms which are their out-of-school experience, a wholly different mode of work and its relations is being gradually devised for those who are designated unexaminable. The power commanded by those busy with this design is, as we shall see, considerable, but their prestige is low. These are courses the occasion for which arises dramatically in circumstances of economic crisis, but political fluidity. They don't fit the dispositions of usual curricular allocation, and only swim up from deep curricular waters when politics can no longer be neglected, but must be transposed to the ideological realm.

They do pose, of course, critical questions about what education is for; what the worth of a human life in our society is. Each subject or area, as I have argued, has an answer to that question couched in its own terms, and the answers change with history. The history which is life in earnest corrodes the old hierarchies, and the answers to the question 'what's it all for?' have to change, or – as happened to Latin and Greek – the subject gets stranded and left behind. Subject-areas rise and fall not so much according to their merits, but according to their creative capacity in accommodating the troublousness of the times within the frames of their ideology. If they tell too sharp a truth, they are rebuked; if they tell a good tale, complicated, but ending happily, about how to recover the good old days for science, for man, or for God, then that's just fine.

6
The Social Mobility of a Subject

The hierarchy of factors that exacts change from areas of the curriculum is not easily diagrammatized. Certain kinds of curriculum handbook are much given at this point to a set of interlocking circles like the Olympic flag, which are as conceptually vacuous as it is possible to be, particularly when they are marked solemnly 'knowledge' 'culture' and so forth, and are much set about with dotted margins outside which monstrous powers called 'change' or 'society' prowl in black letters with many arrows darting at the circles, but themselves hemmed in by nothing but the acute limitations of two dimensions.

This book is of a sufficiently Marxisant persuasion to admit that it loads one factor in the hierarchy much heavier than the others, and that factor is the uneasy conceptual duo, the systems-and-relations-of-production. These, whatever they are, hugely inflect the 'classification and framing', the power and prestige, the totality of relations in the curriculum. But the excursion in the last chapter into the theory of ideology should illuminate just how tricky a process it is to account for changes in the curriculum. The decline of Latin and Greek by 1919 was no doubt overdetermined by the expansion of state education, by the rise of a new segment of the bourgeoisie to academic power professing the ideological strengths of a different class culture, by the triumphant advent of a monopoly capitalism and its conglomerates – Wills tobacco, Brunner-Mond, Firth-Vickers, Handley Page – insisting on a new technical elite from their local universities, by the deadly slow passing of the Empire, by the proper demands of the working class for a decent and democratic education.

The whole tale can be put together from these prefabricated causes, arranged in a plausible order, and made to fit the unutterably banal generalities of curriculum innovation theory. But, however determined, they were unpredictable in that form. It is only as a history that we can watch the comprehensible decline of the classics. And there too we might pause and wonder about the presence in that immediate past still immediately with us of a powerful amnesia which is not so much a consequence as a parallel force with that well-known actor on the historical stage already introduced in Chapter 1, modernization. Latin and Greek have been more or less scrapped, because they stood on the further edge of the tradition crevasse which opened up in 1918. They went down slowly: Latin was still a compulsory O level for admission to Cambridge in 1955; but they went because they had no sufficient answer to any of the historical factors listed with sloganeering bravado in the last paragraph. Their humanizing claims had been wrested from them by English literature, their training of the mind according to the precepts of the first philosophers superseded by the new mathematical logics of Russell, Wittgenstein and Carnap. The trouble now is of course that their disappearance from state schools and their tiny numbers of students in higher education signify a major act of forgetting on the part of the society. Amnesia is a horrible and frightening condition. A European society which knew no Latin and Greek would be amnesiac, the more so at a time when the recovery of the past has so vastly opened up the world over, and understanding how we got to be the way we are (the only adequate position from which to see what to do next) has been so changed exactly by way of the astonishing discoveries of classical archaeologists, biblical and textual scholars, and ancient historians working on the Levant during the past generation.

The response to the threat of amnesia is to start the equivalent of the World Wildlife Fund, whereby a special subject threatened with extinction is caught and bred entirely in the library-equivalent of a zoo. A new academic profession comes into being: curator of the knowledge in danger of being wiped out of the memory. It recruits from very high-prestige training grounds in tiny numbers. But of course its practices, intensely specialized and hermetic like so much learning, are removed from the main lifestream of the society.

This is not a threnody on broken ways of life. It is a description of how the resources of meaning drain away. Now the still legally empowered meaning-maker of the official curriculum is religion, and it is instructive to plot its history, when faced by the great wilderness of incredulity and incredibility which defaces the century. Religious education itself possesses notable legal power, as every head teacher knows. The celebrated 1944 Education Act requires the school to conduct some form of religious worship and religious instructions, the only subject-area so singled out. In 1944, with victory in the war seeming to be so very much to God's and British credit, and just appeals to the rightfulness of the cause satisfactorily combining religious propriety and patriotism, such a clause looked vastly more justifiable than it does now, forty secularized and multiracial years on. In those days, the classification of what was revealingly called divinity or scripture was watertight and Christian: the Bible was the text at all ages, and the New Testament at least was taught as a true narrative, whose precepts were God-sent and to be followed. Pupils were tested for the straightforward recall of their knowledge of the Bible, and the advance of a final secularization, which Engels had so confidently predicted exactly a century before,[1] was still so diffuse and slow that whatever the degree of sullen or amiable incomprehension and unbelief on the part of the pupils and their parents, Bible knowledge was for the devout strain in the official culture a necessary part of becoming a Christian, which naturally children should be taught, because it was true and because they should learn the road to salvation. For the liberal–agnostic strain, the strength of whose determination to do nothing explains why Engels's expectations was disappointed, Bible knowledge was a necessary part of a worthwhile education, an aspect of the inheritance of English literature into which a student must enter to be counted as educated at all. Either way, the subject remained comfortably within the ample space of the Authorized Version, and was taught as something pretty well immutable (as well it might be).

But it is now forty years since these days were made secure, insular and insulated, exactly because the adversary, the devil, was walking abroad all over Europe. Secularization is still not at all finished, and certainly no Secretary of State would have the nerve to declare religious instruction redundant. Indeed, he would hardly be right: the terrific revival of radical Islam, the recent and colossal surge in recruits to British Catholicism and, on a smaller scale, to evangelism in the Church of England, to say nothing of sectarian successes of a dottier kind from Mormonism to the Moonies all give the lie to optimism on the part of the atheists, but leave the question of what to teach of religion piercing and unanswerable.

To answer at all, the subject had to break its institutional allegiance to the Church of England. The church itself, however, was trying to accommodate the same splitting social strains as the subject in schools, and living within the deep irreconcilables of commitment to the revealed truth of God inside a society possessing no language except Christianity to express its Christian unbelief, but retaining its continuing devotion to some kind of sanctity in the central questions and ceremonies of life, it had to provide a serious answer to the question, 'what is a human life worth?' at the occasions of birth and death. Both church and curriculum had to encompass this question in such a way as to defuse three very touchy and explosive charges. The first was the danger of the ultimate detonation of the force of atheism, which would displace both institutions to a marginal terrain visited only by tourists and educational custodians on Sundays. The second was the enormously disruptive force of other religions flowing into the country as immigrants: from Italian Catholics via the Greek Orthodox members of the Mediterranean countries and on to the many and factious adherents of Islam and their old enemies in Hinduism, concluding in the Far West with the boisterous ostentation of new Rastafarianism, all watched sadly and tranquilly by long-standing exiles in the churches of Judaism and Buddhism. The facts of conflicting belief and the keen danger of racial warfare demanded of the home church, and its teaching, major concessions about tolerance, the relative nature of the revelation and of truth itself, and a thoroughly tolerant liberalism which really made that much derided doctrine live up to its own profession. The third force, another bastard child on one side of the hungry generations just listed, was the new theology within the church itself. The names of Tillich, Bonhoeffer and their unchurched Christianity were given popular rating by Bishop John Robinson in 1964.[2] Their device for restoring Christianity to everyday life was to empty it of historical and intellectual content, and ask the Christian to bear witness to his or her Christianity by the fullness and holiness of being and bearing, since, as Robinson briskly vulgarized it, we may 'Let God be the name for whatever is of deepest significance in Life'. The trouble with this remedy for doctrinal conflict and social irrelevance is that it can only work in a practical way in circumstances of high historical drama. As MacIntyre ironically notes,[3] Bonhoeffer could bear, as he heroically did, Christian witness in a Nazi prison; it is less clear how to do the same thing as a rich stockbroker in Virginia Water.[4]

To define Christianity as a state of being removes the difficulties with truth and dogma, and also answers the question of how to be a Christian during the week. You behave much the same as everyone else, but more seriously and in a quieter voice, in order to indicate humility. But the repudiation of dogma leaves belief with no religious specificity; the gap is then filled by morality. This had to be the answer for religious education. Its study of and recommendations about action become ordinarily moral, and because conscious of the teachings of liberal morality, these were largely grounded in strictly interpersonal dealings and attempts to devise techniques for what are emetically known as life-skills, in order to ensure the sufficiently frictionless dealings of class with class, and both with other races. In a dozen worthy ways, religious education bereft of a curriculum turns to the encouragement of understanding and sympathy in face-to-face encounters. Heaven knows, of course, these are important qualities left shrivelled and deformed by the way the world goes, but the cognitive vacancy of the teaching materials, together with the hopelessness of designating religious study with no account given or looked for of truth, God, belief or mortality, means that whatever 'life-skills' and 'educating for personal relationships' may do, they accelerate the loss of belief and help to expunge religion, as well as all forms of spirituality.

Writing this way does not constitute a cry for the restoration of Bible-bashing and the proclamation of the one way to salvation. I am tracing, as the chapter heading advertises, the social mobilities of the curriculum. Religious education, following its church, is not so much mobile as vaporized. What can or should be done about it[5] is in issue at the heart of the culture.

On a sanguine view, we shall eventually face the wounds and severances of our experience, and name for what it is our failure to resolve the deep and killing political and moral contradictions in what we teach and how we live — all of which is hardly imminent. Such an act of self-definition on the part of society might enable the slow construction of a secular and socialist ethic which left due space for the constituent religions of its polity, and offered a language for the recognition of these without deranging the civil and civic order. Poland is the obvious example of a social order in which religion is used politically by the people to deny official politics. Iran is the contrast, in which religion, being coterminous with politics, obliterates the necessary polity of tolerance. Both are repellent. It is only in a few corners of developing countries and their specially desperate straits that an admirable juxtaposition of religious and political education seems to have emerged. And they will hardly serve as examples to Britain, or Europe and the anglophone countries.

On the other hand we can anticipate what we are likely to get. And that is the continued evaporation of religious content into therapeutic forms. For the pretty certain evasiveness of the fair-to-middling rich industrial societies before their own lies, hypocrisies and cruelties will lead them to patch up social agreements in terms borrowed from an imaginary and pacific past, which has always had many historical stations, but is often about halfway to the horizon – nowadays about 1959. These agreements made very exclusively by our social managers will then be used as ideal references for everybody, and the great engines of manipulation will continue to organize the world not for an openly held moral and political debate, but for its manipulable assent.

It is in this large context that the social mobility of the curriculum needs to be understood. Religious education is only one, though obviously crucial, of the forms of knowledge (or, again, realms of meaning) that have abandoned content, because the old content would no longer do, and filled the hole up with mere skills and techniques. In this, they blend with the huge tendency of capitalist society to devise ways of organizing agreement to its prior and determinate ends, and to find space for all its members within which they may make themselves sufficiently happy not to challenge those ends, but to leave the system to go on producing whatever it pleases, including its own destruction.

This tendency, naturally and irresistibly, has deeply invaded education from two directions, and teachers have flocked to study the new subjects created by society for its self-manipulation. It is important here to bring out the full, conscious ingenuousness of my critical analysis. For I will be reminded that the business of counselling and the necessity of studying and improving administration have arisen because ours is a society which, having recently progressed from barbarism, has to find ways of bringing often obdurate and always bloodyminded delinquents within the adjustments of society.[6] Furthermore, it is merely sensible to acknowledge not only that our society is bureaucratized, but that this process has brought great benefits in efficiency, social justice, the elimination of want, illness and public danger, and that not to study it for its greater improvement is irresponsible.

Now both reminders are true. And it is further true that our encounters with the public bureaucracies of health, welfare, production, travel, communication and education constitute our public lives: our public self is defined in relation to these institutions, so to turn and accuse the practices of counselling and of administration as being the complementarily private and public mechanisms of the manipulation of consent to incontestable ends is to sound naively ill-at-ease (or Luddite) in what are infallibly classed as the realities of the modern world. Subsequently, you meet the charge of Utopian (another familiar dismissive), if you suggest the possibility of a profoundly different, free association of men and women in forms of production immune to the techniques of manipulation and the management of assent.

Management indeed turns out to mean persuading others to agree with a more or less good grace on ends which are systemic and unavailable to question. Technique and skills are key words in these trainings, never judgement or reason, nor admiration nor disgust. Indeed the strange ring of this latter coinage takes the measure of its exclusion from the vocabulary of social (and therefore moral and political) arrangements. Such concepts denote, at least in their earlier sense, a moral meaning whose reference could be settled by appeal to an impersonal rationality independent of personal preference.[7] Quite rapidly, the complex but consistent advance of the doctrines of the unfettered non-social self (radical personalization, the freeing of the self from all structures), the detachment of the true person from the occupation of social roles, and the making almost synonymous of the expression of personal feelings with the structure of morality – the moral theory known as emotivism – all served to bring about a social order whose principles of cohesion are no longer open to critical reflection and dissent, but are consequently irredeemable, though constantly changing.

For the free self, possessing as it does no theory of moral value beyond its fulfilment of its own feelings, has no teleology, or scheme of admirable human purposes. Radically individualized as it seeks to be, it possesses neither politics nor civics, nor of course the politeness and civility which derive from the same urban root, but are now reduced to the trivial details of a class-assessed niceness. Deprived of a social theory, the self takes its ends as given by the power of superordinate systems: in the case of Britain in 1985, a failing, but still fleet, portly, arrogant and unchallengeable capitalism. Management becomes the refinement of techniques for ensuring complicity in its systemic ends (think of the well-named arbitration and conciliation services devised for settling industrial disputes). Counselling, a process in education reserved for those who in one way or another have been chewed up and spat out by the system, becomes the administration of similar techniques which console or in other wise (at times pharmacological) sedate the victim over his or her anti-socially lived disappointment. Emotional satisfaction, however, is now too high on the shopping list of all good consumers to be laughed off it, and counselling for an adequate dose of such satisfaction is now the pastoral half of systems maintenance, and a new and stongly expanding section of the curriculum. After all, these are the only ways to sort out a world in which morality and politics are subjective and immune to reason. It is your business, as both manager and counsellor, to persuade those who disagree to see reason, but reason then turns out to mean the reasonableness of giving way to superior power.

At this point, the honest counsellor or the pastoral head of the third year bursts indignantly in to say that finding something for his emotional satisfaction is not why she spends hours fishing William Brown out of the juvenile court for assault. Absolutely not. My point is at first sight the simple and familiar reassurance that awful as William is, the system and the place are at fault in being at least powerfully responsible for making him as ghastly as he is. The point at second sight, however, is that it just *is* both its meaning and function that therapeutic counselling, once it leaves the psychotic ward for the counsellor's office, is the highly personalized arm of a total control system, even whose minor and modest officers like the head of the third year have no criteria of personal worth, meaning or virtue, other than their own effectiveness and efficiency, kindly as they always are (as according to programme they *must* be). They do their duty by the criteria of bureaucratic authority, which on this showing, as MacIntyre says, is 'nothing other than successful power.'[8] That duty turns out to be part of a moral-political structure of manipulation and management in the name of the compliant hedonism which subtends the inhuman goals of endless production. This extraordinary rise to prominence of manipulative techniques and what once was carelessly called 'man-management' is one measure of the controlling the curriculum is asked to do.

The same is even more thoroughly true for the complementary arm of therapeutic and management curricula, which is the study of administration itself. Now especially at the present, one supreme criterion of bureaucratic efficiency is its alleged cost-effectiveness, and the study of management is now directed towards the competitive capture of resources and devising means of putting them to efficient ends.

> Every bureaucratic organisation embodies some explicit or implicit definition of costs and benefits from which the criteria of effectiveness are derived. Bureaucratic rationality is the rationality of matching means to ends economically and efficiently.[9]

MacIntyre points out that we owe this maybe overfamiliar thought to Weber (even though it is not the giant Weber, but wizened nonentities who are the men actually studied in so-called business studies, in and out of school), but he goes on to put an asseveration borne out by both research and everyone's everyday observations, that all senior managers justify their authority by influencing the motives of subordinates, and ensuring that subordinates argue from premises which will produce agreement with their own prior conclusions. Any school head of department will jump to recognition of that process. The manager's function is 'that of controlling behaviour and suppressing conflict in such a way as to reinforce ... bureaucratic authority'.[10] Oddly enough, this is even true in those schools that have taken in and been taken in by theories of organizations and their collective sentiments advanced by such agencies as the Tavistock Institute.[11] For the slow public exposure of inner feelings advocated by these theories are made with a view to the ultimate control and containment of difficult conflicts. They are not to do with the rational discussion of what the good life of a school or a factory should look like. They have no political morality, but a preference for this dissolution of principle.

The manager wants a curriculum therefore that teaches him how to persuade people to accede to organizational ends not accessible to criticism or alternative. The counsellor devises one in which the discussion of personal satisfaction and values is completely central, but without conceivable resolution in an inherently social and strongly characterized life, since its ends are already decided upon by the regulative machinery of the bureaucracy. The counsellor is the bureaucrat's odd-job woman. Her contingent defence is that she, at least, is in direct touch with what each of us is taught to see as a fact, and that is our position as an autonomous moral entity. She is stuck with protecting that small redoubt by advocating the techniques of adjustment and of self-expression, which are the self-congratulatory description of the manipulation of others. But her experience requires her theory to stand that close to moral facts.

Not so the senior or middle manager. He disclaims fervently and explicitly any relation to morality, at least of an imperial kind. It is his business (*sic*) and his duty to ensure the maximally effective administration (the phrases offer themselves) of the means and resources available for the bringing about of ends always chosen somewhere else: by the local authority, by the society, by the Minister. He wants to construct a curriculum that will continue the effortless separation of means from ends, define all problems as soluble technically or by the sensitive application of skills, precisely because he has effected the precipitation of morality from his own domain, which is the rational, accountable (key word), professional (ditto) and effective control of the system which he serves. It is wearisome to have to keep saying it, but the practitioners themselves insist in such assured accents that *they* are self-aware, self-critical aspirants to competence in an unavoidable action, that I have to say again of many managers beyond, but particularly of vice-chancellors and University Grants Commissioners, of principals of colleges and headteachers and deputy heads, that what they have to do is contrive manners to manipulate large numbers of people to do as they are told according to means the managers cannot handle and in the name of ends which few people would support.

To bring off this monstrous and well-named confidence trick, the managers must devise consultative techniques and skills of referral and delegation which are validated by an unrecognizable spectre, the expert, and could only be generated by knowledge which is unobtainable. The making of the subject has to rely consequently on what are reassuringly called case-studies, which might be of use if what they were was careful history or intelligent fiction, but which are used predictively or exemplarily when all they, in turn, really are, are superstition and folklore. Nothing wrong with folklore, of course, as we must nowadays all say; but they don't justify a subject, let alone the subject's power.

For the manager's authority to be justifiable in the language of present bureaucracies, he must be intending to organize his institution according to ends which he sufficiently endorses. In order to do this, he must intend to manipulate others according to his own purpose (whatever his disclaimers). To open things to the possibly different and indeed destructive purposes of others is to relinquish claims to his effectiveness. Happily, such extremities rarely arise, if only because senior managers talk mostly to middle managers, and the common interest of this whole new class[12] is in maintaining the illusion that sanctions their power. Of course, when things come out their way, they will cheer themselves around and up by saying that the stamp of their own authoritative rationality is on this happy event.

These are the practices, complacencies and self-deceptions of what are so accurately called, especially in the case of head-teachers, civil servants. (For such figures to be neither civil nor servile requires the unusual latitude now only conceded to primary schools, conventionally marked by a worthy, affectionate, but absolute mindlessness.) They are circulated in the curricula of management courses and pollute the work of ancillary departments such as drama, a subject whose chronically low status caused its members to seize on the new usage of 'role-play' and 'life-skills' in the management sciences to promote their own indispensability. The deadly banalities of the management consultant and the technocratic expert are universally deployed to justify arbitrary closure, redundancy, the dereliction of building (plant, as they say), as well as the gross, philistine and self-seeking foreshortening of a humane education. We all of us have innumerable such stories to tell. But through it all, with unshakeable self-satisfaction, the managerialists pursue their unimpeded way, entitling new courses 'the management of contraction', 'the organization of decline', or most risible of all, 'falling rolls'. The inanity of the disciplinary diction should have been enough to kill it off. Stuck with a latter-day and pretentious account of the policy sciences as being capable of bringing about rational progress and the accurate predictions which would permit this consummation, no senior manager ever has recourse to such traditional concepts as wisdom, sagacity, utter accident, sainthood, passion, tragedy, historical understanding. No curriculum advises middle managers to pick at random from Hegel, Turgenev, Dickens, Kierkegaard, Einstein, the Buddha, Aristotle, Prince Kropotkin, Hannah Arendt, Rosa Luxemburg, Chinua Achebe.

I do not for a moment deny that we must administer our society. But whatever version of desirable human relations we advance, our administration can only be grounded in the wisdom, maturity, learning, recklessness and intelligence with which we use the specific kinds of human knowledge that we have. To use intelligence upon such subject-matter is to devise a fiction the *form* of which will be congruent with the forms and materials of human life. Such forms have included proverb and saw, as well as allegories of chance, fictions and narratives of endeavour, and even case-study; but there is no substitute for the sort of reflexive thought and inquiry now called critical theory, of which the most usual and useful version is, simply, history.

There can surely be no management theory that is not flagrantly manipulative and no less flatly obligated to self-contradiction. All managers' purposes will always be thwarted and resisted not only by their subordinates' insubordination, but also by their creativity, for which routines cannot be planned. If managers then say, as they fatally do, 'Ah, but we seek only to balance routine and creativity, to enable initiative *and* predictable efficiency', their own persuasive skills intoxicate them, just as they are supposed to. What they exercise is arbitrary power, and the distinguished advance of their subject is merely a measure of the credence given to that power by their society. In its old sense, their only skill is Rhetoric.

It is at this moment that history is brought forward to stand, if not for queen of the curriculum, then as its magus. Now for anything to count as a subject not of the curriculum so much as of inquiry itself, it must possess cognitive content and substantive evidence. In the case of psychiatric therapy, these are provided by the history of the patient; in the therapeutic and bureaucratic subjects, there are no provisions made for what the philosophers of science call counterfactuals (examples that rebut the theory), nor for conditionals (what if something different happened?). The same defect terrifyingly afflicts so-called war games, even in their maddest flights to worst-case instances. At the same time, management theory in the personal or the institutional domains has no critical history, no method for asking, as we all *do* ask in the course of ordinary lives, 'how on earth did I get to be in this mess?' Devoid therefore of principle to guide reflexively understanding backwards or thinking forwards,[13] it is condemned to be the prisoner of its own endless circulation of the present; the purported agent of change becomes in thrall to its own hidden purposes, the warder of changelessness.

The same could not be true of history either in logic or in experience. Of course it is clear that plenty of people lie about history for their own grisly ends, and it is also clear that, in Quine's phrase, '*all* theories are underdetermined by the facts'.[14] Telling a history therefore leaves ample room for partiality, log- or drum-rolling, sentimental twaddle, and downright propaganda. The stern self-image of the historian as the value-free judge of the value-free facts is as big a fiction as the disinterested manager of effectiveness, as all good historians know. The point about history is that we all have one, and therefore can if we are of a mind to and *have* a mind to, check and criticize the history we are told against the one we have lived. It is in this sense that history is logically reflexive. At the same time, the story of history depends on life-in-earnest, and although within and without this story there are no facts which are not inscribed with values, there are determinable events and actions whose truth may, ideally speaking, be established. The way it is usually put is to say that the historian verifies the facts and then interprets, the interpretative frame being subsequently brought up to the true facts and screwed round them for the sake of museum presentation.[15] It seems far better to say that the historian who is in everybody as each of us battles to make sense of our lives, tells and retells, criticizes, edits and confesses a dialectically renewed narrative, whose actions and reactions (as we may say, instead of riding high horses over the facts) are given sequence and meaning and revision according to the beliefs and purposes which the interested agents saw then and see now in them.

This is to put things in an introductorily abstract way. But the present history and historiography of Britain is the best short illustration, in schools, in universities, on television, in the culture at large. The history we told ourselves for half-a-century will no longer do and was always disgusting. It told, as everyone over the age of 40 knows, of a country unequalled in its benignity and resolution, which brought gradual emancipation to its own people and the benefits of both industry and democracy to the Empire it ruled with a firm, wise hand. The tale told of a loyal and utterly adequate military quick to resist the always malevolent piracies of other countries, to defend the weak, and to keep a just and due order in what were thought of as its rightful possessions.

The author of this tall tale was Whig imperialist, and in the present openly contentious climate, he is still doing a brisk trade. But there was always a different history in circulation, much of it necessarily oral, some of it as in the working-class autobiographies I have mentioned,[16] successfully ignored in the list of set books, but still there as a very different version of the narrative, in which the oppressed classes only won any kind of freedom by their own dauntlessness. And as the imperial history went sour, a much glassier eye was turned upon it by novelists like Nadine Gordimer and Paul Scott[17] and historians like James Morris,[18] who were trying to square their own credulous but vivid idealism for what was best in British imperialism with the reality of dire snobbery, venality, cruelty and corruption in its mighty decadence. Meanwhile, the post-colonial states themselves set their new clerisy the task of writing a history and a literature from the wrong side of the imperial police, and in promoting black consciousness, Pan-Africanism and Pan-Indianism, told their own gross falsehoods and in turn violated their own minorities, until once more, in Nigeria, Bangladesh, Zimbabwe and elsewhere, the clash of personal history with official History took place not on paper, but in the streets and in the bush.

The whole action has been muted in Britain, as one would expect, but no less important.[19] Put in a synopsis, we could reasonably say that with the reality of equal treatment and common purpose embodied in the Second World War and made visible in the triumph of the Labour Party in 1945, a sufficient number of young historians turned to the old interpretation of British history in order to subvert it with a new account of what came to be called 'history from below', a new narrative in which the people of England who had been entirely excluded from the drums, battles, kings and constitution history of the old days would be given back a history that returned to them an honourable past with which to live in the present. These men, notably Christopher Hill, Lawrence Stone, Trevor Aston, began from the sixteenth and seventeenth centuries and what Hill renamed, Marx in hand, the English Revolution, bringing out of the historical dark the masses of chiliasts and millenarians, Levellers, Diggers, Muggletonians, who gave the Commonwealth its radical and egalitarian energy and who went under in the landed class settlement of 1688.

This new history placed the motor of change in the class struggle. It went on to find the many different documents that would reconstruct the life of the subordinate class. In this its practitioners were aided by similar developments in France, where the post war historians of the great journal *Annales* also brought Marx and Bloch up to the details of domestic, local, class and political life all over France. They worked in the relative miniature of particular towns (Beauvais, Rennes, Plodemet) and in the huge design of Fernard Braudel's 'total history', *The Mediterranean in the Age of Philip II*,[21] which called on the fullest definition of dialectical materialism in order to include a historical geography, economics, theory of uneven development, and a history of relations of production in hamlet, farm and family.

Braudel may be said to have recast his academic subject. But at the same time, the labours of intensely local historians like W.G. Hoskins[21] brought to light the forgotten lives of obliterated villages and read back the making of a people from the living details of its landscape. He was joined in an adjacent field by Peter Laslett,[21] who worked to reconstruct the daily life of ordinary seventeenth century families, rich, poor and middling, in terms of what they ate, how they brought up their children, how they married and with what settlements, how they died. There is no need to go further into the making of an extraordinarily rich and careful historiography to vindicate the claims that the work put history back into ordinary life, but within a large narrative, explaining so far as it could the disappearance of places, the deaths by starvation, the conversion of souls, in terms of a far larger political economy.

Perhaps the clinching works in this great rewriting took as subject the second epochal upheaval of actual British history since medievalism, the advent of industry, well called the industrial revolution. Working, like the historians of the seventeenth century, from local records, parish registers, magistrates' reports, broadsheets and newspapers, police reports and illegal minutes, E.P. Thompson and Eric Hobsbawm[23] brought back to life in the present the agitators, demonstrators, footpads, highwaymen, paupers and rick-burners who made a culture of class resistance out of those crucial years. It is not too invidious to speak of E.P. Thompson's masterpiece, *The Making of the English Working Class*, as being like a great romantic-Marxist novel of history, in which the years from the naval mutinies of 1794 to the Reform Act of 1832 are populated by a series of working-class heroes, many of them anonymous, who not only won bloody ground from the class enemy, Old Corruption, but brought their own people to a consciousness of their huge strength and resolution. Thompson and Hobsbarm, in turn, have been followed by historians whose records of resistance and creativity come up to the present by collecting orally the reminiscence of the originals, and restoring judicious memory to its rightful place in the conversation of culture.[24]

I write, it is plainly audible, an encomium. But this history gave a whole education system not only the tools of discovery (and the discovery of history is, to say it again, self-discovery), but the crossing of biography with the larger, more destructive and creative forces which can only be seen through the lens of theory. Primary schoolchildren working on the parish register and counting and dating the gravestones, secondary schoolchildren asking their grandparents about the Blitz, undergraduates busy with *Hansard*, *The Times* and *Reynolds News* are alike occupied in reclaiming a past which is capable of being made their own and yet with every re-presentation (the tense is important) is directly open to critical revision and the consequent learning of dialectical knowledge: that is, knowledge which only signifies as such in virtue of its difference from what it is contrasted with.

History is offered as the object-lesson of how knowledge and learning work upon each other to produce an education worth the name. My potted history of History is not sentimental, it is a song of praise. More than that, it indicates a praxis capable of realization at every level of education, and lifts the word education out of its deadlier resonances onto the plane of edification and of human flourising.

7

Class and Culture

Liberation and control, management and resistance, these are the inevitable plays of forces within the mobility of our industrial and class-defined societies. The story of the stories is bloody in all senses, as partisans of different versions try to gain sway for their side; revolution and counter-revolution are merely the names historians themselves have given to the men and the moments at which the machine gun became a more telling way of telling the tale of the society in question. Nor is this a melodramatic way of drawing attention to what has been persuasively seen as a class-struggle in the classrooms. Only one thing is more certain – to say it again – than that there will be no social revolution in Britain, or the United States, or any other country normally and complacently[1] listed as one of the Western democracies, and that is that if there were, the Right would win. In Britain, it would be highly unlikely to be typified by mass rallies or parades of tanks, but far more probably by what E.P. Thompson has called[2] 'steady, vegetable pressure' by a state power grown to an exceptional authoritarianism in a hothouse of economic forcing, and – as Fascism must be – amply supported by a popular mood.

This being so, the class-struggle of the classrooms is not at all a clash of historical titans, nor even recognized as such by many of its protagonists. Those who do, as I shall suggest, give its contradictory, tussling shapelessness a simplicity and starkness of silhouette which has its pictorial attractiveness, but which quite fails to fit the much messier facts of life themselves merely outlined in chapter 1. And yet class is the grammar whose rules enforce the conjugation of our curricular verb according to which children are sent to study pure maths, or business studies, or commerce (typing and shorthand).

So we can repeat the platitudinous premiss of social theory since the great contrapuntal duo of Marx and Mill first set themselves to write their contrary economies in the middle of the nineteenth century, that class is 'the dominant cultural category'[3] of our societies, and our societies may be neither understood nor governed without it. But what does it mean to say so? If we go no further than a round up of staffroom folklore about class, we are likely to be able to group what people fairly crudely say into the following fairly crude sectors of that left-to-right continuum which is drawn with such facility to fix in a single axis all the political positions of an antique polity.

First, there are those (conservative, let us say, with a small c) for whom the model of their society is as a sufficiently steady, occasionally and frighteningly tottering building with spacious and ill-kept accommodation in the basement and on the ground floor, where poor and black and working class live, and a limited succession of floors above that, in each of which the available space is progressively more comfortable and rich in its appointments as it is less crowded in its population, until we reach the grand rooms at the top, furnished with great desks, opened into by immense, discreetly closing mahogany doors and occupied by a very few, dignified men in pin-stripe blue suits. Within this house is a single, hand-driven lift, to which access is only granted to those universally and unenviously acknowledged to be meritorious enough. Such people may subsequently and by their own energies alone cause the lift to rise to the spacious summit whose long, penthouse windows look out upon the kingdoms of the world and the glory of them. This is the house of meritocratic Jack, whose fiction,[4] not without its truth, is that worth in society is that of personal attributes, which should be rewarded according to their inherent value as well as their value to society, and that social structures should be allowed to evolve according to these immanent energies. Let us name this old headteachers' and principals' home from home, the meritocratic-conservative hotel.

Second, there are those whose metaphors for society are synonymous with their metaphors for class. These are the 'radical personalizers', whom we met in Chapter 4, and without too remorselessly insisting that they pay for irony at their own expense, we may call them liberal individualists, or Nietzsche's children.[5] They too tell a fiction which it must be the business of liberal democracies to keep credible and therefore in enough cases true, and according to which class is a dead weight of chains,

fetters, balls and gyves, whose archaic historical symbolism makes
a prisoner of the individual beneath them. It is, then, the
self-creative purpose of that individual so to remake his or her
consciousness that the dead past's dead weight is thrown off in an
act of will determined by the energy of the subjectivity, so that
what remains and is there to grow into fulfilment is unmarked by
its class inheritance, freely and purely itself. Such adjurations may
at times be incongruously heard from certain schools of feminism
who declare allegiance to Marxism, but whose real emphasis is on
an existential act of self-determination, brought on by seminars
and rituals of transfiguration. Given Marxism's view of itself as
the one true science of humanity in the modern world, there can be
little room or relevance for such narrowly subjective moments. But
the best programmes for re-education which, in this example,
address themselves to women's consciousness[6] are far more
conventionally of that wide constituency in the society which
invokes as master-meaning in the value-system the journey to
self-discovery and the achieving of self-fulfilment. Nobody is any
the worse for using Marxism as a name to advance the claims of
liberal and Romantic individualism, but it is as well to be clear
that this is what is happening. A large number of meaning-minders
in the cultural industries who offer a radical and often valid
critique of class in society have no theory of class beyond its
actuality as imprisoning, and personal redemption as always being
within the capability of the individual, if only he makes sufficiently
strenuous efforts at self-education to merit it.

The third common-sensible account of class has taken much
more solid account of Marx-derived theories of class, and is much
more inclined to offer an image of class not in terms of the shaky
building which houses all of society, nor as a heavy encumbrance
bolted onto individuals by their natural enemy, Society, but rather
as the dynamic source of historical energy which powers *all* the
actions of social agency and is therefore the source of the
unintended and uncontrollable motions of structuration which are
history in action and life in earnest. This distinctly abstract way of
putting it implies no particular endorsement of this third assortment of images for an everyday theory of class. But as the terms
'dynamic', 'energy' and 'power' indicate, they do have some
account of the force of destiny, some way of acknowledging that
individuals live their society right through themselves, their lives

and bodies; they do not merely experience it as oppression (although of course it may be that alone), nor as residence, but as conflict, friction, the ceaseless chafing of an engineering in which they are part, which will no doubt wear them out and break them up, but without which nothing at all would move and they would be inert fragments in a stopped story.

Perhaps the mechanical metaphor tells us something about its provenance. Marx himself wrote[7] of the relations between economic base and ideological superstructure as though the former (the systems of production and their intercalation of capital with labour) were the vast machines in some underground powerhouse which drove all the little mechanical figures on top through the motions of civil society: the law, the military, art and science, education, religion, domesticity. Marx himself, like all of us, took his most compelling metaphors from the dominant public practices of the time, in his case, capitalist technology; indeed, it is a datum of his own analysis that he was bound to do so. Inasmuch as more or less Marxisant criticisms of education have been the source of some of the most vigorous and progressive ideas in the field for the past twenty-five years, then it is worth illustrating this variety in two brief instances which bear particularly on the analysis of the curriculum: the Althusserians and, less precisely, though a bit offensively, the New Left Hegelians.

Louis Althusser, born in 1920 and now sadly confined to a mental home because of his apparently murderous bouts of depression, stands best to exemplify his own influence. That influence may be readily traced in a clutch of recent primers.[8] But Althusser addressed himself directly to theorizing the leadenly anaesthetic properties of a French education which he sees as the state's own processing apparatus functioning always on behalf of the elite bourgeoisie (the social-analytic vocabulary of English cannot do without the French conceptualizations) in order to ideologize and inculcate a mute, quiescent acceptance of the way of a world ruled by its present rulers. We have already glanced at the theory of ideology, and in a now widely invoked formula, Althusser wrote[9] of 'ideological state apparatuses', largely encompassing the whole educational system, which functioned as printing machines whose inscription of dominant ideologies upon helpless individuals left them incapable of voluntary agency. At the same time it reduced them to bearers of ideological standards, emptied historical momentum of their will and their very presence, and made of history 'a process without subjects', in which juggernaut structures clashed at night out of their own formative and dialectical drive.

The theory is subtler than this rather crass synopsis makes it sound. It enables a theory of social-personal formation which gives proper place to the notion cheerfully propounded by this book, that individual identity assembles itself out of the inevitably ideological narratives which cultural structures spontaneously produce as the expression always of human interests and their interested parties.[10] But putting things thus certainly domesticates the harsher edges of Althusser's distinctly ruthless view of human inaction. He was, we should recall, writing from a Paris in which a cadre of severe and ascetic *maîtres à penser* [11] (and he the least of them) set themselves in about 1960 or so to repudiate the doctrines of classical humanism, deny the central images of Man as the agent of progress which the human sciences of enlightenment would help to bring about, and dissolve what his colleague in the enterprise, Jacques Derrida, later called 'the metaphysics of presence',[12] which the grim old bourgeoisie keeps in trim to disguise its entirely partial privileges.

In spite, however, of these seemingly remote and academic lucubrations, the Althusserian model of class in our terse review of class and the curriculum has its short significance. For he insisted, in the company of others, that education was a process which only seemingly could be said to lead to individual enhancement and self-awareness, but which in the harder way of social things really taught pupils to stay quiet, do as they're told, and more largely, to accept with docility the world they step into as adults. Althusser was then faced with the entertaining indignation of very large numbers of his teacher-disciples, who furiously denied that they were no more than carriers of ideological radiation to dissolve any resistant marrow in the pupils' bones. Under this attack, he devised the useful, though very approximate notion of 'relative autonomy', subsequently and rather more tightly theorized, as we have seen, by Basil Bernstein.[13] This left teachers some space for political and intellectual manoeuvre, and uncoupled the flatly one-to-one connection between economic base and ideological (that is, educational) superstructure which Engels wrote into official doctrine after Marx's death. Such a connection is the surely far too simple-minded foundation of even such a powerful book as *Schooling in Capitalist America*,[14] the main assertion of which is that schooling is no less and no more than the manpower-training-and-providing machinery of capitalist society.

Relative autonomy is the slogan, rather than the concept, which releases teachers from the rigid determinism of this description, and allows them a degree or two of critical freedom.

It is never a view to be paltered with, even though, as Marx himself observed, to become aware of the limits on your imagination is to move them, and therefore to understand that too much of your teaching day is taken up with holding pupils to the bureaucratized lines of arbitrary work is to become capable of not doing so, and opposing the imperative that you should.

This is the shadowy realm in which, as I have quoted Anthony Giddens as saying, structure produces agency which reproduces, in a changed form, structure. In a more homely idiom, we can only do what we do according to the rules and conventions of the place; but when we do so, we may change them as we go. As the observations on selves and identity in chapter 4 insist, no one can make themselves an identity *outside* social structures, but equally it is extraordinarily difficult to distinguish spirit and culture, an essential life from what life makes of it. Wherever the knife falls between shadow and act, it never quite cuts at just the point where structure and agent, or society and the spirit, truly meet. Psychologist, linguist, sociologist, political scientist and novelist are all trying to throw their intellectual net over those moments and make them universals.

This chapter-long inquiry into the reality and elusiveness of class can hardly do more than point out the difficulty as a central conundrum in the human sciences, although it is of course no accident that this huge question arises so bluntly and disobligingly in connection with the official knowledge-system of society. The magnitude and density of the issues released by the question of how structure turns into action, or in a more staffroom diction, how class organizes both the knower and the known, are staunchly faced in a well-known book which may be listed as a product of Althusserian inquiry without its ever falling into the more plonking versions of mechanistic explanation. Paul Willis's *Learning to Labour*[15] takes the most recalcitrant boys of the school-leaving year ('the lads') and alternates vivid ethnography with structural explanation, whose import is that such boys, cheerful, truculent, anarchic and resigned as they are, learn thoroughly the superordinate lesson of the curriculum as being that it is work itself which defines their week, their year, their life, that further it is pointlessly allocated in fixed and necessarily boring quantities by superiors from whom the only self-authenticating escape is to dodge or skimp what is given to do, and replace it with directly remunerative and subversively illicit alternative production. Thus and thus the lads learn to labour and not to labour, to endure dead routine and to keep as much of the profits as may be feasible without trouble from authority.

These are the homely and economic class lessons of old England. But Willis's book intends no simple minded victory for Althusser's grim theorists.[16] For as every teacher knows, as that first-rate film *Gregory's Girl* so touchingly brought out, he and she piously work and think with him and her in the same work-endorsing, work-dodging rhythm. The teacher in charge of the metalwork rooms and the antique Morris Minor engine does repairs for his friends and neighbours with payments in kind or out of kindness, while he allows the lads themselves to mend unlicensed motorbikes on the quiet and off the syllabus. The third-year head cooks the books and the law in allowing her tiny bunch of incipiently delinquent girls to evade the dance and movement lesson which they hate and are very bad at, in order to practise the hairdresser's and beautician's art in the toilets as the only job they have a hope of getting, as the only pleasure they have in awful homes and dreary schools, and as a reasonable way of keeping them quiet anyway. It will not do at all to come down with a radically sanctimonious thump upon such versions of pastoral care as covert forms of 'social control'.[17] These practices are not forms of control, they are forms of *life*.

It is, of course, the rigidly fixed nature of the whole scheme which makes its critics so impatient, and this fixity characterizes even the subtler formulations of new Marxism. Such theory has become a badge of dissent worn by those who wish, admirably enough, to delay, qualify and deflect the undoubted inclination of schooling in capitalist modernity to plan production of smiling, polite, obliging, compliant little bearers of a changeless social order situated in the lotus-land of about 1960. But few of them take seriously the Arctic immobility of their pet spokesmen. Thus

Nicos Poulantzas, defining the location of class as found in the struggle itself, a definition given by Marxist epistemology, goes on with necessary generality to say:

> Social relations consist of class practices, in which social classes are placed *in oppositions*: social classes can be conceived only as class practices, these practices existing in oppositions *which, in their unity, constitute the field of the class struggle.*[18]

'Practices' become synonymous with relations of production and the situation of struggle in the realm of everyday life, because such life in class society simply *is* a matter of class-struggle. So whatever you think you are doing – resigning, giving up, getting tired, or merely dying with a little patience – the significance of structure is such that intentional action is impossible, and your own sign is that of struggle. It follows, for this dogmatism, that 'social classes coincide with class practices, i.e. the class-struggle, and are only defined in their mutual opposion'[19] . . . and 'in this sense, if class is indeed a concept, it does not designate a reality which can be placed in the structures; it designates an effect of an ensemble of given structures, an ensemble which determines social relations as class relations'.[20] If, indeed! Well if it is, by this token class is entirely caused by the interlocking dynamics of a historically singular, but ubiquitous mode of production, and then what is both vindicated and abused as functionalism comes into play.

Functionalists, whether under that or more everyday titles, claim that all social behaviours similarly function to maintain the system of that society, and that understanding social action is a matter of inserting that action into the structure of society in order to see what it does to maintain that structure. Conversely, it may be removed from the society and understood by asking what its absence would do to unsettle that society such that the behaviour's restoration (or its creation in the first place) enables the machine to function better or indeed at all. Thus, even ceremonies that turn the world upside down (as teachers coming to school on set days of the year – 'for charity' – dressed exaggeratedly as schoolchildren in gymslips and long black-stockinged legs or crammed into grey shorts), such ceremonies by definition function to maintain a systemic structure which without saturnalia would have no disinhibiting release of tension or dispersals of unspoken resentment at the necessities of authority. In the revealing cliché, this 'safety valve' view of the social machinery is a routinely familiar reference to functionalism. It may come in many political colours,[21] but for our immediate purposes it is its Marxist guise which has both disguised and discovered the art and craft of the state as it devises education and culture for the liberation and control of the people, intended or unplanned.

But whatever the discrediting of Marxism and the alternatives, it is probable that the mental modes of all teachers – and, most likely, of all citizens – will continue to include the house of class, the lone ranger *and* the Left functionalist. This being so, what more accommodating, discontinuous, but also experienced theorization of class will do to explain by redescribing the pervasion of the curriculum by the fact and values of class formation? Looking for a different model in the natural sciences to the old brass and iron steam-engine, which for Marx and Engels both symbolized and *was* the agent of alienation and accumulation, working always for and against men, we may come up with the metaphors of a particle physics, in which class is a field of force whose wave functions pulse down the channels of production, investment, labour, and so on, and whose highly various, systemic, but unpredictable atomic life is carried in the realms of family, friendship, school, cultural form, and as many other charges of electro-social life as you care to name. Some such formulation has the merit of acknowledging both power and pervasiveness, as well as inertia and chance,[22] and also acknowledges that fields of force have their own rules, but are at the same time subject and object of study. They may be harnessed by those who know their working, and given specific, alterable purposes.

My illustration (the metaphor purports no more than that) arises from two longish essays with which the piously political student might begin practical reasoning about class.[23] Both heroes, E.P. Thompson and Jean-Paul Sartre, are intensely practical in their reasoning about political life,[24] to the extent of famous interventions in the living praxis of their day – Thompson's intervention being indeed still very much alive, in the movement for European nuclear disarmament. In their writing, both emphasize the interconnectedness of individual life with a larger social life, itself a commonplace enough thing to do, but both seek to bring out the quickness and vivid spontaneity of that individuality, its distinctiveness of silhouette and of effectuality, as well as its atomic self-sufficiency, the degrees of freedom which allow a mass to become just that: a bloc of discrete, active, but causally inefficacious motions of indifference. When activity-in-indifference characterises large groups, as for example when internal events cause mass, but separate response — a torrent of refugees from a bombed city, or crowds of unemployed across Britain — then Sartre identifies this as 'seriality' (his coinage): a continuous, multitudinous situation of passive or oppressed helplessness. Against *and* within these motions of creative individuality and the seriality of (causally speaking) passive co-existence, Thompson reaffirms the necessary *fight*, that compound of bloody-mindedness and the will to freedom, of independence and leadership, as well as (less attractively) of organization and ruthlessness, which compose class solidarity.

As the two activists (*sic*) think of it, a militant class is, in Sartre's words, never 'simply embattled, nor simply scattered in its mass passivity, nor a bureaucratic machine (as in political political parties). It is a multivalent, mobile *relation* between these different forms of practical life.'[25] And he precedes Thompson, though in a very different language, in reminding all social thinkers-and-actors that the many forms of practical life 'cannot be enclosed by any single category of interpretation'.

Seriality becomes solidarity, and dissolves back again; these are the rhythms of history, in its homely and its historic forms. So it was, say, in Prague in 1968, the process being helped along by Russian tanks; on my reading of British history, so it was in Britain between 1943 and 1947. Either way, both seriality and solidarity may find either their life or death in the spontaneous actions of 'bonded groups' (Sartre's phrase) or in formal institutions like political parties or schools.

Perhaps these metaphors may prompt a richer vocabulary of class analysis in the conversation of the curriculum, for the obviousness of class advantage, hypocrisy, mercilessness and apathy is all the more painful to point out as it is denied, ignored or neglected by teachers of every kind, from infant schools to universities. Yet it is class which organizes who does which subjects in what numbers at every level of education. That same process of organization and selection determines admission to the privileges of the professions (the mental forms of production) and to the less obvious rewards of semi-skilled labour (the manual). These things are everywhere known and bitterly commented upon,[26] but almost changeless in the proportions of reproduction. It is always worth insisting upon them, and ensuring that a still popular sort of falsehood, that everybody can 'get on' and 'do well' and reach the top of every tree if they have a mind to, is regularly put down by new figures confirming the old truth, that Britain is a monstrously and arbitrarily unequal country, and that such unforgivable injustices flout the first principles of a decent moral republic.

These circumstances are the results of policies and structures of access and admission in education – of, as they say, input and output. But class is no less present in all that happens to the curriculum in between. It is there, if you want to see things that way, in the very presence of the teacher teaching the class-inflected definitions of the curriculum to working-class pupils who, in the relevant phrase, just don't want to know. Truly enough, as I have noted, there is a dire tendency among teachers to combine in their picture of the good life as realized in the curriculum those qualities which put so many of them where they are: obedience, faithful repetition of all they have been told, docility, quiet, hard work, stifling small-mindedness and attention to unimportant detail, respectability. These are some of the moral and intellectual attributes of the European *petite bourgeoisie*, and malediction comes easily to all radical tongues when they are named.

No doubt there is truth in such charges. Teaching has long been the avenue of social promotion for working-class children with the wits and the opportunity. To obtain that promotion, they had to do as they were told, and if so-called reproduction theory has anything in it, it is (to compress drastically) that educators seek to make students in their own image. Now critics of teachers and teaching who hold this view – and all rational people must be alive to its frequent accuracy – have been at pains to point out that, for instance, even in the most liberally self-conscious classrooms, the teachers do most of the talking.[27] They have picked up Bernstein's famous distinction between restricted and elaborated codes, in which the former modes of speech are context-specific, personal, allusive, disjointed and concrete, and the latter generalized, abstract, sequential and complicated. In his wake, they have suggested that teachers speak the latter, 'educated' code, and working-class children fail so frequently because they can't make the conceptual, as well as the linguistic shifts (and the one failure because of the other) which are required of them.[28] And thereafter, these critics have gone on to suggest that a petty-bourgeois teacher population selects and advances those children with nice manners who smile politely and write clearly, and ignores, bullies or puts down all the others.

By this stage we have travelled out of the realms of inquiry into class towards the mean streets of everyday abuse. Well, abuse has its justified targets. There are indeed battalions of teachers, in the deep complacencies of universities as well as the dismal mediocrities of many primary-school classrooms, whose effective preferences for cowed submission and leaden, truculent concessiveness are actualized in curricular practices best vivified in Michel Foucault's analysis of the ideal modern prison,[29] in which the warders' surveillance of the prisoners would be made total, and therefore totalitarian.

No one can ignore the deep drives of industrial culture towards what Poulantzas calls 'the exceptional State' and its 'populist authoritarianism'.[30] Indeed, it is the whole purpose of this book to call such teachers as read it to the standards of resistance to these dreadful and dangerous forces. But the last enemy is not the first, and in criticizing the class formation of teachers and its effects in the ideological distortions of the curriculum, it is important to be sure of where real power and its menacing coercions lie, as opposed to the trivial irritations of manners and morals we happen to find unimportantly limiting. This distinction comes out with massive inescapability when we turn in the next chapter to consider the 'modes and relations of production' as these issue in the making of work by the systems of the curriculum. But for now it will do to say not only that it doesn't much matter if teachers still tend to send girls to home economics and boys to metalwork, or if they pretend that writing poems is creatively self-fulfilling when several children find it very boring, but that such actions are hardly expressions of a class hegemony whose universal saturation ensures that class values, class organization of knowledge and culture, and ultimately class retention of capital and production are kept where they are.

There are, after all, *values*, not merely class values. The value of severe and lonely dedication to the creation of a painting, a performance of a Mozart piano concerto, a piece of philosophic inquiry, unites Cezanne, Solomon and Wittgenstein in what it is dumbly incomprehending as well as wrong to call a class activity. Without such austerity, there would be no art nor thought, and without these no history, only the repetition of inanity. By the same token, the virtues are virtues, not modes of class oppression: the compassion and gentleness shown by Jesus to Mary Magdalene, Cordelia to Lear, Bonhoeffer to his Gestapo captors, are themselves virtuous. They are not class property, any more than they are only Christian; they recur in classical Greece, primitive East Africa, contemporary Buddhism. Courage is courage in the battle of Bataan, before Agincourt, at the Hot Gates.

Opposing the deformations of class in the curriculum is a deeper matter, therefore, than taking the side of the students against the teachers because they, like your parents, are the ones who are there and get upset, whereas the ideological state apparatuses and their policemen are hard to find and somewhere else.

Sometimes the depths are perfectly clear. When all is said and done about the class favouritisms implied in particular ways of teaching, it is surely the case that, as never before, the British primary and secondary-school systems are the sources of decisive social progress, even at a time when progress itself has such a threadbare referent. It is argued[31] that the pedagogy of discovery and of self-pacing, the curriculum of concept-building and thematic fields of study, are peculiarly congruent with ideological tendencies and social relations of the meaning-minding industry as presently disposed in the various cultural bureaucracies of church, education and media. Their preferences are for loose, informal modes of control, for 'persons' rather than 'characters', as I put it in chapter 4, for ways of knowing rather than states of knowledge, for delaying the divisions of intellectual labour in the interests of fluid agglomerations of cultural reference (politics, art, science, gastronomy, travel, humanitarianism, sexuality). All these, the case goes, are best suited to their own children and their social advance.

It may be so. But it is also true that the threats to educational freedom and the reality of repressive control are rather less marked[32] in the amiable excesses of infant-school finger-painting and secondary-school sessions on personal relationships than they are in the dead ends of the Manpower Services Commission and the various efforts now being made to run secondary and further education from the Department of Employment. There are no doubt severely *intellectual* strictures to be made of bits of awful curriculum; some have been made here already. But those have only at several removes a relevance to questions of class. Indeed, at a time of such lowering and ungenerous uncertainty, it is worth reaffirming the great contribution made to the sum of human happiness and freedom, especially if freedom is thought of less as a right to individual space and more as a virtue, by the development of the comprehensive school for children from the age of 5 to 18. That development is still in its babyhood, in places hardly begun, but starting from the straight abolition of the eleven-plus selection examinations, the legal insistence that all but the fee-paying handful of the nation's children go together to school through the same gates, followed by the enormous extension of both study and opportunity – of subjects, equipment, travel, and methods of teaching – the changes in schooling reflected in the rewriting of the whole curriculum have made unmistakably for a better world. In the teeth of continued and dreadful ignorance, bigotry, illiteracy, and the rest, the citizenry as never before can speak up for itself, knows more of the great world and respects what it does not know, refuses servility and loves freedom, honours culture and tolerates variety in ways which still give meaning and believability to the great project of human enlightenment and emancipation.

Of course, such boldness of affirmation risks shouts of derision at a bareness of face which to the old self-appointed guardians of culture is synonymous with cheek. And of course these embodiments of progress may have all kinds of things about them which we don't like. Children may so far have learned, as teachers claim they intend to teach, to think for themselves, that they get up and leave the classroom. They may have won for themselves the knowledge that some hands in the curriculum dealt to them are part of a pack of lies. Maybe this and maybe that. But in so far as the intentions behind the move to comprehensive education in schools was that all children should be given access to common culture and a curriculum as realizing a shared, mutually accessible picture of the good life, then – allowing for the slow historical construction of all new institutions – those good intentions have not been dishonoured, and the best teachers who may without priggishness be said to act as the conscience of the institution have surely kept their faith with and in those ideals.

Looking on the bright side has its presumptuousness, no doubt. But it doesn't win or lose the day for progressivism. The all-important significance of class is not only that it is so ubiquitous and material a fact of life in Britain and the world, that nobody can understand what is going on without some picture of class, but much more that the effects of class are to have wounded and poisoned so many lives in such irrevocable ways. The point of this short tour of class theory is, as ever,at once theoretical and practical. It is to indicate that the picture (or theory, if that seems preferable) you have of how class works, frames and directs what you will do about it. My brief apostrophe to the victories won by and on behalf of teachers and pupils in comprehensive schools (which, to say it again, denotes both primary and secondary) connects theory with practice in the easily forgotten platitude that political and moral gains, like military ones, have to be held onto and renewed. Given that class is the mobile, elusive, but invasive thing it is, then like power itself class may be transformed in one social action on behalf of the good life and its truth and beauty, while at the same time it reappears elsewhere with its new mutilations and imprisonments.

This is indeed the process of our history, and it is formally and repetitiously inscribed in the curriculum. Indeed, the making and remaking of any curriculum is a collective, but also contested act of cultural revision. In the view of the comprehensive curriculum as well as that of polytechnics and even the corners of some universities, which I have taken, for the present chapter, from the sunny side up, this revision as it has been conducted over the past thirty years or so has consistently, though fumblingly, sought to rejoin lived experience to offical knowledge. That is to say, as the temporary surges of feeling came through from a working class only just counted into the benefits of capitalism, teachers responded by altering the structures of recognition extended to their pupils. Where once the school had insisted on the absolute-ness of the boundary between school and out-of-school, between street wisdom and book wisdom, between speaking properly and talking like a lout, an entirely new, irregular, but vigorous movement began to acknowledge the culture and experience which the children brought with them so inalienably in order to attach it to different forms of knowledge itself, and the purposes and actions which are the end, the telos of knowledge.

So, speech changed. Talking improperly became limitedly possible. Especially in primary schools, the child herself moved forward on the plane of reception; she was put in a slightly larger, more prominent space in which to make some shift at creative action and a personal discovery of the world in her own language. What she wrote, she wrote 'in her own words'. When she measured the playground and counted gravestones, devised histograms of passing traffic and built a collage with her friends from her table, whatever the sentimentalities and trivialities of some of the work done, such a curriculum enormously extended the purchase of her own experience upon the inscrutability of learning.

There is no need to rehearse the various, polemical, and often moving literature which has been a sign of these times. But a personally chosen, memorable handful will perhaps do something to bring out what I am trying to name: the strenuousness of physical, moral and intellectual effort which men and women put into the battle to make sense of their lives, and then, most moving of all, the way in which at the right time, in an indeterminate place, these efforts rise above the merely personal and surge into a common stream. When Brian Jackson and Dennis Marsden[33] wrote the small history of their associates' experience as working-class boys who passed the eleven plus and went to Huddersfield Grammar School, they showed in a vivid tableau the way the school first put down and then tried to wipe out the experience those boys and girls brought with them; and they restored to life the intransigence with which some at least resisted their orders. When Richard Hoggart[34] described the working-class life of the Hunslet he grew up in – when indeed in almost as good as a book[35] Brian Jackson copied him – he not only restored to value the class life he so richly described, he extended recognition to a whole treasurehouse of recorded value which all children of the 1940s brought to school – comics, thrillers, the Light Programme, the Home Service, the sentimental song and the stand-up comedian – and insisted on its shaping spirit and memorable force, as well as on the spirit and force of all such experience in the lives of all children. When David Holbrook wrote his significantly titled *English for the Rejected*,[36] even when the Royal Commission delivered up its muffled prose under the chairmanship of John Newsom,[37] a new educational constituency had been named and, if at times condescendingly (this is England (*sic*), after all), recognized as having, in the phrase, its own life to live.

This is what I mean by cultural revision. It transpired in the Newsom Report and in the Plowden Report three years later on primary schools. It issued in such successful curricular projects as the Schools Mathematics Project and Nuffield Science, in *Science 5–13*, and a dozen others whose advances and withdrawals may be read in the very formation as well as the publications of the Schools Council.

Any such tide comes in on a very uneven front. As tides will, it goes out again. But the tide metaphor will not do to describe the doubling back and forth of historical progress and regress. It will not do to say, with the new Marxists,[38] that the educational changes I have summarized and applauded are no more than the machinations of social democracy trying to make the world safe for post-1945 capitalism. Class, as I have remarked, is inseparable from power, and power is not just the ability to coerce in either two or three dimensions the wills of others:[39] it is what it says it is: power, the essence or force which is effectual, the nature of causality (or efficacy) itself.

There is no need for this to sound melodramatic. This side of warfare, history only moves very slowly and, as we might put it, in its own time. But if the changes in the curriculum on behalf of a slightly less lethal class system which emerge from recent British history may be seen as energetically willed, voluntary and worked for, they have to operate in the field of structures – structures of regulation, production and systematization – which have *their* deadly and inflexible presence.

8
Work and Meaning

I have spoken much in these pages of structures, and as many people have noted, the word and the concept are fatally liable to merely modish use, as well as implying a real existence out there, instead of its having a strictly metaphoric life identifying otherwise nameless and uncontrollable eventualities.[1] But it is in speaking of the structures of economic production that the idea has one of its strongest applications. As we have noticed, the value, meaning and functions of work itself are taught to and learned by children from the moment they enter the reception class, and days are divided into worktime and playtime. From the age of five, the deep distinctions between work and leisure, production and holiday, weekdays and weekends, clocking on and off, productiveness and unproductiveness, conscientiousness and sloth, all come to shape not only the innumerable individual identities, but our profoundest sense of space and time, continuity and culture themselves. Indeed to complete education is to enter the present as an adult, and such entrance is marked by stepping over the thresholds of production into the society of other free, productive men and women. Of course, as we see around us every day, many of those thresholds either give onto tightly locked doors or open into derelict premises, but the effort to keep that entrance to work universally open remains the central, collective enterprise of the society. To have work is to ensure your own freedom.[2]

For work to be work it must be contained within the recognized structures of the mode and relations of production. It must be made visible and given value as production by its actualization as a commodity. Only then is it official work, and gathered as such into the relations of production which define social life. Within capitalism, these mean that whatever commodity is produced, including the so-called invisible commodities of the service industries – driving a truck or a train, working in a bank, mending teeth or lecturing on ancient history – that commodity must be defined according to the criteria and categories of profitability, productivity and efficiency. Once a social practice is organized in such a way that the time it occupies may be divided into remuneration and surplus-value (Marx's phrase), then that time encloses the occupation as commodity, and separates labour from capital accumulation.

In his famous formulation of these processes, *Capital*, Marx himself simplified the argument by speaking always as though the commodity were a palpable, manufactured product which, as he saw it, the slightly crazed brain of both worker and employer thought of, fetishistically, as possessing value in itself and not just for its social uses. In a famous passage, he wrote:

> A commodity is therefore a mysterious thing, simply because in it the social character of men's labour appears to them as an objective character stamped upon the product of that labour; because the relation of the producers to the sum total of their own labour is presented to them as a social relation, existing not between themselves, but between the products of their labour. This is the reason why the products of labour become commodites, social things whose qualities are at the same time perceptible and imperceptible by the senses . . . To find an analogy, we must have recourse to the mist-enveloped regions of the religious world. In that world the productions of the human brain appear as independent beings endowed with life, and entering into relation both with one another and the human race. So it is in the world of commodities with the products of men's hands. This I call the Fetishism which attaches itself to the products of labour, so soon as they are produced as commodities, and which is therefore inseparable from the production of commodities.
>
> This Fetishism of commodities has its origin as the foregoing analysis has already shown, in the peculiar social character of the labour that produces them.[3]

It isn't a satisfactory account, unspecific as Marx is about what it is which does the 'presenting' of the sum total of their labour to all men, and so presents it moreover as at once a social relation and a *thing*, with its curiously autonomous life. And Marx has been subsequently and seriously criticized, even by economists much influenced by and sympathetic to his thought, for precisely this crucial notion of 'surplus-value' and its operational slipperiness.[4] But the importance of the passage as of the book is that it shows believably how a very particular, not at all inevitable system of providing for human needs becomes a structure of meaning which attaches men to things, in a telling phrase, in spite of themselves.

By 'mode of production', Marx and those who follow his analytic lead mean the economic system dominant in any one society which seeks to create and distribute abundance. It is a phrase by means of which to conceptualize not whether a particular economy is, say, dependent on extraction from nature (mineral or energy mining, for instance) or on manufacturing, but rather the ratio of subsistence to surplus, of use to exchange (and profit, if any), of money to its reproduction, and all of these ratios at *any* point of historical development, not merely at that point at which money is replaced by capital. Now the 'relations of production' are conceptually inextricable from the mode. For the mode sets limits to the ways in which men and women may associate with one another as they pursue their vital interest in food, shelter, property, freedom on behalf of themselves and their families and friends. Most simply, once the mode of production operates with the categories of capital and labour, and the drive to accumulate begins, then classes are alienated one from another, and workers alienated from work. Capitalist relations have begun.

The magisterial reach of this theory is clear. It accounts for some of the deepest conflicts, contradications and pains of contemporary experience. It places the acts of production at the centre of that experience and brings out that failure to fulfil which makes us strangers to ourselves, and fixes them as inevitably contested, in so far as the pointlessness of profit accumulation for others rides our acts of making and makes us their slaves.

Putting things like this is only possible, of course, in an analytic framework that sets itself in opposition to the totality of what it analyses. But opposition entails position. In other words, Marx, like any other critic of the industrialization he first identified as capitalism, at least in a full-blown theory, has to situate himself somewhere else in order to gain leverage on the object of his criticism. He stands on the foundation of two traditions: from the first, enlightenment position, work is criticized as having lost the creativity and potency of self-fulfilment, which Marx's very various Victorian contemporaries located either in the medieval guilds and their crafts or in the practice of the artist, the very type of free, useful and humanly enhancing production. From the second position, however, hugely more long-standing, work is Adam's curse, the condition of his discharge from the Garden of Eden and the enduring burden of a humanness severed from beatitude.

Either way – and few Victorians, certainly not Marx himself, distinguished between their dual inheritance – industrial work was what had come to deprive men and women of the living connection between them and their creativity, the connection broken in the theodicy of the Fall before which, either in Biblical truth or mythical longing, the provision of subsistence was entirely harmonious with the rhythms of nature. Alternatively, industrial work was what, in its killing repetitiousness and clear severance of the 'hands' from head and heart, had sundered – through the agency of the boss – the maker from the made, the whole person from the activity of creative work.

This is the long appeal to an ideal of work as self-sustaining, fulfilling, slow, rhythmic and true, to which Left and Right alike appeal[5] from the early nineteenth century until a present in which teachers of all kinds seek to keep apart in the minds and efforts of their students work which is satisfying, true and creative, and labour (best seen in exams) which is repetitive, uninvolving, false and deadly. The distinction between live work and dead labour is Hannah Arendt's,[6] but it is implicit in all criticisms of what happened to the daily work when industrialization took over.

Of course, it is an act of hysterical self-obsession to suppose that the possibility of eternal indolence has not been a transhistorical fantasy, as all myths of Paradise, in which work is so ambivalently present and absent (is harping work?), testify. Equally, however, it has been methodically underlined in the last chapter that transhistorical values take on their distinctive historical character and outline. Work is a human condition, but who on earth ever came to think that it could possibly be a good thing in its capitalist version?

Trying to explain work in its typically capitalist origins, Max Weber[7] propounded the famous thesis that Protestantism, in both its Calvinist and Lutheran versions, obviously shifted the locus of grace and redemption from the church to the individual. In spite of insisting on the arbitrary nature of that redemption, placing the individual soul in such a bright, universal light gave to all actions an equivalent potentiality, either as a source of damnation or grace. Any sin might be *the* sin which damned a soul. Any virtuous action might redeem it.[8] It is therefore hardly surprising if, in the attempt to take this chance of grace, the most vigorous adherents of a doctrine with no hierarchy of well or evil doing, but only a belief in the power of actions to change the world, one without (furthermore) any ritual of absolution, should have evolved a mode and structure of being in which conscience-stricken rectitude, brief, austere self-examination and ceaseless activity were predominant. Weber then suggests that as the contextual and dogmatic beliefs dissolved under the impact of science and its 'disenchantment of the universe', the formal structures remained as the necessary poles of being within which a man kept himself upright. The character of the capitalist was made within such frames of being.

Weber's has been an extraordinarily popular thesis, so much so that the phrase 'the work ethic', compressed from the title of his great book, is habitually referred to as the prevalent meaning of the labour culture, whenever anyone puzzles over what to do with the unemployed or seeks to explain how it is that some people simply renounce the contemplative virtues and work pointlessly on. Like Marx's theory, however, but on a larger scale, Weber's has great gaps, or rather, is one-legged. He is doubtless right to return the power of *ideas* back alongside economic production itself as the motors of history, but he gives no sufficient account of the genesis of classes nor of the actualities of cruelty, unhappiness and oppression, which are at the humanist heart of Marx's thought. Neither man in practice properly credits human beings under capitalism or any other industrial system with their undoubted powers of resistance, of making concessions and compromises which also leave them room of their own to move, of evading and dodging the points at which coercion hurts in order to do and to make do for themselves.

The drive for a totalitarian control and surveillance of the minds of men and women seems at times — and nowadays is one such time — to be coterminous with modernization.[9] And yet the supreme theorists of modernization, Marx and Weber, never see the facts of an alternative life, a counterculture, simple expressions of the episteme in all human lives which, as naturally as breathing, seeks and finds corners for its freedom. There is no complacency in this. The corners made available for such freedom by concentration camps, or even the officially benign institutions of modern bureaucracies like schools and hospitals, are not very great. The unforgettable point of, say, Solzhenitsyn's great novella about the Gulag, *A Day in the Life of Ivan Denisovitch*, is that we make the best of them.

The mention of schools brings us back to the curriculum. For this short history of work as meaning, in which Marx and Weber are the first, essential teachers, still has a little way to go. Both thinkers knew that the values and meanings to which people give their lives are, because of that significance, the site of bloody disagreement. Of the two, Marx both weighed the costs of that disagreement, in terms of terror and bloodshed, and was more hopeful about the outcome. Still speaking from a tradition that reached back, though the Enlightenment and its faith in progress, to the Christian and Greek formation of ideals that nominated, in Aristotle's word, *eudaimonia* or human flourishing as the goal or telos of a man's life, Marx wrote his critique of capitalism from an ideal of undivided human creativity, the happy operation imagined by both Aristotle and the Romantics. The defeat and supersession of capitalism was the biggest step towards achieving that ideal. Teachers may have learned some such lesson more from folk-memories of what Wordsworth and Ruskin or, further back, Thomas More and St Benedict may have said, than from fierce old Marx and the besotted optimisms of Rosa Luxemburg. But the notion of human flourishing lives on in the far from empty appeals made in the curriculum to happiness and satisfaction, and to the epistemic trigonometry of that flourishing: freedom, fulfilment, and self-critical awareness in *praxis* and *poesis*, action and making.

Weber, on the other hand, had a bleaker and more sombre view of the developments of industrial production. Glancing aside at the Marxists of his day in Germany, when the attempted social revolution of 1919[10] failed and Luxemburg was murdered with Liebknecht, he observed thinly, 'They summoned up the street. The street has dispatched them.' He not only had no great faith in any social movement; he saw the march of modernity as advancing more and more completely with the bureaucratic forms that had become the inevitable expression of the advent of the state, and further considered that the only opportunity for making things a bit better lay in ameliorating the working of those bureaucracies according to the criteria of efficiency, and a rationality which strove always to adjust ends to means in some more or less adequate fit. The characteristics of the good bureaucrat might then make the depredations of a blind state and ignorant masses slightly more orderly to live with.

In effect, Weber provided in fine detail a map of the very relations of production diagrammatized in Marx's mode of production. Taken together, they show us the way of the working Western world since 1900 or so. More bureaucracy, no revolution: the organization of consciousness[11] deceives all parties. (Until, of course, it reached Tehran, when the Ayatollah, as I remarked, rebutted Weber's predictions and dispatched him with Marx to the attic of history.) The trouble is that the slogans of a mindless individualism, as set in bold type for the banners of the tabloid right, have turned 'bureaucracy' into a swear word. Nobody on the sane side of idiocy, however, can suppose that Western societies could possibly function without bureaucracies, and those remaining few whose enthusiasm it is to imagine them no longer in function, have no picture of a redeemed society capable of taking decisions, defending itself, caring for its sick, raising its children, and burying its dead, which does not require a scientific administration and a handbook on how to run it.

Weber wrote the handbook.[12] He saw that bureaucracies must have a purposive rationality expressed first, in the equitable treatment of all clients, secondly, in an efficient knowledge of the files and perfect accuracy of record and retrieval, thirdly, in anonymity in the referral of cases and an infallible routinization of their handling, and lastly, a clear subjugation of means to ends, of process to aims and objectives. And as Peter Berger ironically sees, these ways of sorting experience are now part of all our everyday experience, not only in our necessary traffic with public life – banks, doctors, police, supermarkets, schools – but also in the way these impinge on the everyday living – keeping the deep-freeze full, getting the children to school or ourselves to work on time, keeping out of the red on the current account, paying bills and remembering favourite programmes on television. All experience is partially bureaucratized, for better as well as for worse.

Admittedly there is some difficulty in recognizing the moment at which the shaping of experience, identity, time and decision moves from mere regularity and routine to becoming bureaucratized. Perhaps we can say that the passage is made from routine to bureaucracy when the agent treats another subject (feasibly including himself) as a *client* or, in the revealing term, patient; when formal records and files objectify everyday arrangements in a transferable form; when time dictates the action and not the action the time.[13]

These termini may serve to mark the moves to bureaucracy in formal action. As the Bergers bring out so well, bureaucratic habits deeply penetrate and reshape the modern consciousness. What they do not bring out is the connection between these shapes and pervasions and the relations of production which are controlled and made systematic by the special forms of modern bureaucracy found in those great institutions of modern capital, the corporations.

It isn't quite enough, however, to say flatly that some bits of bureaucratization are good for us and some bad. The official symbols of liberal individualism are such that the notion of bureaucratic organization and its central structures of formality, anonymity, efficiency, justice and regularity are thought of as in themselves deadly and inhuman. Anyone who insists on their proper working can be dismissed as one of the faceless and repressive automata who people Kafka's *The Trial*: creatures whose only purpose is the purposeless maintenance of their system and the eradication of human inconsistency. Consequently, the new developments of bureaucratic systems into the forms of managerialism and counselling that appeared in chapter 6 have to present themselves as warmly and sympathetically concerned with individuals in order to achieve people's compliance.

Such self-presentation works all the better if its practitioners believe in it. So, teachers will organize the curricular culture of schools, self-deceivingly confident that creative activity (art and craft) is not less so for beginning prompt at 9.30 a.m. and going on until, although impossible to stop before, 11 a.m. when it's playtime. ('Play, boy', Estella and Miss Havisham commanded Pip.) The kindly headteacher of a devoutly progressive, childcentred primary school, conscious of his personal care and, indeed, generalized affection for his children, cannot without pain see the files and times of school life as the agency of state bureaucracy.

His difficulty is, however, only the start. Anybody might reasonably agree, after a brief dose of Weber, that the rational adjustment of means to end in the name of efficiency is imaginably a help towards the good life in industrial flourishing. They might reasonably go beyond Weber, with the help of Kafka's warning and recent political history,[14] to make a strong separation between the bureaucratic and the informal realms of life, more or less in parallel to the distinction between public and private life, and the latter as being the domain of all that is informal, flexible, warm, sympathetic, creative, and so on. Something can be made of the argument; it is the way in which most of us hang onto meaning in private life, both at home and at work. But it suppresses the fact of dominance by the public over the private (a dominance inscribed in their lexical meaning). We have rather to think of all lives, in and out of production, as conducted in a *milieu* in which means-end rational planning only applies to specific and short-term problems.

It is, however, the dominating premiss of bureaucratic planning that *all* thinking is defined as amenable to means-end rationality. That is to say, there is a law of its motion which drives together within its own effective field all the activities of its milieu. We may risk a proposition: that bureaucracies are intrinsically driven to attain hegemony over all human action.

If this is thought too near the view of the *Daily Mail* or the worthy headteacher, perhaps it may be more politically astute to say that in the tense, gigantic dialectic between individual liberation and industrial production released in Europe at the end of the eighteenth century, bureaucracy represents an always veering effort on the part of the state to mediate between the two poles, mutually repellant and attractive as they are. It cannot be doubted that veering at the present time is all the way of the systems of production.

It is a loss of balance widely felt, but little grasped. In school life generally, the change in pressure comes through as the weight of committees, of increases in record-keeping, in the minor, irritating, but ceaselessly fracturing interruptions of the day: the dreadful bell, the special appointments, the movement of equipment, the checking of stock, the allocation of resources, the public address system, the notes and chits, the sanctions and punishments, the assembly. But the pressures upon the curriculum of bureaucratization are felt, as it is the point of this chapter to show, with profound and enfolding power as – once more – mode and relations of production. What then comes though is a particular account of work, work for its own sake and organized in these ways because those are the ways which turn doing into production. In a celebrated paper, E.P. Thompson[15] provided an early history of the tropes which accomplish this conversion, when he identified the moments in the seventeenth century when capitalism combined with Protestantism to make time itself into a commodity which should be *spent* valuably, not wasted, and thereafter the way in which the image of the clock ('clocking on') came to dominate production. It did so symbolically as well, even to the extent of clocks and watches becoming the talismans given in honour of the service rendered by those retiring and as a token of their prior gifts of the time of their lives.

The turning of time into a commodity ('overtime', 'part-time', 'time-and-a-half') has been going on since then, and the fitting of time to space in order to provide a unilinear calculus of reward is now a commonplace of educational production. It is most ostentatious in examinations, where the production of set quantities in set periods is what is required, produced and examined. Even when schoolteachers themselves rebelled in the name of non-productive *poesis* and, after the Beloe Report of 1961 and the early Schools Council examination bulletins, moved some examining towards the submission and assessment of coursework folders, bureaucracy and production exerted their logic. In order to regularize production and make assessment just, anonymous and efficient, teachers had to organize techniques of statistical moderation,[16] worked out in endless hours of committee discussion, and issue definitions of quotas and types of production – essays, projects, experiment reports, 'oral talks' *sic* (not more than ten minutes), notes, poems. The same principles hold throughout the curriculum. At tertiary levels, the production of coursework and answers for three-hour examinations is organized by the same inevitably bureaucratic principles. The striking difference is that so very few university examiners (colleges and polytechnics are better educated) have any knowledge of parametric statistics. Singled out for stardom by its purity, they continue to believe that the first-class honours award is identifiable in terms of incontestable qualities rarely to be found in contemporary decadence, and perfectly immune to the demands of a curve of distribution.

These myths are noticeably strong in university humanities departments, but they are present everywhere: over here, amongst teachers who mark down the mock O levels in order to make the pupils work harder: over there, in polytechnic modular courses, where tutorial timorousness in anticipation of the external examiner, custodian of both comparative and absolute standards, causes all students to be awarded a lower second.[17] As most myths do, these seem to obscure the facts of life, in this case that examinations are best understood as boundaries marking access to the next stage of education, and therefore as stages of allocation at the appropriate age (16, 18, 21; O level, A level, BA) in the required numbers for further training or its withdrawal.

Given the mostly arbitrary, but drastic significance of examinations, it is not surprising that their ideological and legendary mass is as great as it is. In representing the culmination of years of work, they enforce the imperatives of work at all previous stages. Given also that teachers made their own mobility out of working hard for examinations, they vehemently endorse what in any case the whole culture teaches: that to become a citizen, a home-owner, a parent, a grown-up member of the world, you must join the society of freely productive men and women, and produce with them. So all children are made to produce, preferably in quiet, and largely by themselves, for it is taken for granted in individualism that that labour is best which you do for yourself, and which when completed is your own property, not to be shared, collectively produced, or stolen (copied from). Such work is also best if it is produced in measurable amounts ('You've done a lot this morning, Garry', and the old *canard*, 'No need to read PhDs, just weigh them'). The rates of production are then subjected to innocent forms of operational research, and the natural way for these to be controlled is in the bureaucratic mode. Hence, pieces of work must be finished by Friday, or by the end of term, must be handed in on time (unless you have a note of exculpation from parent, tutor, or policeman), must represent enough bulk for the time spent, must be all your own — with the possible exception of art which can be occasionally collective, the occasions being school plays or concerts, the odd mural, a magazine.

It is hard not to smell the presence in all this of the deadly machinations of F.W.Taylor and 'Taylorism', the time and motions techniques first devised to accelerate beyond belief the mass production of Ford cars in the USA of the 1920s. Versions of Taylorism, [18] and then later revisions which brought to bear the tenets of a liberally inclined industrial psychology, were the intelligible and widespread expressions of a monopoly capital competing fiercely with itself to ensure that no resource, especially wage-time, was wasted. It gave severity and discipline to the novel forms of an efficient bureaucracy. In state or private capital corporations, those techniques emerged (between 1920 or so and the present day) that fix the terms of planning for production, define the meaning of efficiency as cost-effectiveness, and ensure that the multiple division of labour, but the denial of interdependence, characterize all production, including intellectual production. The anthropological PhD, the primary-school zoology project and, supremely, the increasingly successful efforts of the Manpower Services Commission to control the curriculum, and therefore the lives of an insurgent age-group, are all alike subject to these vastly inclusive processes.

What is more, these processes of necessity frame the minds which do the planning. It is a valid criticism of industrial society that it turns all human activity into the solving of problems which, when once named and defined as problems, are then amenable to the development of techniques which gradually overcome them. A question is not on this account an attempt to direct inquiry and discover the telos;[19] the self-confident, science-minded theoreticism of the rational planner must pose questions capable of defining realizable goals, goals which in turn may be reached by technical, foolproof means.

Well, any fool may use a technique, helped out where necessary by operational managers. The curriculum, as another product from the systems of production, is naturally available for rational planning, since its aims and objectives are determinate and definable, and techniques may be found to attain them. Such has become the conventional wisdom of education's administrators, and as only to be (rationally) expected, curriculum and staff development are linked in the planning of all up-to-date institutions; a manager manages everything and everyone according to their 'needs' and the objectives of production.

The wide, enveloping tendency is totalitarian, even if in a very genteel, vegetable sense. It may be that economic production is humanly improved by these disciplines; it is certain that in all our public life bureaucracy will and must continue as the only mechanism we have for controlling the enormous potentiality for misery, epidemic, destruction and disorder our mass society might realize any day. But – to go no further – the complex milieux of domestic, educational and welfare life should be vividly alive to the mortal dangers of means-end planning, the irrelevant application of cost-effective criteria, the technicizing of both poesis and praxis in the human capacities for creation and action.

If, as I propose, the curriculum as a product is more like a work of art than a manufactured item, it is a work of art like a cathedral or a city, rather than a painting or a concerto. In other words, it is a collective, historical expression of men's and women's purposes and preoccupations, and inasmuch as the word expression connotes a single historical moment, it is also the tradition and ground which make purpose, making and thinking themselves possible.[20]

For no one can intelligibly say that they have aims and objectives in building a cathedral or a city. Or indeed a novel or painting. They are purposive actions with 'unevisageable ends'.[21] To perform them, we standardly look back to see how we got to this position in the first place, and for this short historical reckoning, move forward to make the step. Such thinking is directly contrary to the approved lessons of design theory and the managerial sciences. It has inherent inclinations towards the philistine, the complacencies of common sense, towards (alas) conservatism. These can be avoided with a proper intelligence, as we shall see in chapter 10. But the lived criteria of 'seeming right', of properness and propriety, human suitability, of delicately recognized desires, of practical usability and likely pleasure at beauty are the conditions of art. And if these sound too comfortable, then comfort in the biblical sense of solace is not much in evidence in our relations of production, and in any case I subjoin to the notion of good art the rather more terrifying requirement that it be virtuous and truthful about life as it is lived, and life as it might be lived better.

The curriculum as a work of art has a tale to tell of a better life as well as one to tell us of what and how we do now.

9

Values and the Future

It has been continuously argued in this book that the curriculum should be understood as an ensemble of stories told by one generation to the next about what the possibilities are for the future and what it may be going to be like to attempt to live well at the time. But although I have made blithe play on many occasions with the term 'the good life' and although – Richard Briers and Felicity Kendall notwithstanding – I use the term quite unironically, it would be irresponsible to pretend that the phrase connotes a shared picture of things. Indeed the whole point of my military metaphor at the beginning of Chapter 1 was to show that different world-pictures are fought over continuously, and that this struggle over meanings and values is inextricable from the struggle over territory and wealth. But because the whole curriculum, from that of an infant to that of a doctor, from cradle to grave, is securely settled as, above all, official and at the same time assented to, then we have in it a statement of the instrumental and the expressive realms of the society. That is to say, the curriculum is both the text and the context in which production and values intersect; it is the twistpoint of imagination and power.

Neither this way of putting things, nor the recommendations I shall want to make about the content of the curriculum should be taken to imply that I think that what is taught in schools, colleges, polytechnics and universities is the most important aspect of a nation's life, and that changing them means changing it. The most virtuous curriculum in this world would not prevent of itself our being blown into the next one, if those in power had a mind to it, or no mind with which to stop it. None the less, unless our assorted and disunited nations devise a rational and virtuous science of human affairs – R.G. Collingwood's noble phrase, which I have so much invoked and to devising which he gave his life[1] – then the human prospect is fairly bleak. Given also that it is the business of an intelligentsia to imagine the good life and to teach how to lead it, then the national curriculum certainly begins to loom as large in importance as, say, television newspapers or other instruments of public communication.

Indeed, it *is* one such instrument itself, and as the striking title of the well-known research reminds us,[2] it is one to which every citizen is required to be, with however impaired hearing, audience for 15,000 hours of non-returnable life. Moreover, it is an excellent premiss of liberal or social democratic societies that the content, form and organization of the curriculum is constantly open to public debate, and in point of fact, that debate is regularly and quite decently conducted. Primary schools run parents' classes to learn the new maths, older parents come loyally together with teachers to try to prevent sixth-form work and syllabuses disappearing from their schools, and polytechnics have been known to incorporate students in curricular review and (as they say) evaluation.

These are a few of the signs whose signified reality is the mildness and docility of the society, no doubt, as well as the successful ordering of a cultural consciousness by the dominant interests – that saturation of the *Zeitgeist* named in a rather blank and baffled way 'hegemony' by its enemies. But the reality includes the widespread sharing by the constituency of British society, its many overlapping minorities and its fluid coalitions, of the main principles and politics, the meanings and metaphysics of the national curriculum, however incoherent and inequitable these undoubtedly are.

Understanding the curriculum of British education is therefore to understand a text and texture of social meanings at their most open and readable. But it is also to construe a multivalent and ambiguous text, whose ideological structure is at the same time arrestingly firm and monolithic. In a valuable metaphor, this humdrum, municipal, but solid edifice occupies and holds the wide middle ground of society.[3]

The phrase was first applied to the analysis of television news magazines, where the standing of the presenter – the William Hardcastle, Robin Day, Alistair Burnet and Ludovic Kennedy figures – became such as to guarantee the impartiality of coverage in the programme, together with its judiciously representative mediation on behalf of each of us, the common citizens, as we face up to and interrogate the inadequacies, mistakes and vanities of our rulers. Kumar's convincing case is that such programmes search for the middle ground of social exchange, a geography by definition away from extremes and planted comfortably in a position across the middle of the road whence, the hope is, it will cause all the traffic on left and right to swerve into the ditch. The trouble with the metaphor, as with the politics, is that the middle ground won't hold, as the end of an epoch cracks the highway right across. Plenty of people, television presenters included, go on driving across the bumps and holes as though nothing has happened, and a lifeless assortment of clichés are to hand which partly acknowledge, partly deny by their casualness the real state of affairs; fingers in the dyke and paper over the cracks serve well enough, in a short interview, to keep the old bus on the road.

But Kumar notes that in order to hold this gregarious ground, the agencies of public communication have to widen their exclusion zone enormously. If the nation's broadcasters claim to speak peace unto the nation, as the old nine o'clock news slogan more or less put it, then peaceful speeches had to include as many people as could reasonably be thought of as, in turn, constituting the main membership of society. Those excluded had to be outlaws. But it follows that if views about our life and times are increasingly fractured and contested, then to hold the middle ground you must include a lot of people you would rather exclude. That is, your very principle of solidarity drives you seek controversy in a doomed attempt to resolve it by hearing both sides of the case (the constitutional, but spurious myth of 'balance'), and by asserting a reconciliation found by presenter-knights Robin Day or Alistair Burnet exactly on the fulcrum of the counterposed positions: left v. right, management v. labour, war v. peace, men v. women. Hence, Kumar concludes, public debate on key social issues, as conducted by the BBC and the ITA, is driven veeringly down a spiral of controversy and conciliation in the search for an irrecoverable community of political assent.

I think it is possible to prefigure the whole cultural framework of 'stories we tell ourselves about ourselves' as similarly a holding of an ideal middle ground where most of us are supposed to live, publicly and privately. Kumar, in other words, gives us another homely, intelligible and comprehensive way of understanding ideology and its workings in many different quarters of social life.

I shall apply the notion to the curriculum, but perhaps it brings out its domestic strength, as well as throwing into a kind of relief the way in which the unofficial curriculum of television shadows, extends and echoes the official curriculum of education, if we enlarge the focus of Kumar's concept to take in all television narrative.

We can then see its subtlety and flexibility in acknowledging potential exclusions and even outlaws breaking away from social solidarity (whole peoples at a time, as with the nationalist surges in Wales and Scotland, and the unfinished battle of Ulster). Television narrative constantly recognizes new groupings, and — by giving such groups space in the texture of national narratives — assimilates, perhaps sedates, and sometimes liberates such groups. Thus, soap operas about amiably dotty punks and student revolutionaries (*The Young Ones*, itself a friendly placing title), about single women making their own, post-divorce professional and sexual career (*Solo*) or the same women fluttering safely on the married side of the same sort of life (*Butterflies*), about Geordie workmen finding employment on the other side of the EEC (*Auf Wiedersehen, Pet*), about the wretchedness and splendour of black ghetto life round the dole queue (*Black Joy*), even about the bitter tensions and murderous vengeances of fidelity in the six counties of Northern Ireland (too many Wednesday *Plays for Today* to recollect), all these varied expressions of new, often unsettling group life in contemporary Britain appear in 625 lines and dazzling colour in order to renegotiate the terms of our membership of its society.

The edge is taken off the unsettlingness of these stories by the dazzle of colour television; as every good painter knows, it is very difficult to prevent dazzle becoming either glamorous or nostalgic. But to put things a distinctly functionalist way, it may plausibly be claimed that the range of narrative on television about the multitudinous forms of the good and the bad life in our Britain helps a country *recognize* (the key verb) its own tolerable variety, and therefore helps to keep it tolerant, as well as sympathetic, even compassionate, understanding, mutual, perhaps friendly.

The discordant ring of this insurance company list of the cardinal virtues — mutuality, friendliness, assurance, protection, relief, benefit — declares its lack of harmony with the real, grimmer virtues of our streets: endurance, bloody-minded independence, scepticism, loyalty, dogged pride, kindness. Television, as we might expect, uses soap opera to soap over the lacerations and wounds of a class-hostile life. One of its main qualities is, in liberal society, certain to be soapiness. But the curriculum – the story of the subjects – has another set of tropes which, while quite unable to assume salvation or to prevent the end of the world, may at least hold up if the world ends. And in any case, its more settled (conservative, if you like – how could it be otherwise?), less febrile, local and domestic temper and circumstance immunize it against the demand for news (which must be new) and entertainment (which mustn't hurt) that belabours television. With the best and most radical will in the world, education systems are, functionally *and* intentionally speaking, providing for the reproduction, in some recognizable and therefore conservative form, of contemporary society. It is therefore the duty of teachers in virtue of their role – a moral and a sociological point – to make their necessary changes within a pretty stable and solid framework. By its social definition, a state school cannot train the revolutionary cadre.

Not many teachers would put things in these terms, and are quite right not to do so. But the structure of their daily lives is such as to prevent most of them being *required*, precisely by the public definition of their role and its duties, to endorse a mindless conformism and an obtuse bureaucratic correctness. The tendencies are there, of course, and more marked always in some roles rather than others: it is no accident that headteachers and their deputies are so much miscalled by their staffs for pettifogging triviality of mind, structural timidity before their superiors, and the dismal extinction of their imagination. Similarly, it is not unjust to say that, as professions, the reproduction of themselves by university and polytechnic law departments and schools of medicine is typified by narrow self-protectiveness, by the dull turning into technique and technology of the baffling complexity of human actuality and encounters, by simple greed, pretentiousness and witch-doctoring. These hideous strengths are those of the politics of special knowledge as mediated by the power of the present forms of bureaucracy. But they are escapable: change social structures, and you change what they make people into.

People – in this case, teachers of all kinds – have their own intransigence, and (like children) do not need quite so much care and protection as the self-importance of the very earnest is apt to insist. Indeed one essential way to understand theory and practice in the curriculum is to study the many forms of subversion and resituation necessarily performed by all teachers on all aspects of what they teach. The uniform and unilinear diagrams of curricular instruction give no play to these wide margins of inevitable creativity in everyday teaching. The creativity may be all the wrong way according to the flow charts, it may indeed be less cheerfully interpreted not so much as creative play and more as downright error, or quite unintelligible. But this is the nature of human communcation, which is not to be mapped in the more simplistic forms of the communication handbooks onto a neat little tree-diagram. Supposing it can be leads to one of the more chronic expressions of banality in present-day management, that human problems are a result of 'lack of communication' or 'information leakage', which would go away if communication were improved or restored or otherwise mended by a plumber. Human attention is not like a wheel, turning over and over on the ground of its study, touching at every spot. It is more like a child on a walk, running, skipping, stopping to look closer, coming back over the same ground for something left behind, going on again with strides of varying pace and length. Indeed the old clichés of the school report reflect just this metaphor: 'she has made great strides', 'he has difficulty keeping up', 'his attention wanders'. It is worth adding that a child on a walk isn't only a metaphor, but is the realization of human attention itself.

The complex play of human attention and its infinite capacity for perhaps creative misprision[4] is one powerful guardian of freedom against brainwashing. It is also the provocation of good curriculum planners, who long for the unattainable perfection of fit between their aims and the students' learning. It is cheerfully declared hereby that such a fit is impossible, and would be lethal if it were possible. Let us return instead to the notion that the curriculum, in all its conceptual and unsystematically varied hierarchy of learning, teaching, knowledge, praxis, skills, has stories to tell the world of its constituency, and that these, takeable in many different frames of mind, are marked onto the vital map of human interests.

I shall further say that such a map has five realms of value,[5] each realm lived according to the particular, history-bound absolutes or master-symbols of an epoch. Now it is the claim of this book that we stand at the gate of an old epoch, and as new epochs will, the land outside the gate looks like a wilderness. The evidence is all about us, quite apart from the fact that we have to hand the instruments to make the new epoch into the most literal wilderness the world can imagine. That evidence reposes in the distinctly material ways people have of choosing and living their values in terms of what practices and possessions they really hold on to; what changes they make at those points in their life where they are touched most nearly; what they want for their children; what they will give up.

Whatever people do, for good or ill, they do it within these following essential orientations and vital interests: in time, to their past, present and future; in space, to property and sexual relations; everywhere, to the knowledge of death; and all of these as known and lived through the singular lenses of the master-symbols of the day. The curriculum as the most stable meanings-bearer of a secular society must carry a sufficiently coherent organization of each realm of value, both internally and in relation to all the others. It is plain that such coherence is now largely absent, and that the whole structure is fractured down every join.

Consider how the messages and enigmas of the curriculum place a pupil in time. There is a dead rationalism which supposes that all the information of the curriculum should be entirely lucid. It is wrong. Any knowledge system must have its ratio of mystery to message, or else the unsolvable conundrums of experience are subjected to the fatal techniques of algorithmic thought. When I speak of coherence, I do not mean that a curriculum should be without its mystery, only that the mystery should be settled in life itself and not in the mystifications of what we may well call the showmen. Now to be placed by your parents and teachers in time is not, as the time-line[6] of the primary-school history project confidently proclaims, to situate yourself neatly on the moment at which an orderly past produces you, on your way to occupying an orderly and continuous future. Finding yourself a place in time depends on a large number of factors of the kind that impinge on the exceedingly chancey nature of identity as we reviewed it in chapter 4,[7] and provide that elusive essence with bits and pieces of place, nation, myth, morality and behaviours to attach itself to.

In this always provisional process, the story of the past, as I have been at such pains to emphasize, is strictly crucial. For the epoch now ending so slowly, the past has been surpassed, but mythologized behind a faintly golden haze. That is to say, the past is what we have left behind in order to attain our present freedoms and comforts, and its trajectory is understood by having led in a more or less deliberate development to a present in which the old miseries and brutalities have been eliminated. Surpassing the past, in a necessary pun, leaves us also able to honour its great heroes who made the present what it is, but whose like we shall not look upon again. This is the ambivalence of the past's meaning for us: things were bad in those days, of course, but those were also the good old days whose central figures took part in decisive and heroic battles titanically above the puny deeds of us, their successors.

This avenue upon the meaning of the past is open in many textbooks, but is most widely and handsomely visible in assorted revaluations of the past performed in the more durable of television serials. In the globally popular *When the Boat Comes In*, the poverty and bitter inter-class rancour and inequity of 1920s Tyneside were vigorously portrayed. We are well past all *that*, was the clear political message. At the same time, the simplicity of the political silhouettes – the Rolls-Royce, the blunt, dauntless, trenchant working-class Labour Party man – make it easy to feel and say that at least you knew where your loyalties were in those days, and what the enemy looked like. There is nothing like a reliable enemy and a pungent theodicy for making sense of the past and yourself.

When the past arrives at the present, it is simply converted as meaning into the opportunity for production. Chapter 8 had much to say about work as the central meaning of the so-called 'labour culture', and the individual, indeed the nation, situate themselves in the present by working. It is through working in the present that time is given structure and then allocated to the past, a process controlled, as Keynes theorized, by the handling of money, and its containment of our great expectation of life through the keen excitements of saving, accumulating and spending. The present is the space in which we produce and are paid. The future is then the time in which we will spend and consume. It means what it does as the land of future plenty, a plenty purchased out of what we produce at work now (that the exigencies of credit constantly bring the aspired-to and enviable future nearer and nearer is only one of many disintegrations in the allocation of time).

It is obvious that the curriculum carries and expresses its specific versions of these very generalized meanings. The tight connections between schooling, employment, the forms of study and the methods of assessment are both taken for granted and pretty well understood; what needs a renewed emphasis is how completely (and how partially: plenty of children and students expect not to get work or, if they do, to dislike it) individuals and classes are constituted as people doing time by their access to work. The strong ceremony of the parents' evening in primary or secondary school, or of registration at the technical college, displays in its most ingenuous and touching encounters how it is that forms of work animate and embody the hopes of the future, and the hopes *for* the future. Parents ask about their children's prospects with a strained love and anxiety going far beyond the notion of financial reward, profound in its significance as that is as a meaning-giver to the uninflected passage of time. Getting the right qualifications for admission to a good job is, then, the point of education and its curriculum, and even when this harmless ambition is unloaded of its commonplace snobberies about 'getting on' and 'doing well', it is still an authentic and powerful source of energy and resource of value. As I insist, every subject tells a story, and the best-loved story is the one that connects conscientious study to social promotion and satisfying production and service.

It is perhaps to toll a surly, sullen bell to claim, as I want to do, that the curriculum formalizes and indeed teaches, at least implicitly, an attitude to death, given that it is so important to all of us that death be itself believably transcended beyond the individual end in the good of those we love and care for. One's own death, at least in the offical tales of school told to children, which decently canonize our very best impulses and qualities, is assured of its meaning as a memorial in the future lives of our prosperous, happy, protected and well-loved children. The length of a generation would seem to be, in the global danger and local uncertainty of modern life, the sanest measure of choice and consequence. To ignore the consequences of action which put the first generation of children at risk in the name of distant future benefits is to lose hold on the only safe moral scale we have. (Such ignorance was at the heart of the dreadful and murderous Khmer regime, starting a new world in Cambodia with Year Zero). Well, the curriculum tells quietly its worthy tales about the memorializing of our parents and of the teachers who, ideally, stand beside our parents, in the bright hopes of better futures.

If there is sentimentality here, then that is a quality which is deplorably lacking in all but discussion of primary education. Stories of progress and modernization, of individual creativity and fulfilment, of co-operation and mutuality, of productivity and obligingness, are all variously told by the teachers and what they teach. However distantly, the bell tolls for all of us in each of them, in their images of praxis and poesis, of gift relationships and, in the reiterated phrase, human flourishing.

And so it is as the curriculum places its students in space, especially according to the coordinates of property and sexuality. (The closeness of the two is brought out by the convincing feminist critique that what has been wrong between men and women since capitalism got going strongly has been men's treatment of women as possessions.) Within their many dimensions, boys and girls learn the articulation of a self and a society as they perform the actions of owning and relinquishing; or as self and society shape their freedoms and their dependences. Once again, this is straightforward enough not to need much elaboration. The now substantial literature of gender-definition[8] has much to say about sexuality as shaped by the curriculum, and the definition of knowledge largely as private property is, as we saw, inscribed in the principles of work, particularly at examination time.

The matter is more subtle, of course, than a glance in the exam hall or getting girls to do metalwork will reveal. Property and sexuality are the ground of our spatial being in *any* society, not merely capitalist ones, and what we do about them entails bloody quarrels about the commitment to what men and women really live for. The owner-occupier and the romantic lover are highly specific answers to the questions, where do I live? and whom do I care for? but the questions recur in all human societies.[9]

What is, then, important is to understand how historically specific values transform universal questions into the highly specific generation of answers. For the curriculum as it is represents those answers, always mobile and contested, as they are taught at the end of the eventualities of the present. My contention is that our ending present is also an ending era, and in common with thousands of teachers at all levels I believe that many of the commonly accepted answers to the old questions are incredible falsehoods. But to authenticate this, it is necessary to sketch out the rainbow of our era, and where it ends.

To attempt this in a few paragraphs is only to align some very crude, but not vacant headings. I shall say, flatly, that bourgeois society is ending. This is also to say that the vastly powerful political economy centred on Europe since the early nineteenth century is breaking up. The economic centres of power have been moving west for several decades, but are moving again to the South Pacific. Within this huge and uneven formation, Britain, as the first capitalist and first imperialist nation, had far more in terms of wealth, privilege and power to lose when the balance of things shifted. Since the end of the European Civil War of 1914–18, that loss has been going on steadily, apparent in the erratic alternation of boom and slump, managed or abandoned by its rulers. The terms of that decline and how it shall be endured are the terms of British politics, and its curriculum is an even readier text than its newspapers in which to read how the settlements and treaties have been negotiated.

The arc of the rainbow is not smooth, however. For when the Second World War was over, and the world became divided into its two mammoth ideological alliances, the new political economy led in Britain to a ratification of personal values for which much in the century had prepared the nation. The absence of strong Communist parties with an honourable war record such as marked France and Italy, the purportedly special relationship with the USA, where individualized values had a long record going back to 1776, the strength of domestic and low-key Romanticism, all combined to give a renewed push behind the expressive values still so celebrated by our education system.

We have to call the values individualized in order to differentiate them from their contraries in a more institutional order. Perhaps it makes for lucidity to set out the values in question as though they may be merely counterposed, in order to bring out the emphasis of liberal culture in its official, curricular forms, upon the conscientious, singular, subjectively approved values, rather than those which ask for allegiance to larger structures and institutions. Indeed, we can say that British society, like all others in the West, is remarkable for the present porousness of its institutions, their loss of holding power.

INDIVIDUALIZED	INSTITUTIONALIZED
sincerity	goodness
honesty (truth to self)	truth
freedom of choice	duty
integrity	loyalty
dignity	honour
rights	right
fulfilment	asceticism
experience	endurance
independence	humility
freedom of being	obedience
passion	wisdom
morality	politics

To talk of values is not to cut off discussion about the so-called instrumental side of life, in the curriculum or in production. That is to assume the truth of the fact–value severance that it is part of the business of this book to deny. A value is merely the organizing concept which identifies a field of activity or practices as making sense and being worth while. By this token, all human activities are values-impregnated, and cannot be interpreted without them. They would simply make no sense. My assertion is that in the forty years since European and Japanese Fascism was defeated at least in its military uniforms, British society has taught itself in its classrooms and on its television screen that the good life is lived by the left-hand list of qualities, and in any conflict between the two, preference should go to the first. In other words, this is the specific structure whose ideological premises give their present actuality to our human preoccupation with past, present and future; with the space of property and face-to-face relations; with the circumambient globe itself.

And it is the globe which has begun to resist them, to turn monstrously upon them and crush their ruthless hedonism with the elemental necessities of earth, air, fire and water. For the conjunction of the values I have named with the drives of capitalism has produced what is neutrally called consumerism. This drew on the centuries-old habit on the part of men to regard the earth as an inexhaustible bank of resources, his own space for the exercise of his demands. As long as technology remained slow in its advances, the globe contained the demands. Once technology joined with the triumph of capitalism, it became clear across a century or so that the globe's tolerance of its exploitation and pullution had rapidly approaching limits.

This is an argument which has made extraordinarily rapid headway in a very few years. Of course, the spoliation of the earth has been horribly visible for a century in the filth of industrial cities, the ruinous erosion of arable land and pasture in America and Africa, in mere starvation, and the poisoning of the habitat by the chemistry of both war and peace. But it is fair to claim that only recently have suitably authoritative sources[10] pronounced on the precipitous danger of these circumstances. What is then really remarkable is that, thinking only of our smallish subject and its province, the warning has been so quickly heeded and absorbed. The growth of the happily renamed life sciences and the advent at all levels of school of subjects such as environmental sciences provide the readiest, most widely discussable example of the way the old value-system and its vigorous hedonism is breaking up. Of course growth economics are not going to come to a stop. Of course economic development is so uneven, so subject to local caprice and incompetence, that much of the Third World is in no position, short of starvation, but to go blindly for growth, at whatever penalty in terms of rates of interest and the new imperialism of aid disguised in the godless alliance of ruling elite and international corporation. Of course.[11] But it is still amazing that, all over Britain, children, students and teachers are so rapidly well informed and anxious about the ruin of resources. That they are is evidence of how the school and higher educational curricula have done their considerable bit towards discrediting the beautiful people.

For the post-1945 scheme of the virtues is crumbling fast. Work, as I have said, is less and less likely to provide a dominant meaning in people's lives, or not as tied to profitability, to mass unemployement, to making destructively useless products. The future can no longer be promised to the present by prosperous parents, and the past has many mansions, some of them morally much more admirable than the present, or the sombre-looking future. Institutional virtues a long way from either Nuremberg or the Holy City look to have their attractions.

Neither revolution nor moral regeneration impends. Things look bad rather than better, and in any case only the most febrile commentator would speak of 'new moods of realism' and other clichés. What we can say, however, is that the breaking of the old world picture makes it increasingly clear that the curriculum must treat morality and politics directly. While it is certain that, for a season, the difficulties of recovering political consensus are insurmountable, and that therefore there will be no agreement on a curriculum embodying a single picture of the good life, there is no way out of this quandary through the amiable evasions of liberal pluralism or philosophical relativism. A decent curriculum and its honest toilers will have to engage with an adequate scheme of human desire, and a fairly stern sense of physical necessity.

10

The Language of Politics in the Conversation of Classrooms

As soon as anybody mixed up in education takes the risk of speaking of the good life, a chorus of obloquy is likely to go up. For all its present manifest failures, liberalism is still the official intonation, and one extensively declaimed, of classroom and lecture hall. Even the givers of the philosophy and politics seminar, who have begun to take such a risk again recently,[1] only do so gingerly, and their professional obligations to think about the conditions and nature of virtue in the republic have been little met for a very long time.

For the loose premiss of liberalism is, of course, that nobody has any right to tell anybody else what to think, but that, since the central good of human life is individual freedom, which is exercised in the making of choices, the good life is best organized by clearing as large a space as may be cleared for the choosing activity, compatible with not infringing the choosing space of others, and validated by more or less optimistic trust in the innate goodness of people. If, however, that trust turns out to be misplaced, liberalism still upholds as a paramount good the freedom of individuals to go to the bad, as long as that is their choice.

The consequence of this in the conversation of classrooms, as in that of the civil society, has been to attenuate to the point of vaporization the ideas of the good and the true. If the good life is what you lead as a result of your free choices, then what is good for you, while not being good for me, is indisputable, can only be known by you, and cannot be taught. The compliance of such a world-view to the irresistible but inexplicit invasions of consumerism was mentioned, though untheorized, in the last chapter. For now, there is little need to go beyond pointing out how completely people have acceded to the notion of the good life purveyed by television glamourizations, in and out of advertising, because the area of human choice has been successfully allocated to the purchase of consumer commodities, from houses to holidays; in the world of domestic subjectivity, liberal individualism and the life of the limitless desires of the consumer go comfortably together. For the 75 per cent of the British adult society in employment, there is much to be said for this private, mobile life and its satisfactions: the car; the camper; the decent garden; the package holiday to the kind old sun; the modish, informal clothes, themselves forever quoting the ideal informalities of a healthily sporting life, on the ski slopes, at Le Mans, at the country club. In an incomprehensible world, private politics on the scale of your own and your children's lives are defensible (you can vote for its providers) and morally palpable. I have no wish to deny the delight and attractiveness of such pleasures, nor to limit access to them in the name of asceticism.

But the life-weaknesses are obvious. Not only will the globe stop supporting such easy-going extravagance: the petrol will run out, and the limitations of poverty will spread; but also the pleasures themselves are socially limited. Lying on sunny solitary beaches is what Fred Hirsch[2] calls 'a positional good'; however, it stops being a good if the beaches are polluted by a filthy sea and covered with too many people. Not only do these objections thrust their way into the private, mobile lives, but the way of life itself is morally repulsive in its disregard for any scheme of the duties that have to be set against such privileges, a disregard on which it is only too likely that the less privileged will want to take their vengeance.

Such maledictions over the consumers' instantaneous gratifications are familiar enough and cheaply bought for a *frisson* by the social conscience-striken segment of the meaning industry. The real costs would only be paid if anybody tried to act upon such a different view of the way the world ought to go.[3] But the cerebral displacements attendant upon taking quite so heavenly a curricular view have been criticized already. The classroom point, like the political one, is blunter. It is this.

The mobile, private consumer's view of life simply *is* the unacknowledged good life of contemporary liberalism. The hold of the consumer's heaven upon our imagination is very powerful.

The classroom and the political criticisms that have got through the private enclave of consumer mobility are the ecological critique, and the less focused, but numerically vast resistances of the peace movements and of feminism; the three taken together presently constitute in Britain a momentous and diffuse surge in popular consciousness against the dominant forms of rationality, action and purpose. These arguments, however, have to get through assimilably; that is, the criticisms are largely to be understood only in so far as the liberal frame of mind absorbs and decodes them. Thus the ecological critique impresses people as a threat to their present homes and lives, not as a statement about the interdependence of a world which in any case is moving its attention to the South Pacific. If the notion of a positional good had any acceptance, naturally enough it would intensify the competition to gain one such good, rather than induce a universal acceptance that such goods must be equitably shared and conserved. If someone can afford the last country cottage, then he or she will buy it, not leave it to the so misleadingly named National Trust.

Similarly, the best way to understand the meaning of the one unmistakably non-routine public movement of the day, the peace movement, is as the private individual's display of his or her public powerlessness and the terrible menace each sees as looming over private freedoms; to signify this, all wife, husband, lover or child can do is bear visible witness. Their sign is to be seen in their quiet helplessness. The feminist mode of opposition is also an individualist one. Their case is correctly and with justice understood by most people as for greater space for the exercise of personal freedom, and more opportunity to gain the political power which decides on how such space is portioned out.

These three overlapping pressures of public consciousness upon the received definitions of the free, fulfilled and self-aware individual living the good life according to his or her good luck each constitute a radical criticism of the way of the world, especially in its capitalist formations. But each of them is still refracted through the data and precepts of liberal individualism which, lacking as it does any sufficient theory of human interests attached to a realistic classification of desires, can do nothing much about the state of the nation beyond loose moral exhortation of a deeply unattractive sort to raise niceness to others to the level of universal principle. Each contribution, from the ecologists, the feminists, the disarmers, involves drastic and accurate criticism of things horribly wrong in British society; for good measure, I should probably add to the list the vigorous critics of the evil and deep-seated racism now boiling up in Britain, but in spite of so much busyness about multiracial education in local authorities, liberalism is hard put to it to situate the very idea of racism in its scheme of things, and has consequently failed so far to acknowledge its poisonous presence.

Indeed, the present treatment of multiracialism would serve as an example of the difficulty of coming at agreement about common desires and interests, and framing these envisageably in a form of life. Since it is a worthy premiss of liberalism that you must not tell people what to believe and how to think, but that they must be left to make up their own minds, it can only be possible to consider multiracial education in schools as an individual issue in which different social lives may be studied (for example, as different religions) and from which, it is vaguely hoped, an undifferentiated relativism may be somehow inhaled by students. (The issue doesn't arise in universities, since they are habitually blind to their own structural racism, except in the few honourable cases of single scholars,[4] who opened up the study of the origins and reality of British racism.) By relativism, as I have said, I mean the view that all world-views as between societies or even as within individuals are adjusted to fit distinctive circumstances, for judging which there is no common court of appeal, and therefore nothing to be said about different ways of life, beyond that they work satisfactorily in the circumstances.

Hidden in this perspective so far as it applies to whole societies is often an unrecognized functionalism, or (to repeat) the view that everything in a society functions to maintain that society on its own terms. Hidden in this secondary view of separate people is the doubtlessly fairminded attitude that others have their own, unknowable motives and what impels and organizes them in their world need not at all be what impels and organizes oneself. Either way, actions, beliefs and behaviours are only intelligible as relative to their own context, within which they function to hold those different from ourselves in truths-for-themselves which we may not share, but which are strong in their own validity.

It is a powerful argument often dottily applied.[5] Its strength and truthfulness are that there are indeed many different forms of life and good lives across the world, and it sounds a convincing moral precept that you should not judge what you do not understand, even less that you should interfere with it from outside. There are powerful counter-arguments to the effect that transcultural claims on common humanity give each of us authority not to condone a practice which is plainly inhuman, and the obligation to try to prevent it if we can, especially if its victims within the culture just as plainly think the practice is as horrible as we do. The dottiness comes in at the point at which people not only claim that any practice or expression or belief may be valid for the practitioner, that there is no agreement possible on any moral or political values and ends, but indeed that goodness and truth reside in their being strictly good-for-you or true-for-me. Both claims are absolutely relativized and stand on the self-contradiction that they make absolute the principle of relativism, which is that nothing is absolute.

The deep obstacle which this inevitably confused and widespread habit of mind set up, even among well-meaning teachers intent upon educating children decently, is that they cannot get beyond this variegated relativism, compounded with the justified fear of the totalitarianism implied by too-ready use of the word 'indoctrination', to a discussion of what a feasible human flourishing could look like in the future, and what interests and desires really are basic and what are changeable. There is a fear of agreement on moral ends which derives from the unexamined notion that individuality, resting upon the free exercise of choice, must further rest upon moral pluralism. So in curricular planning, as in classroom discussion, the right to be wrong – or, as it is more genteelly put, the right to your own opinion – is volunteered as an ideal in such a way as to expel the truth as a controlling concept. Of course, in the real life of classrooms, children are told to shut up and listen to the facts in order to reproduce them in their examinations, but I am invoking the implicit ideal of communicative rationality as shaping the form of the curriculum, the context of its learning and teaching.

It is important to get clear that I am talking about the universal models of what it is to be rational which the whole curriculum endorses, and not just about what happens in the discussion lessons of the humanities. These models are endorsed as much by the primary-school project as by the university physics laboratory. Indeed, given the enormous public prestige and visibility of physics, its account of rationality and relativism, truth and *telos*, is omnipresent and all-powerful. Physics is of course a hugely self-confident field of study: together with certain kinds of biochemical inquiry, its dominance of university study is assured and absolute: it commands the research grants, the numbers of appointments, the social elites of the academies. It is largely ignorant or contemptuous of the recent relativizing and sociologizing of its knowledge base, because its triumphs have been so incontestable.[6]

Those triumphs have depended upon a methodical separation of the facts and values of the world, which was historically grounded in the founding of empirical inquiry and philosophical science in the eighteenth century. But as has been repeatedly declared in these pages, the division of thought and experience into reason and emotion, calculation and imagination, fact and value, becomes irreversibly established as what ontology is, during the settlement of bourgeois society in Victorian Britain. Pure science instructed technology, and technology suffused the culture with the belief that science dealt with the objective world of facts, but that its strictly disinterested purpose was the enlargement of the field of knowledge for its own sake, and not the organization of its inquiry for human benefit. The benefits might accrue, certainly, but they were subsequent to the business of enlightenment.[7]

Such a method of defined rationality itself according to its own, collegiate success. Hypothesis-making, evidence collection, verification by experiment; classification, counting, formulation of laws; these became the dual process whereby reason itself sought and found knowledge. Since values are by this canon separate from facts, and since facts are objective, it follows that values can only be subjective and impossible to agree upon. Rationality and values are themselves sundered, and there can therefore be no way of resolving disputes about values rationally. Opinion is the individual's sovereign. Only if the human sciences can obey the adjurations of Carl Hempel and Ernest Nagel,[8] and make themselves formally, conceptually and methodically, members of the physical sciences, can politics become a rational subject. But they cannot.

It is well-known how extensively this position has been

attacked, both in the name of a dissolution of the fact–value distinction, as well as in fully documented claims for the status of a reflexive and critical human science well able to stand up for itself in a third realm of knowledgeability that breaks open the antinomy of subjective and objective. But the grim old picture of the factual, infallible and omnipotent science prevails. The liberal belief in the autonomous individual and the scientific faith in empiricism combine in the doctrines of moderation and balance, evidence-counting and observation. There is in such a world no form of rational praxis (only the impulses of psyche and structure) and no inquiry into the good life, unless it has what cannot be granted to it, problems and techniques.

This can only mean that questions about how to live must be placed in the rough and reach-me-down calculus of utilitarianism, which science allows as the making of the best of a bad job. Utilitarianism as a social philosophy[9] holds that, in a mass society, questions of public policy can be resolved by reducing all questions to a calculation of the outcome of political actions in terms of the material benefits it will bring to given proportions of the population. These benefits are laid along a single scale of materiality, and the numbers they affect are measured. Policy is then decided upon according to Bentham's slogan 'the greatest good of the greatest number'.

In Bentham's time it was a radical doctrine. But it is quite unable to handle incalculable but vital concerns of human being. It has no picture of human flourishing beyond the material welfare which, however important, is *not* synonymous with happiness, let alone virtue or *eudaimonia*. It is the utilitarian calculus, ratified by a bourgeois society under the lights of liberalism and scientific empiricism, which is now breaking down so vastly. In the not unimportant corner of human desires and interests marked 'the curriculum', what can be done about it? How can the state of affairs even be talked about?

The first help I offer comes from the study and the content of British television. For a start, British television provides much of the subject-matter of everyday conversation as well as being a very substantial and audible part of the whole conversation of the culture. Let us get the disclaimers out of the way first.[10] Of course there is awful rubbish on all channels; of course the family quiz and the competitions can make any remotely sensitive person shrink with embarrassment; of course tired old scented soap operas on the sexy or on the sugary side are deeply lowering in their top-rating success and stomach-turning in their popularity; of course the suppression of certain intractable political subjects like Northern Ireland and the fixing of the fight in any trade union dispute violates natural justice and demeans intelligence; of course Mrs Whitehouse is sometimes right about disgusting movies and all of us are right to recoil from the silliness and nastiness of the latest dose of the horrors. No discussion of television can start without a due declaration of one's own taste, judgement, immunity to its insidiousness, diminishing use of its programmes, preference for older, established cultural genres – book, piano, art gallery.

Once that is done, however, perhaps we can see and hear in television what it tells us of ourselves. In my earlier extension of Krishan Kumar's argument that broadcast political discussion intends to 'hold the middle ground', but that such an intention of itself pushes such programmes onto controversial terrain, I suggested that the whole ideological field of broadcasting is mapped onto the programmer's sense of that field of the culture that is permitted public legitimation and expression. The narratives of television act as integuments, holding together the many pieces of the culture, and because the medium is so fluid, swift and responsive, it can do so in many different voices. Subjects can come up in the conversation of culture and be admitted to broadcasting very quickly; once admitted, the same topic can be very variously treated – as material for drama, as issue in the public forum of the studio audience, as comedian's joke, as the vehicle for a serial, as documentary.

Much has been made of the difficulty of breaking open the frames and conventions of television. The so-called 'tyranny of the slot', which dictates length of programmes as well as time and cost of preparation, date of screening and so forth, processes dense, subtle and delicate human experience into routine and rapidly assimilable forms. The conventions work to exclude the unsettlingness of the best art, the chiasmus of aesthetics and morality present in, say, a great novel, but smoothed and plasticized by the modes of camerawork and the manners of actors and actresses. None the less, its relative openness, the very operation of its modes of production, which make it an entirely unpredictable agent of both liberation and control,[11] its amazing quickness of ear and eye and responses, its obsessive self-discussion, the sheer bulk of its provision, all make television a powerful curriculum builder in the society, both senior and junior to education.

Both institutions organize a medium of public communication. Television obviously has a great deal more glamour (always a tricky concept) especially among schoolchildren, but education has more direct power. Both command between 5 and 6 per cent of the gross national product. Television's fleetness in devising new agenda is vitiated by its transience; it is driven always to seek the new. Education's comparative dullness and stolidity is compensated for by its stability, the settled nature of its knowledge and its discursive practices. But each sets the curriculum of the other, and neither may be understood without the other.

Such understanding needs to go deeper than a list of contents, though this would be a start. Trying, for instance, to match the forms of television science to the science of schools and universities would not win the battle for either, but would bring out their sturdy reciprocity. Science comes in many forms: lecture courses like Jonathan Miller's *The Body in Question* or Bronowski's famous *Ascent of Man*; magazine programmes like David Bellamy's or James Burke's; regular documentaries like the incomparable rivals, *World About Us* and *Disappearing World*; lastly, but perhaps best, dramatizations of famous careers in the history of science, like the magnificent *Voyage of Charles Darwin*, which brought to exact and vivid life the patience as well as the reach of Darwin's genius, and both the historical context and physical endurance of his adventures in Christian heresy, world geography and sea-going actuality. These are essays in a humanist science, and no one could doubt not only that they are deeply edifying but also that they arise from the official curriculum of our education system. They are mapped onto the culture in a way that endorses it, certainly, but also makes possible criticism of a science taught and philosophized as though it all took place in Karl Popper's laboratory,[12] and not in the battle to work out answers to questions which declared themselves in the case of Darwin and in that single mind as a deep life-question which could not be put in any propositional form.

A history of television history would similarly include admiring reference to the 26-parter on ITV *The World at War*, a vast revision of the Anglocentric view of the Second World War, which drew on remarkable finds amongst abandoned newsreel footage left in their cans by all the combatants. A parallel inquiry might turn to the hardly less drastic revision done on the British Raj by the dramatization of Paul Scott's quartet about the British withdrawal from India, *The Jewel in the Crown*. The two examples serve to do no more than indicate how important to the understanding of national identity such an enterprise would be.

But the tropes and tones of television are no more varied than those of classrooms, only more ephemeral in content and less stolid in manners. What is more important is the implied conversation of television culture, and what its ideal speech-situation, or in other words, its implied model of the best, most sympathetic, respectful, disinterested and egalitarian exchange of human knowledge, wisdom and counsel would look and sound like. The phrase 'ideal speech-situation' is generally credited to Jurgen Habermas, and he set out its conditions in my paraphrase as follows:[13] first, that truth or validity are the object of all discussion; secondly, that no force is exercised, other than the force of the better argument; thirdly, that we seek to exclude all motives except the motive to discover the best argument for what may be called valid (and true).

It is this picture of the conversation of culture which needs to be held over against the vapidly judgementless holding of the ring of argument, in which the professional broadcaster (or the teacher) merely acts as broker-umpire at the assertion of contrary points of view by opposing parties. This is the balancing act which expels truth and merely draws conclusions that sufficiently mediate different views in a passable compromise. All that is sought for in such negotiations is agreement, a sufficient correspondence of interests. This is the management of consensus.

There is quite enough of this kind of thing in schools, as on television. It represents the worst kind of threat to truth and therefore to virtue, but also to the rationality that must have truth as its first principle of mind (as justice, for Plato, is the first principle of the republic). And the broker's balancing in turn threatens the idea of democracy and our political obligation towards it,[14] because, in the event of irreconcilable disagreement, there is no court of appeal (all opinions being equally valid), and it follows that someone must be autocratic, probably with the help of policemen.

On the other hand, even if it looks an ingenuous thing to say, the ideal speech-situation is, ideally, invoked by all good lessons and seminars, and is broadcast widely by the whole montage of both television and the curriculum. Each, that is, lives in the reciprocities and exchange, the dialectical juxtapositions of form and content, their inevitable reflexivity in the play of subjects over subjects, which together make up the texture of their narratives. The whole curriculum, like the whole programme system of television, may be taken to contain as immanence the ideal speech-situation, which is to say, a conversation whose politeness embodies the best political language of the day. A conversation, however, is not just itself; it is *about* something. Ideally, again, it is about the good life. The best parts of television and the curriculum have this subject-matter in common, and, with Aristotle in mind, we could say that the good life is not something you plan (nor conceivably could plan), but what the good man lives, only known fully for itself when it is over.

If I am right, it is possible to learn a rational and admirable mode of thought from the intercalation of these official and unofficial curricula, and while learning it, so join a conversation about how to live which may be accurately called political. The obstacles are frightful, of course, both in terms of the ordinary noise coming from Vanity Fair, which drowns that conversation, and from the deadly but astute enemies of the people, who have accepted that the end of the twentieth century is a very dangerous place, but who are prepared at whatever risk to bend those dangers to their own advantage.[15] But so far, the small voices of the conversation of culture in the best classrooms, seminar rooms and television studios remain just about audible.

The unpredictable play of liberation and control in these places is in part structural, in part intentional. I have vigorously named the defects, hypocrisies and contradictions of liberal society, but its continuing strength is, as Bernard Williams puts it that:

> *to someone who recognizes the ultimate plurality of values
> ... there are such values* ... Put in that blank way, [such a
> truth] can be taken to speak for an objective order of values
> which some forms of consciousness (notably the liberal form)
> are better than others at recognizing. But that way of putting
> it is very blank indeed. It is more illuminating in itself, to say

that one who properly recognizes the plurality of values is one who understands the deep and creative role that these various values can play in human life. In that perspective, the correctness of the liberal consciousness is better expressed, not so much in terms of truth – that it recognizes the values which indeed there are – but in terms of truthfulness. It is prepared to try to build a life round the recognition that these different values do each have a real and intelligible human significance, and are not just errors, misdirections or poor expressions of human nature. To try to build life in any other way would now be an evasion, of something which by now we understand to be true. What we understand is a truth about human nature as it has been revealed – revealed in the only way in which it could be revealed, historically. The truthfulness that is required is a truthfulness to that historical experience of human nature.[16]

Now the curriculum is *intended* by its many authors to express these truths in its forms and narratives. But its structural strength upholds the same freedoms.[17] That structure of its nature generates reflexivity; the states of knowledge and ways of knowing are not yet separated from one another, although the accelerating drives of the divisions of labour in our society tend more and more to make them so. Each realm of meaning, in Phenix's useful phrase, can play upon the other in ways capable of altering them or of producing new theories.

I mean this on behalf of all those joining the political conversation. This is not abstract talk about high theory in the upper air. The essential form of all learning (all learning about life, that is) is a narrative. All narratives might have ended differently. The human mind in virtue of possessing an imagination can experiment with different endings. A schoolteacher working against the grain of a syllabus out of natural bloody-mindedness, a small child busying away with her own bit of botany, or one of the lads wrecking a lesson by his murmured insolence are all providing themselves with a different narrative, a momentary living of a theory about how the world might be made to go in a different direction.

Not much to build on there, except that absolute indoctrination is impossible without the aid of drugs and torture. But people are

all too apt to heed the worst voices, and however much the
different narratives of the curriculum ensure a continuing criticality, criticism in itself is only the exercise of freedom, it is not
freedom directed to any purpose. Since I am much preoccupied
both with understanding how the entire curriculum works *and*
with directing it to better ends, it will be useful to identify some of
the voices which speak among its many messages, and consider
how they may be received in such a way as to become effective.

For any message to be understood, there must be some kind of
fit or common focus between the two frames of mind in
communication. A successful lesson is presumably one in which
the fit is more or less complete; where the teacher's frame of
feeling and structure of intention coincides with the feelings and
motives of his or her audience as praxis. 'Encoding' and 'decoding'
are mutually transparent. Each process may be thought of as built
upon common structures and meeting in medium and message, as
in figure 10.1, in a model of the mass communication transaction.

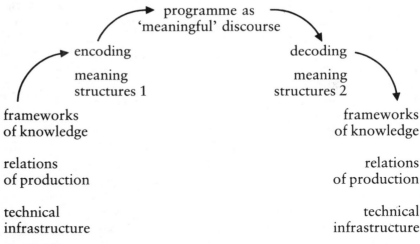

Figure 10.1   A model of the mass communication transaction

Perhaps this language is unnecessarily abstract.[18] The technical
infrastructure of the classroom or seminar room is first given by its
immediate technology – tables, display cases, blackboards, VTR,
and so on – but beyond that, by the technical production of the

institution's own life through books, the reproduction of paper, telephone calls, typing, all the apparatus through which work is done and by which it is actualized. (In the case of a television programme, this infrastructure is easier to see: it includes the cameras, the recorders, the radio and recording apparatus.) By relations of production is meant most of what I have already written about work and its meanings: the hierarchies of pacing, sequence, collaboration and study in the transmission of education. With embodied meanings, we come of course to the central preoccupation of this book, a term which I have used more or less synonymously with value, taking both words to be the concepts which identify a field of activities as visible and valuable, and not therefore intelligibly subsequent to technical modes and relations of production as Marxists would have it, since they must be logically prior for there to be some such activity in the first place.[19] And although we have learned that concepts are the interweaving of their usages, and that therefore the practice of an economic mode alters the meaning we attribute to it, all that follows from these minor reflections is that embodied meanings are inscribed in every stage of encoding and decoding (or meaning something and understanding it), and that whatever meanings and values there are, they can only be *for* somebody and *in* a context.[20]

I want to propose that there are three such fields of meaning which may be heard among the many voices on the different wavelengths of the curriculum and of television, and that all three are ideally understandable to any member of British society of whatever sex or racial origin or social class, even though it must naturally be true that each will be differently spoken or heard, according to the presence of whichever sex, race or class. The three are: usefulness, humanism, criticality.

Each of these insulates the field of meaning within education as opposed to production. Now it has been a main premiss of this book as it is a truism about society, that education is distinct from production. Indeed it is a main point of educational discourse that it keep its account of its subject-matter in an ideal state. It is a condition of science itself that, in the search for simplifying and ordering the impossibly recalcitrant facts of life, it must constantly remove itself from the immediacy of those facts in order to devise the most concise description capable of formulating (*sic*) the facts. By the word 'science' here, as elsewhere in these pages, I intend what the philosopher of the eighteenth century intended, the space and standing of all knowledge and the knowable.

In one of the most famous and purest examples of idealization in this sense – that is, making the material into idea – the equation $E=mc^2$ represents the equivalence of energy to mass, when mass is annihilated at the speed of light in empty space. From the equation, itself derived by Einstein from his own theory of relativity, glowed the hideous detonations brighter than a thousand suns, as well as the so far contained and smouldering peacefulness of the world's nuclear reactor stations. No one, however, could think of the equation as *close* to the seething invisibilites of the electronic interbombardment which is both mass and energy. Its success as theory is a necessary (though not sufficient) consequence of its economy and beauty, both of them in turn consequences of their intensely idealized formulation. Originally hypothetic, the metaphors of this symbol were none the less capable of application to reality. Like any true narrative, they passed from hypothesis to theory through the frame of experiment.

On the argument of this book, these are the motions and emotions of all cognitive effort and effect. It is also my argument that they characterize all stages of thought, and their assorted logical forms. Indeed, rather than arrange these spatially, as educationists in ivory towers as well as ministries have latterly told us to do,[21] let us go back to adapt and paraphrase R.G.Collingwood in one of his earlier books (1924) *Speculum Mentis, or The Map of Knowledge*. There he sets out what is at once a hierarchy and a chronology of the forms of knowledge. According to this chronology, all societies begin the metamorphosis of experience into knowledge through art. Art is the first means human beings devised for idealizing (in the strict or philosophic sense) the facts and events of life, in order to make them stand still long enough to be tested and used as instruments for the interpretation and control of that life.

In his argument, Collingwood writes of the whole scale of civilized development in terms of each stage of thought, and the conceptualization followed by the control of the world which each made possible. He further insists that each stage is superimposed upon its predecessor, so that the initial form of thought, art, is not only the necessary beginning, but remains as foundation and immanence in all subsequent thinking and in the knowledge which is secured.

The moral of this is both social and personal, and it is brought out in the most practical way by the everyday life of primary schools. Whatever else may be goofy or wrongheaded in the usual primary curriculum, its teachers have got hold of Collingwood's point, that thought starts with art, and that without the arts of story and symbol, rhythm and form, the children can hardly learn to think at all. The practical emphasis of most primary classrooms on painting and modelling, music-making and music-listening, story-telling by teacher and children, in books or drama or movement, carries the marks of grace, even when these activities are as dire as they can be to all but the parents. Hence the whole emphasis of this book on our telling stories of so many kinds (every picture tells a story), on, that is to say, framing things in a narrative.

It is, however, the awful mistake of liberalism, as I have argued, to suppose that any story is as likely to be true as any other, indeed to attenuate truth itself, as I have argued, either to what happens to be agreeable to think ('true for me') or to any comfortable-looking midpoint between the extremes of opinion. But art combines as naturally as may be the love of beauty with the search for truth, as Aristotle impressed on us against his master Plato's judicious banishment of the poets from the republic.[22] Even that same art of the primary school, in writing, music or modelled forms, seeks not only to tell a tale, but to tell the truth. By the same token, the humanities discussion class for the school-leavers and the philosophy seminar on abortion at the university have in common and immanent in their practice a model of the ideal speech-situation which I have already invoked and Habermas has codified.

In a high-handed passage of his splendid novel, *The French Lieutenant's Woman*,[23] John Fowles makes the doctor Grogan, who in his crusty, vigorous, slightly provincial and bibulous way stands for the brotherhood of scientific inquiry, tell these (as we say) home truths to the hero, Charles Smithson, himself a slightly dilettante, but honestly intellectual Darwinian:

'You believe yourself to belong to a rational and scientific elect. No, no, I know what you would say, you are not so vain. So be it. None the less, you *wish* to belong to that elect. I do not blame you for that. But I beg you to remember one thing, Smithson. All through human history the elect have made their cases for election. But Time allows only one plea.' The doctor replaced his glasses and turned on Charles. 'It is this. That the elect, whatever the particular grounds they advance for their cause, have introduced a finer and fairer morality into this dark world. If they fail that test, then they become no more than despots, sultans, mere seekers after their own pleasure and power. In short, mere victims of their own baser desires. I think you understand what I am driving at — and its especial relevance to yourself from this unhappy day on. If you become a better and a more generous human being, you may be forgiven. But if you become more selfish ... you are doubly damned.'

In the teeth of the facts about cynicism, callousness, incompetence and indifference towards the best meanings of the country's education, it is still both possible and necessary to affirm that the *structures* of both making and thinking in our education, however distorted and debased their practice may sometimes be, entail that the space and conditions in which the truth may be found, beauty made, and goodness defined, are always kept open. And in its much more fluid, electronic and ephemeral way, the same is true for television, becase British television takes both form and content, structure and essence, not (as in the USA) from the dominant power of capital, nor (as in the USSR) from the power of the state, but from education, as both institution and discourse.

Education maintains, by means of its curriculum and in spite of education, the twin discourses of truth and freedom. Such are, in liberal or any other kind of society, both its function and meaning. I prefer to put things this way, rather than to praise mere rationality, because the terms truth and freedom, understanding of which is a precondition as well as the structuration of rationality, alert us to those great names as the necessary virtues of education as well as of educated men and women. Against old-fashioned liberalism and (indeed) on intelligent behalf of the human future, I would want to claim, as before, for freedom the standing not merely of the condition of individual action[24] (freedom *from* wanton constraint, freedom *to* act as one chooses in self-definition). Rather, let us say that to live, in thought and action, as a free man or woman, is to live one of the virtues.[25] By the same token, for living freely to be virtuous, it follows that the agent, whether an individual or an institution, must stand uncompromisingly on the side of truth. Indeed, the free man is, by definition, truthful. It is hardly surprising that a book such as this on the curriculum moves towards the conclusion that all children and students should be taught to be good and to tell the truth.

The pious resonance of this excellently Victorian admonition rings no bells for any particular secretary of state, however. Teaching virtue and truthfulness is always likely to make things uncomfortable for the system of structural lying built into the political negotiation which defines the intersubjectivity of the culture. Indeed, a main characteristic of many official statements issued by Elizabeth House is that they seek the complicity of the education system, especially by means of the curriculum, in the official and constitutive discourse of state lies and propaganda.

Resistance, I have claimed, is inscribed in the structure of pedagogic discourse itself, and the justification for this mouth-filling phrase is that it signals the formal separation of *all* educational conversation from the business of production.[26] Production being what it is under the pressures of locally failing capitalism, that separation creates the margin of a few degrees of freedom, and the structural space whose presence ensures the impossibility of indoctrination (which is the pedagogy of the infallible deduction). Of course there are circumstances – writing this book is one example, putting on the school play or concert is another – in which pedagogy is forced into production, and schooling becomes creative work. When this happens, as anyone who has been a teacher knows, the dangers increase with the exhilaration. What is being made is new; it is not the recontextualizing of the already known. It is therefore an instrument of praxis.

The distinction needs developing. Pedagogic discourse (teachers talking teaching) in order to be capable of critical analysis has to become, as I have argued, 'idealized', which is to say turned into usable, testable, formulable metaphor. It has to be kept as clear from experience (the materials of real life) as possible, compatible with that experience remaining in its reach. It occupies the realm of the imagination. But in that realm, critical analysis is only enabled if critical thought comes up with what the philosophers call counterfactual conditionals, which is to say, that we play the game of 'just suppose . . . ' and imagine feasible alternatives that could as well be the case as what is. To move into the imaginary is to create new worlds: the acts of criticism and creation stand in an essential relation to one another, forever spiralling from one to the other in the essential motion of thought. To imagine freely is a partial definition of the practice of education (as opposed to schooling). At the same time, free imagining becomes merely fantastic and enervated, unless it maintains energizing contact with the real.

When this contact fails, we lose ourselves in daydreaming, the private novels of the powerless whose imaginative life is their consolation for their incapacity to direct anything in the real world to their purposes. Such fictions, widespread in the controlled helplessness of so much modern life, are theories of a kind with no empirical content. Their standing as truth (and not many people believe that they *are* true, of course, not even their eponym, Walter Mitty) is perfectly unaffected by facts and events. In so far as narratives or educational discourses are all imagination, they are ineffectual. They mirror the real, but they cannot affect it. This is what it is like to be stuck in an ivory tower.

A theory of practice [27] is what it purports to be: a discourse which re-situates the real in the contexts of the imagination, and in so returning the facts of life to the field of possibilities from which they came, makes those facts resume their shadowiness so that they may be seen again as given the force of actuality only by chance and contingency. The interplay of criticism and creation is, then, the theory of practice and the disturbance of what Bourdieu calls the habitus, which is to say, the system of durable, transposable dispositions which works as the generative basis of structured, objectively unified practices.

Such and such, as Kipling endearingly observed of the Python, is the way sociologists always talk, but the frightful and aridly necessary abstraction of their speech is also an example of what I am discussing. Only when we can imagine a habitus, will we understand how dispositions are made systematic by the order of schooling, and become the basis of how people really live. All too readily, that is to say, most children learn terribly well to do as they are told, and most students are dismally adept at keeping the imaginary well away from the real, at accepting that criticism has no purchase on creation, and that both discourse and habitus are changeless forms for the reproduction of that timeless entity, bourgeois society. Since a sizeable proportion of those students who spend longest learning the pedagogic discourse become pedagogues in their turn, it is hardly surprising that what teaching does to teachers, as David Hargreaves unforgettably wrote,[28] is to make them boring, exhausted and hate the job. More subtly, I may repeat an observation earlier implied, that because teaching has been a safe and steady avenue of social promotion throughout this century, and rewards in education largely go to those who politely repeat after the teacher what the teacher has said, the fractions of the working class and the *petit-bourgeoisie* (especially their daughters) who are the teaching force are heavily weighed down by the durable dispositions they have acquired towards docility and intelligent conformism. So many in the staffroom lack either solidarity or critical resistance (bloody-minded teachers rarely become headmistresses, do they?), and show a deeply ingrained preference for petty private rivalries allied to a killingly small-minded individualism.

Not much light or space in such a habitus. Against its narrow constriction may again be set the structural advances made possible in the discourse of education by extensions in knowledge and by the changed place of these in both the politics and hermeneutics of inquiry. As I have so much protested, the moves against the deadly dogmatism of the hunters and gatherers of numbers, against ludicrously oversimple models of human behaviour, and against the lethal reductions of utilitarianism have gone a long way. The criticism and creation of learning in its long historical progress themselves give the discourse of education its power of liberation. The shock waves of these against the solid walls of the late capitalist habitus is one engagement in the civil war whose battlefield I began by describing.

I listed rather cryptically three linguistic weapons with which teachers and pupils in different parts of their being might arm themselves on behalf of human freedom. There were: usefulness, humanism, criticality. I spoke then of these, in a clumsy metaphor, as being voices broadcasting on the wavelengths of culture, continuously available to any audience which could tune in. Each carries its own version of both truth and goodness; each, in other words, is necessarily teleological; it has human ends and improvements, the betterment of the world and the perfectibility of man in view.[29]

At this concluding stage of my argument I want to bring my three weapons — sword, chalice and golden orb — into specific relation with *telos*, a view on our human future. Schooling is a small and a large enough subject to spend a lifetime on, and the curriculum — what we learn and what there is to learn — is the official point of going to school, college or university. Now it is clear that the curriculum, which is the heart of education, increasingly fails as a means for binding our children to life. Its structure of values cannot do this, because the view of life those values frame is no longer believable. To put the same point another way, the theory of life implied by so much of our curriculum does not fit the form of how we actually live. Hence managerialism and therapeutic counselling are dreamed up in order to persuade us that lies are truth; the process of persuasion has naturally to begin with those who will teach us how to be managed.

The best of our teachers, and of our students too, know that our curriculum cannot 'bind them to life'. What they can then do is tune themselves to what is useful, what seems likely to serve a human future (humanism) and what enables critical resistance (which is at the same time the creative imagining of alternatives). This selection among the wavelengths goes on as teachers and students alike pick out the usefulness of, say, these novels as opposed to those, or given the chance, of learning Russian instead of Spanish. Usefulness in this sense is not the same as practicality; it is as useful to be able to mend an old car as it is to be taught *Timon of Athens* instead of *The Winter's Tale*. Both may be made different use of, in the present moment of history. Either takes the strain of that history better than some of the alternatives. So, too, with a humanism which no longer looks much like Matthew Arnold's, but is still not an empty concept, whatever the French *maîtres à penser* say. A workaday humanism leads an honest biology teacher to insist on life in the life sciences, and to spend much time on industrial pollution, nuclear waste and the exhaustion of resourses; a similar humanism encourages a home economics which can propose the usurpation of take-away pancake rolls, sodden beefburgers and the eternal sugary confectionery by decent bread, fresh fruit and the democratic cuisine of the good supermarket – let alone launch an inquiry which had much to say of factory farming, Franju's terrifying movie *Le Sang Des Bêtes*, and the effects of cereal-to-meat ratios on world starvation. A mildly theoretic criticality, of a sort sometimes more evident in the exigencies of a comprehensive-school fifth year than a university seminar in fine art or psychology, makes immediate play with the discrepancy between History and my life-in-earnest, which will eventually be part of a future historian's History of Britain. There is no necessary salvation in criticality; it may be blindly philistine or mostly self-referring. But there will be no future without criticality.

These are forms of the discourse through which the curriculum, and therefore a different future than that envisioned by our present masters, may be fought for. If I also say, as I do, that these small weapons may best be wielded for something that may be described as a socialist view of that future, I hammer no Stalinist anvil, nor fantasize none of the more barmy dreams of anarchism or syndicalism as sung by the initialled sectarians of motley revolutionary groups. It is clear, furthermore, that although Marx was the greatest analyst of capitalism there has been, Marxism as a theory of social advance no longer will grip upon the facts of our society. As that society in its classical bourgeois form breaks up – that is to say, as bourgeois class formations, the stark relations of *rentier* capital to propertyless labour, the long lines of Old Empire, as all these disintegrate and world economic power moves vastly both in form and geography – so Marxism, as a total account of old capitalism devised from within that capitalism in order first to oppose and then to destroy it, disintegrates into its earlier compositions, that mixture of socialist allsorts made up of Owenites, Saint-Simonians, Blanquistes, Left-Hegelians, Chartists and so forth. Lacking any coherent theory, each affiliation then gave its allegiance to some domain of human desires and needs crying for recognition as the social order of mass and free-market industrial capitalism became established. Thinking of those programmes, variously compounded of profit-sharing co-operatives, pantisocratic communes, welfare militants, anarchists, libertarians, and suffrage reformists, we may only see any socialist interest on the part of present-day teachers and curriculum developers as finding rational expression in a combination of altruism with mutuality, of peacefulness with a sufficient independence.

Put like that, a manifesto for the human future would ring with resonant platitudes. I am claiming that, in the present vertiginous uncertainty of the world, its runaway debtors and acceleratingly out-of-control imbalances of payments, its raging and horrible wars, its similarly headlong starvation, the small barony of Britain, certainly becoming modestly but unequally poorer, cannot afford the luxuries of predestinarian Marxism. Thinking about socialism,[30] with no more than a national curriculum in view, commits the teacher-sympathizer to repudiate, especially after the longed-for and terrible upheavals of impossible revolution, the simplified paradises of Marxism. But given the same teacher's clear duty to imagine the good life and to fight against the so simply horrible manifestations of late capitalism both home and abroad, what is to be done, which will be feasible, honourable and effective?

> In the last days, perilous times shall come, for men shall be lovers of their own selves, covetous, boasters, proud, blasphemous, disobedient to parents, unthankful, unholy, without natural affection, truce-breakers, false accusers, incontinent, fierce, despisers of those that are good.[31]

It is only sensible and not at all melodramatic to think that the last days of the world may be at hand, without some huge effort of both will and compassion, the two great elements of humanism, to stop making the weapons of ultimate destruction. But other, less globally final days impend, so long as one looks no further than Britain's minor, but not temporary impoverishment and steep decline in power, and the dissolution of bourgeois imperialist society which has caused it. In these circumstances, the steady-nerved teacher-socialist will take what he or she can from the motley of pre-1848 socialism, and use it to make human and liveable the small space of European Britain and its post-Keynesian systems of production and education. He, that is, will take the stories of the subjects and retell them, in order to give much more room to the meanings of altruism and peacefulness, of independence and mutuality than is usually allocated in present-day environmental science, peace education, physics or machine maintenance.[32] She will take the art of the curriculum and give its symbols and images much freer, bolder and more homely play than is dreamed of among the egg-boxes and tambourines of the present.

It is important to make clear that such a vein of thought and feeling runs deep in radical culture. I am not trying to make something out of nothing. Nor am I trying to do down the great pleasures of private life, the deep satisfactions of consumer living, nor the delights of a well-upholstered leisure life. I am insisting that these may only be enjoyed as part of a worthy, just and generous life, and that it is the function, meaning and duty of being a teacher to think about how this may be done, and how such lives may be made out of the materials of classroom and street. It is not easy to see how to be a teacher without engaging with the strenuously contested, but essential notion of a common good.[33] That good lives in the just, tender-hearted, merciful and generous dealings we may make with our resources – our wealth and our attributes certainly – but also in our membership one of another. In a secular time, it is likely that only some severe, forgiving, dedicated and highly sceptical version of a new socialism will have the language to imagine and the power to manage such a brave, small world. These are indeed the politics of knowledge, and it is still possible to hope that their products will be precious and repeatable versions of human flourishing.

Notes

CHAPTER 1   THE STATE OF THE NATION

1 The argument I borrow is Alasdair MacIntyre's, in *Secularization and Moral Change* (Oxford University Press, 1967).

2 Raymond Williams, *Drama in a Dramatised Society* (Cambridge University Press, 1975), p. 15.

3 Most notably, J. H. Elliott, in *The Revolt of the Catalans: A Study in the Decline of Spain*, (Cambridge University Press, 1963.

4 The documentation of my examples is to be found in Eric Hobsbawm and Terence Ranger (eds), *The Invention of Tradition* (Cambridge University Press, 1983).

5 See, of course, E. P. Thompson, *The Making of the English Working Class* (Gollancz, 1963).

6 Much in this analysis follows Jurgen Habermas, in his *Legitimation Crisis* (Heinemann Educational Books, 1975).

7 Clifford Geertz, *The Interpretation of Cultures* (Hutchinson, 1975), p. 448.

8 The title is Dan Jacobson's in his methodologically (as well as textually) absorbing study of the Old Testament, *The Story of the Stories* (Secker & Warburg, 1982).

9 Karl Marx, *Selected Writings*, edited by D. McLellan (Oxford University Press, 1977), the *'Grundrisse'*, p. 357.

10 In, classically, *Economy and Society*. Weber, famously, is the first and bleakest prophet of the triumph of managerialism, to which we shall return. See especially his essay 'Politics as a Vocation', in *From Max Weber*, edited by H. H. Gerth and C. W. Mills (Routledge & Kegan Paul, 1948).

11 The metaphor was first used by Pierre Bourdieu, in, variously, *Outline of a Theory of Practice* (Cambridge University Press, 1978) and, with J.-G. Passeron, *Reproduction in Education, Scociety and Culture* (Sage Books, 1977).

12 The difficulties of handling poisoned ideas are stirringly listed by John Dunn, in *Western Political Theory in the Face of the Future* (Cambridge University Press, 1979).

13 The title of a now celebrated conference of apostates. See subse-

quently Stuart Hampshire and Leszek Kolakowski (eds), *The Socialist idea* (Weidenfeld & Nicolson, 1974).

14 The phrase is R. G. Collingwood's, in *An Autobiography* (Clarendon Press, 1939). Collingwood believed that history was that science; I have tried to build on his views in my *Radical Earnestness: English Social Theory 1880–1980* (Martin Robertson, 1982).

15 I owe much of this summary of Hegel to Charles Taylor's *Hegel and Modern Society* (Cambridge University Press, 1981), and, in the brief reference to critical theory which follows, to Raymond Geuss, *The Idea of a Critical Theory: Habermas and the Frankfurt School* (Cambridge University Press, 1981).

16 See William Morris, *Political Writings*, edited by A. L. Morton (Lawrence & Wishart, 1973); see also my treatment of Morris, in *Radical Earnestness*.

17 This premiss is quoted from Geuss, *Idea of a Critical Theory*, p. 2.

18 Following Charles Taylor, once more, in his 'Interpretation and the sciences of man', now extensively reprinted, first appearing in the *Journal of Metaphysics* (January 1971).

19 For atrocious memories of which, see S. Humphries, *Hooligans or Rebels?* (Basil Blackwell, 1981).

20 As represented famously in Brian Jackson and Dennis Marsden, *Education and the Working Class* (Routledge & Kegan Paul, 1962).

CHAPTER 2   GRAMMAR AND NARRATIVE

1 See Tom Nairn, *The Break-up of Britain* (New Left Books, 1978).

2 Much documented in S. Hall and T. Jefferson (eds), *Resistance Through Ritual* (Hutchinson, 1976).

3 The view that modernization is the inevitable motion of all societies has been vigorously set back in Iran: Khomeini has more or less single-handedly rebutted Max Weber.

4 The classic analysis of these two traditions of inquiry into metaphor, while favouring the transparency side, is Max Black's in *Models and Metaphor*, (Cornell University Press, 1962). For the cloudy, or hermeneutic view, see Paul Ricoeur, *The Rule of Metaphor* (Routledge & Kegan Paul, 1979). A widespread examination of metaphor in all forms of science, human and natural, is provided in the anthology edited by Andrew Ortony, *Metaphor and Thought* (Cambridge University Press, 1979).

5 See R. R. Bolgar, *The Classical Heritage and its Beneficiaries*, (Cambridge University Press, 1954). The structuralists, especially in France, have returned the study of rhetoric to the centre of the human science by their emphasis on language rather than man as the subject of study.

6 Thus, F.R. Leavis of Dickens's *Hard Times* in *The Great Tradition* (Chatto & Windus, 1948).

7 A notion which T.S. Kuhn makes almost synonymous with narrative. See his *The Structure of Scientific Revolutions* (Chicago University Press, 1962).

8 It is done for us by Stefan Körner, in *Categorial Frameworks* (Basil Blackwell, 1970).

9 The conditions for realizing ideal language are sketched in Jurgen Habermas, *Legitimation Crisis* (Heinemann Educational Books, 1975).

10 I take the substitution of 'edification' for 'education' from Richard Rorty, *Philosophy and the Mirror of Nature* (Basil Blackwell, 1981), and am grateful to him for the chance to escape the more dire impress of education with a capital E, as well as the case for an iron epistemological philosophy.

11 By Pierre Bourdieu, as noted in *Outline of a Theory of Practice* (Cambridge University Press, 1978) and elsewhere.

12 Innocent proponents of this view, who have none the less influenced formal thinking (for want of a better word) about knowledge and education, are best represented by Paul Hirst, most accessibly in *Knowledge and the Curriculum* (Routledge and Kegan Paul, 1975).

13 Coming in that order, in the history of all subjects. The process is entertainingly described by Frank Musgrove in *Patterns of Power and Authority in English Education* (Routledge and Kegan Paul, 1969).

14 Karl Mannheim first drew attention to competition in ideology in his example, generationally, in *Essays in the Sociology of Knowledge* (Routledge & Kegan Paul, 1952).

15 Here and afterwards used in T.J. Arthur's edition (Lawrence and Wishart, 1970). It is relevant to remember that *The German Ideology* was written with Engels during 1846–7, and never published during the two men's lifetimes. It is not therefore a systematic work, and certainly not the procedural handbook some later Marxists have used it as.

16 Perry Anderson 'Components of the national culture', *New Left Review* vol. 50 (1968), reprinted in *Student Power*, edited by A. Cockburn and R. Blackburn (Penguin, 1969).

17 Most popularly in the anthology edited by M.F.D. Young, *Knowledge and Control* (Routledge & Kegan Paul, 1972). The criticism in the same terms of primary-school pedagogy was made by Rachel Sharp and Anthony Green, *Education and Social Control* (Routledge & Kegan Paul, 1975). The best of a now substantial reading list is Michael Apple, *Ideology and Curriculum* (Routledge & Kegan Paul, 1979). See also his *Education and Power* (Routledge & Kegan Paul, 1981).

18 Notoriously, the poorest white families have the highest proportion of single parents. See Peter Townsend, *Poverty in the United Kingdom* (Penguin, 1979), especially chapter 7.

19 *German Ideology*, p.64.

20 I have no wish to make Paul Hirst the villain of liberalism. But he conveniently expresses the classically liberal view of education as the successful deployment of a freely choosing rationality in the domains of knowledge, a view which prefigures the ideal speech-situation of most classrooms.

21 This is the classic theory of semantic difference proposed by Fernard Saussure, in his *Course in General Linguistics*, edited by Charles Bally and Albert Sechehaye (McGraw-Hill/Collins, 1974), part I, chapter 4.

22 The whole summary of historical partiality in these paragraphs is a sort of nursery Hegelianism. It derives from Charles Taylor's tips in his *Hegel and Modern Society* (Cambridge University Press, 1979) or, for those who want the original, J.W.F. Hegel, *The Philosophy of History*.

23 See Clifford Geertz, *The Interpretation of Cultures* (Hutchinson 1975), especially 'Ideology as cultural system'. See also my *Ideology and the Imagination* (Cambridge University Press, 1975).

24 John Fowles's wholly admirable and classic *The French Lieutenant's Woman* (Jonathan Cape, 1969) boldy makes the Darwinists, and by implication, the feminists, torch-bearers of the new science.

25 Just how differently science has been done in the East is brought out by Joseph Needham in the greatest work of scientific history ever written, *Science and Civilization in China*. My own glimpse of this giant work was gained from the anthologized version, edited by Needham with Colin Ronan (Cambridge University Press, 1978).

26 M.B.V. Roberts, *Biology: a Functional Approach* (Nelson, 1971).

27 James Watson, *The Double Helix* (Weidenfeld & Nicolson, 1967).

28 Thomas Kuhn, *The Structure of Scientific Revolutions*.

29 see Habermas, *Legitimation Crisis*, pp.102–10.

30 The best such parody is Ernest Gellner's of the linguistic philosopher, in *Words and Things* (Penguin, 1959).

31 See Rorty, *Philosophy and the Mirror of Nature*. *Radical Philosphy*, a journal of faintly *samizdat* air and presentation, has done much from junior establishments in the hierarchy, especially polytechnics, to alter the stereotype described here, and to push philosophy back towards the insistent unacademic questions about meaning in life, good and bad societies, acting and living well.

32 Quoted from Stuart Maclure, *Educational Documents: England and Wales 1816–1968* (Methuen, rev. edn, 1969), p.159.

33 For the history of late-eighteenth-century poverty, see E. J. Hobsbawm and G. Rudé, *Captain Swing* (Lawrence & Wishart, 1969). For

the significance of the late-eighteenth-century bread riots, see E.P. Thompson, 'The moral economy of the 18th century crowd', *Past and Present* 50, 1971.

34 Richard Hoggart *The Uses of Literacy* (Chatto & Windus/Penguin, 1957) pp. 37–8.

35 For a useful selection from their relevant writings, see Peter Keating, *The Victorian Prophets* (Fontana, 1978).

36 A vivid synopsis of such an essay is to be found written by the man who, in his lifetime, was best equipped to try it: Raymond Postgate in his introduction to *The Good Food Guide for 1965–66* (Consumers' Association with Cassell, 1965).

37 All given classic but novel relocation in the narrative of E.P. Thompson's *The Making of the English Working Class* (Gollancz, 1963).

38 All documented in the self-explanatorily named *The Invention of Tradition*, edited by Eric Hobsawm and Terence Ranger (Cambridge University Press, 1983).

39 It is my point that this is a long-standing human faculty, a view powerfully supported by Dan Jacobson's *The Story of the Stories* (Secker & Warburg, 1982).

40 It is a claim upheld by much recent historiography, best exemplified by Stefan Collini, John Burrow and Donald Winch, in *That Noble Science of Politics: A Study in Nineteenth Century Intellectual History* (Cambridge University Press, 1983).

41 The reference is to Richard Rorty's now deservedly celebrated *Philosophy and the Mirror of Nature*, which tries to do away with philosophy as the agent of a realist epistemology. I shall come back to the question of what realism means in chapter 4.

CHAPTER 3   THEORY AND EXPERIENCE

1 As, with distinct partiality, John Dunn does in 'Practising history and social science on "realist" assumptions', in his *Political Obligation in its Historical Context* (Cambridge University Press, 1980).

2 T.S. Eliot, 'East Coker', part II, in *Collected Poems and Plays* (Faber & Faber, 1976), p. 179.

3 The phrase is Louis Althusser's in *Lenin and Philosophy* (New Left Books, 1977).

4 E.P. Thompson, *The Poverty of Theory* (Merlin Press, 1978), p. 356. This definition is fairly criticized by Perry Anderson for its lack of an operational taxonomy, in *Arguments within English Marxism* (New Left Books/Verso, 1980), especially chapter 3.
Compare also Pasternak's novel *Dr Zhivago*, where the grim, but sympathetically treated revolutionary, Strelnikov, tells Zhivago that in

revolutionary Russia the personal life, the individual life of the feelings, is over and done with.

5 I hope this very crude and foreshortened summary of Karl Popper's description of scientific method in *The Logic of Scientific Discovery* (Hutchinson, 1959) will serve the purpose of this chapter sufficiently.

6 The historical record is valuably, if uncritically summarized by A. N. Whitehead, in *Science and the Modern World* (Cambridge University Press, 1938).

7 T.S. Kuhn, *The Structure of Scientific Revolutions* (Chicago University Press, 1962). John Ziman, *Public Knowledge* (Cambridge University Press, 1972), and *The Force of Knowledge* (Cambridge University Press, 1976).

8 Gödel's Incompleteness Theorem is illustrated in many hues by Douglas Hofstadter in *Gödel, Escher, Bach: an Eternal Golden Braid* (Harvester Press, 1979).

9 A very partial history of its career is given by Marjorie Grene, in *The Knower and the Known* (Faber & Faber 1965).

10 I owe the idea of knowledge as a product being like a work of art to my friend, Gordon Reddiford. Taylor was celebrated in song and story for first working out in intense detail the methods of mass assembly, in which each worker performs thousands of times per day one single brief action. See Harry Braverman, *Labour and Monopoly Capital* (Monthly Review Press, 1974).

11 A good phrase coined by F. Phenix in *Realms of Meaning: a Philosophy of Curriculum*, (McGraw-Hill, 1964).

12 It is put with a dogmatism at times proper, at times merely supercilious, by Roger Scruton, in *The Meaning of Conservatism* (Penguin, 1980).

13 A singularly critical history of these relations is offered by Jurgen Habermas in his *Knowledge and Human Interests* (Heinemann Educational Books, 1974).

14 I keep using the time-honoured phrase, map of knowledge, with a particular eye on R. G. Collingwood's use of the phrase in his book of that name, *Speculum Mentis* (Clarendon Press, 1924), to which we return in chapter 10.

15 I extend my own definition here, as taken from *Ideology and the Imagination* (Cambridge University Press, 1975).

16 DES *Statistics, Yearbook*, 1979, 1980. The comparable ratio in, for instance, civil engineering is $1:18$. The university *teachers* of the humanities are largely male, however.

17 I am relying on a phenomenology of the imagination which I try to portray in my book on children's fiction, *The Promise of Happiness* (Cambridge University Press, 1981).

18 They are called, of course, preparations *against* it. But see Geoffrey Barraclough's *From Agadir to Armageddon*, Weidenfeld & Nicolson, 1982) for chilling parallels with 1911–14.

19 Readers familiar with Richard Rorty, *Philosophy and the Mirror of Nature* (Basil Blackwell, 1981), will recognize my indebtedness with the first three names. The others are my idiosyncrasy.

20 Heidegger, *Basic Writings*, edited with an introduction by David Krell, Routledge & Kegan Paul 1978, p. 383.

21 Unforgettably parodied by Paul Jennings (via Sartre) in his essay on 'Resistentialism', reprinted in *The Jenguin Pennings* (Penguin, 1962).

22 Heidegger, ibid. pp. 383–4.

23 R.G. Collingwood, (Clarendon Press, 1939), *An Autobiography;* reissued, with an introduction by Stephen Toulmin (Oxford University Press, 1981).

24 Collingwood is a good example of what Bernard Williams means by the term, in the title essay to his *Moral Luck* (Cambridge University Press, 1981).

25 I have written at some length about his life and work in my *Radical Earnestness* (Martin Robertson, 1982).

26 Collingwood, *Autobiography*, p. 114.

27 Edwin Muir, *Autobiography* (Hogarth Press, 1954; Metheun, 1968), p. 48.

28 It is Alasdair MacIntye who suggests that within the terms of present ethics, the only virtue (and the ethical life for MacIntyre simply is the pursuit of virtue) is to live as continuous a narrative, which one can then be proud of, as possible. See his *After Virtue: A Study in Moral Theory* (Duckworth, 1981), especially chapter 15.

29 Storm Jameson, *Journey from the North*, 2 vols (Collins/Harvill, 1969; Virago, 1984); Vera Brittain, *The Testament of Youth* (Gollancz, 1942; Pan 1980; Virago, 1984); Naomi Mitchison, *You May Well Ask: A Memoir 1920–1940* (Gollancz, 1979).

30 Ezekiel Mphahlele, *Down Second Avenue* (Faber & Faber, 1956).

31 I take this point from Bernard Sharratt, in *Reading Relations* (Harvester Press, 1982), p. 313.

32 First published in 1848; valuably republished by MacGibbon & Kee in 1967.

33 I rely here on Amelie Rorty's anthology, *Identities of Persons* (University of California Press, 1976), especially the paper by Derek Parfit.

CHAPTER 4　　IDENTITY IN SELVES AND SUBJECTS

1 I follow Derek Parfit in this argument as rejecting common-sense accounts of identity, and going for a more slippery and less reassuring

philosophical account. See his paper, 'Lewis, Perry and what matters', in Amelie Rorty, *Identities of Persons* (University of California Press, 1976).

2 See also Derek Parfit's singular and tremendous book, *Reasons and Persons* (Clarendon Press, 1984).

3 And here I rely on the editor, Amelie Rorty in her postscript to 'Characters, persons, selves, individuals', in *Identities of Persons*.

4 The phrase is Basil Bernstein's, in his *Class, Codes, Control*, vol. III, rev. edn (Routledge & Kegan Paul, 1977), to which I shall return.

5 Rorty, *Identities of Persons*, p.313.

6 Erving Goffmann, *The Presentation of Self in Everyday Life* (Doubleday/Penguin, 1969).

7 I take much of the strictly moral philosophy which follows in definition of individuals from Peter Strawson, *Individuals* (Oxford University Press, 1963), although he is interested in individuals in a more metaphysical sense as well as a technical category.

8 I adjust the title of Thomas Nagel's fine book, *The Possibility of Altruism* (Oxford University Press, 1970), where Nagel indeed argues for its necessity.

9 I am aware that a number of contemporary human scientists, notably Michel Foucault and Jacques Derrida in Paris, oppose what they see as this preposterously bourgeois 'metaphysics of presence' and propose its superannuation. See Foucault's *The Order of Things* (Tavistock, 1970), and Derrida's *Of Grammatology* (John Hopkins University Press, 1976). My nursery riposte would be, 'Man may no longer be our subject, but only men and women can write the new history.'

10 See Robert Darnton's *The Business of Enlightenment: The Publishing History of the Encyclopédie, 1775–1880* (Harvard University Press, 1980).

11 Such as Alec Nove sketches out, in *The Economics of Feasible Socialism* (Allen & Unwin, 1983).

12 Conservatism of a realist kind is illicitly extended into conservatism of a political kind in his essay on these matters by Antony Flew, *Sociology, Equality and Education* (Macmillan, 1976).

13 This is a propositional form of Anthony Giddens's 'Theory of Structuration', as advanced in his *Profiles and Critiques in Social Theory* (Macmillan, 1982) and fully expounded in his *The Constitution of Society* (Basil Blackwell, 1984).

14 Mary Douglas, *Purity and Danger: An Analysis of the Concepts of Pollution and Taboo*, rev. edn (Routledge & Kegan Paul, 1969).

15 Basil Bernstein, *Class, Codes, Control*, vol. I (Routledge & Kegan Paul, 1971), and vol. III. See especially the introduction to volume I, where he describes his first encounter with Durkheim.

16 I simplify drastically here. For the hard argument, see Stefan Körner, *Experience and Theory: An Essay in the Philosophy of Science* (Routledge & Kegan Paul, 1966).

17 As before, I rely extensively on Max Black, *Models and Metaphors* (Cornell University Press, 1962).

18 Memorably indemnified by Ernest Gellner, in his attack on Oxford philosophy in *Words and Things* (Penguin, 1959).

19 For sorting which terms, see the classic exposition in Lionel Trilling's *Sincerity and Authenticity* (Oxford University Press, 1972).

20 In his classic, but often impenetrable study of these processes: Pierre Bourdieu with J.-C. Passeron, *Reproduction in Education, Society and Culture*, translated by R. Nice. (Sage Books, 1977).

CHAPTER 5   ACCESS AND PRESTIGE

1 Jerome Bruner, 'Culture and cognitive growth', in his collection of essays, *The Relevance of Education* (Allen & Unwin, 1972).

2 Bernstein has been rebuked for too much following a Durkheimean or fixed view of the social order, thus underestimating the drive and friction which a more Marxizing model would have provided. He replied to his critics with the concluding essay in *Class, Codes, Control*, vol. III (Routledge & Kegan Paul, 1977), 'Education and the systems of production', adapting his classification and framing analysis in order to correlate classroom practice, economic buoyancy or decline, and method of production.

3 Following Jorge Larrain, in *The Concept of Ideology,* (Hutchinson, 1979).

4 There is a useful short history of the word in John Plamenatz, *Ideology* (Macmillan, 1971).

5 Here referred to in T. J. Arthur's edition (Lawrence & Wishart, 1970).

6 Clifford Geertz suggest the two terms, in 'Ideology as cultural system', an essay in his book, *The Interpretation of Cultures* (Hutchinson, 1975).

7 As has been pointed out, Marxism took essential parts of its structure of theodicy from Christianity. See Denys Turner's powerful attempt to turn Marxism back into Christianity, *Marxism and Christianity* (Basil Blackwell, 1983).

8 The best first guide in a large bibliography is Perry Anderson's, in a commemorative issue of *New Left Review*, numbers 100–1. See also James Joll, *Gramsci* (Fontana, 1980). But Gramsci was writing for an untheoretic audience, and the best place to learn about him is in the original. See Antonio Gramsci, *Selections from the Prison Notebooks*, edited by Quintin Hoare (Lawrence & Wishart, 1977).

9 In his novel, *A Painter of our Time* (Penguin, 1965), p. 64.
10 Notes for the study of which are provided in Karl Mannheim, *Essays in the Sociology of Knowledge* (Routledge & Kegan Paul, 1952),
11 Bernstein, 'Ritual in education', *Class, Codes, Control*, vol. III.
12 Originally, George Sampson's, in *English for the English* (1922), edited with an introduction by Denys Thompson (Cambridge University Press, 1970).
13 I borrow here and later from Steven Lukes's admirable monograph, *Power: A Radical View* (Macmillan, 1974).
14 I have in mind the most difficult parts of Pierre Bourdieu and J.-G. Passeron, *Reproduction in Education, Society and Culture* (Sage Books, 1977).
15 As in J.A. Hobson, *Imperialism*, 3rd rev. edn (Allen & Unwin).

CHAPTER 6   THE SOCIAL MOBILITY OF A SUBJECT

1 As quoted by Alasdair MacIntyre, in *Secularization and Moral Change* (Oxford University Press, 1967).
2 John Robinson, *Honest to God* (SCM Press, 1964).
3 In 'God and the theologians', collected by Alasdair MacIntyre, *Against the Self-Images of the Age* (Duckworth, 1971).
4 Edward Norman has tried to rebut the (largely Latin American) call for a politicized Christian ministry in his Reith Lectures, *Christianity and the World Order* (Oxford University Press, 1979). Peterhouse, Cambridge, is not, however, the most exemplary place from which to argue with such supreme unction for a restatement of a non-social, wholly individual doctrine of grace.
5 The best suggestions, very much under the influence of Robinsonian theology, come from Ninian Smart, *The Phenomenon of Religion* (Macmillan, 1973).
6 It will be noticed that these observations rest on Michel Foucault's historical diagnosis of the Surveillant Society in *Discipline and Punish* (Allen Lane/Penguin, 1977).
7 I once more borrow gratefully from MacIntyre's *After Virtue* (Duckworth, 1981) especially chapters 6 and 7.
8 MacIntyre, *After Virtue*, p. 25.
9 Ibid., p. 24.
10 Ibid., pp. 25–6.
11 Greatly as I honour Elizabeth Richardson's pioneering study of a school under the Tavistock lamp, I think it is open to these strictures. See her *The Teacher, the School and the Task of Management* (Heinemann Educational Books, 1973).
12 As Miloslav Djilas identified it as being in *The New Class* (Allen & Unwin, 1956).

13 As commended in Rudolf Bahro, *The Alternative in Eastern Europe* (New Left Books, 1978).

14 W.V.O. Quine, *Ontological Relativism* (Columbia University Press, 1969).

15 I can't go far into these matters, but what I am saying conflicts with some of the essays in the well-known anthology of P. Gardiner, *The Philosophy of History* (Oxford University Press, 1974). I take much from Roy Bhaskar, *The Possibility of Naturalism* (Harvester Press, 1979), although mine is a very different, much more Aristotelian naturalism.

16 See notes 28, 29 and 31 of chapter 3. The following should be added to this list: William Lovett, *William Lovett: His Life and Struggles* (1860; reprinted MacGibbon & Kee, 1967); Fred Kitchen, *Brother to the Ox* (Heinemann Educational Books, 1959: 1939); James Dawson Burn, *Autobiography of a Beggar Boy* (1855: now out of print); Thomas Frost, *Forty Years Recollections* (Tinsley, 1880).

17 Paul Scott's *Raj Quartet* 4 vols (Heinemann, 1967–75), now made celebrated by its fine rendering on Granada TV, is a striking revaluation of the meaning of the imperial occupation in its most dismal and neglectful years. Nadine Gordimer, in *A Guest of Honour* (Jonathan Cape, 1970; Penguin 1973) seeks impressively to characterize the post-imperial politics of any one of the former Central African Federation countries.

18 James Morris gives a full revaluation of the Empire in his three-volume *Pax Britannica*, rev. edn (Penguin, 1978).

19 The structure of the action is classically analysed by E.H. Carr, in *What is History?* (Macmillan/Penguin, 1961). The history from below may be said to start from Christoper Hill's books *Puritanism and Revolution* (Secker & Warburg, 1958); *The Century of Revolution* (Nelson, 1961); and the founding of the journal *Past and Present*.

20 Fernand Braudel, *The Mediterranean in the Age of Philip II*, 2 vols (Harper & Row/Collins, 1973).

21 W.G. Hoskins, *The Making of the English Landscape* (Hodder & Stoughton, 1955); *The Midland Peasant* (Macmillan, 1957).

22 Peter Laslett, *The World We Have Lost* (Methuen, 1965).

23 E.P. Thompson, *The Making of the English Working Class* (Gollancz, 1963; Penguin, 1968); Eric Hobsbawm, *Labouring Men: Studies in Labour History* (Weidenfeld & Nicolson, 1964) and, with Georges Rude, *Captain Swing* (Lawrence & Wishart, 1969).

24 Notably in the Ruskin College journal, *Socialist History Workshop*.

CHAPTER 7   CLASS AND CULTURE

1 A complacency whose etymology excludes perimeter countries, for instance in the Caribbean or the Middle East.

2 E. P. Thompson, *Writing by Candlelight* (Merlin Press, 1980), p. 201.

3 The phrase is Anthony Giddens's, in his essential primer, *The Class Structure of the Advanced Societies* (Hutchinson, 1973).

4 Classically written by Michael Young, *The Rise of the Meritocracy* (Penguin, 1961). The author is now, symmetrically, Lord Young of the Social Democratic Party and Dartington.

5 This is a rather compressed malediction, expanded in chapter 9. Nietzsche, of course, took his own conclusions with such absolute seriousness that they took away his reason. His descendants, however, are rather less ascetically self-indulgent. See *Beyond Good and Evil* (Penguin edn, 1973).

6 Such books as, first and classically, Germaine Greer, *The Female Eunuch* (Paladin, 1971); Juliet Mitchell, *Woman's Estate* (Penguin, 1971); Sheila Rowbotham, *Woman's Consciousness, Man's World* (Penguin, 1973); Ann Oakley, *Sex, Gender, and Society* (Temple Smith, 1972) are all, in their way, educational handbooks.

7 Most simply, polemically and reductively in Marx, 'A Critique of the Gotha Programme' in *Selected Works* (Foreign Languages Publishing House, Moscow, 1972).

8 For example, Roger Dale, Geoff Esland and Madeleine Macdonald (eds), *Schooling and Capitalism*, second level Open University reader (Open University with Routledge & Kegan Paul, 1976). A. Hunt (ed.), *Class and Class Structure* (Lawrence & Wishart, 1977); Rachel Sharp, *Knowledge, Ideology and the Politics of Schooling* (Routledge & Kegan Paul, 1980); Stuart Hall et al. (eds) *Resistance through Ritual* (Hutchinson, 1976); Mark Levitas, *Marxist Perspectives in the Sociology of Education* (Routledge & Kegan Paul, 1974); and Henry Giroux, *Ideology, Culture and the Process of Schooling* (Falmer Press, 1980).

9 In, first, *Lenin and Philosophy* (New Left Books, 1971).

10 This formulation derives from Jurgen Habermas, *Knowledge and Human Interests* (Heinemann Educational Books, 1974).

11 Now known as the Structuralists: notably Claude Lévi-Strauss, Jacques Lacan, Lucien Goldmann, Roland Barthes, and Michel Foucault (q.v.).

12 Jacques Derrida, *Of Grammatology*, translated by J. Spivak (Johns Hopkins University Press, 1976).

13 Basil Bernstein, 'Education and the systems of production', in *Class, Codes, Control* vol. III, rev. edn (Routledge & Kegan Paul, 1977), and subsequently in 'The stability of pedagogic discourse', CORE 1984 (microfiche).

14 Samuel Bowles and Herbert Gintis, *Schooling in Capitalist America* (Routledge & Kegan Paul, 1976).

15 Paul Willis, *Learning to Labour* (Saxon House, 1977). The subtitle is *How Working Class Kids Get Working Class Jobs.*

16 In an endearing last chapter, he takes the unusual risk for an ethnographer of showing the subjects of his study how he explains their predicaments and occasion. It is no surprise that they think he's all wrong, and Willis is morally and intellectually too scrupulous to summon up the spectre of false consciousness.

17 As the authors accuse their primary-teacher subjects, in Rachel Sharp and Anthony Green, *Education and Social Control* (Routledge & Kegan Paul, 1975).

18 Nicos Poulantzas, *Political Power and Social Classes* (New Left Books, 1973), p. 86, italics in original.

19 Nicos Poulantzas, *Classes in Contemporary Capitalism* (New Left Books, 1975), p. 14.

20 Poulantzas, *Political Power and Social Classes*, p. 67.

21 Classically, in such more-or-less scientifically-administrative versions as that of one of the founders of anthropology, E. E. Evans-Pritchard, *Social Anthropology* (Cohen & West, 1951).

22 Or better 'Fortuna' as Machiavelli would have it. Relevantly enough, Machiavelli is enjoying a revival in current political thought, not least because of the centrality he ascribes to 'Fortuna' – translatable as a mixture of luck, unknowable destiny (as in, 'my lady Fortune') and chance, all of them terms excluded from slightly earlier handbooks of political economy on the confident planning of the globe. See Quentin Skinner, *Machiavelli* (Oxford University Press, 1981) and his paper, 'Machiavelli on the maintenance of liberty', *Politics* no. 18, 1983.

23 The first is E. P. Thompson's essay 'The peculiarities of the English', in *The Poverty of Theory* (Merlin Press, 1978). Thompson breaks open both the functionalists' view of class as stratification (as in geology) and class as abstract historical necessity (as in Marxism). He insists, in this essay and the anti-Althusserian title essay, on the intractability of history as lived experience, and class as part of this dense, enormous process. The second is the vast concluding section of Jean-Paul Sartre's *Critique de la Raison Dialectique* (Le Seuil, 1960) (quotations in my own translation). The best empirical inquires into class in Britain are J. A. Westergaard and H. Resler, *Class in a Capitalist Society: A Study of Contemporary Britain*, (Heinemann, 1975); and Peter Townsend, *Poverty in the United Kingdom* (Penguin, 1979).

24 I try to bring out the methodical significance of this quality of Thompson's in my *Radical Earnestness* (Martin Robertson, 1982).

25 Sartre, *Critique*, p. 561.

26 Starting with R.H. Tawney's *Equality*, now reissued with an introduction by Richard Titmuss (Allen & Unwin, 1964). The next major educational text was by Jean Floud and A. H. Halsey, *Social Class and Educational Opportunity* (Heinemann, 1959). Past inequality in university admission is fully documented in the Robbins Report, *Higher Education*, Command 2154 (HMSO, 1963); in primary schools by Brian Jackson, *Streaming: an Education System in Miniature* (Routledge & Kegan Paul, 1964). Up-to-date figures and arguments include John Goldthorpe, *Social Mobility and Class Structure in Modern Britain* (Clarendon Press, 1980), as well as, stirringly, David Hargreaves, *The Challenge of the Comprehensive School*(Routledge & Kegan Paul, 1982).For the most recent figures on class membership of University admission, see UCCA, *Statistical Supplement* 1984. For more general statistics, see Ivan Reid, *Social Class Differences in Britain* (2nd ed. Grant McIntyre, 1981).

27 Up to 90 per cent in some cases, over 70 per cent in all. See D. Morrison and D. McIntyre, *Teachers and Teaching* (Penguin, 1969). See also Sara Delamont, *Interaction in the Classroom*, 2nd edn (Methuen, 1983) for the instruments of analysis *and* quantification of such findings.

28 Bernstein's early typology is given much more detail and purchase in the modes of Martin Halliday's linquistic taxonomy by R.M. Coulthard and J.M. Sinclair, *Towards an Analysis of Discourse: the English Used by Teachers and Pupils* (Oxford University Press, 1975).

29 Foucault, *Discipline and Punish* (Allen Lane/Penguin, 1977),

30 Stuart Hall's phrase, in 'The great moving right show' (in Pluto Press, 1981). Stuart Hall with Martin Jacques (eds), *The Politics of Thatcherism* (Pluto Press, 1981).

31 Among others , by Michael Apple in *Ideology and Curriculum* (Routledge & Kegan Paul, 1979). The critique is provided with the instruments of analysis, however, by Basil Bernstein in his essay 'visible and invisible pedagogies', in *Class, Codes, Control*, vol. III.

32 Much advertised in Geoff Whitty and Mitchael Young (eds), *Explanations in the Politics of School Knowledge* (Nafferton Press, 1978).

33 Brian Jackson and Dennis Marsden, *Education and the Working Class* (Routledge & Kegan Paul, 1962).

34 Richard Hoggart, *The Uses of Literacy* (Chatto & Windus with Penguin, 1957).

35 Brian Jackson, *Working Class Community* (Routledge & Kegan Paul, 1966).

36 David Holbrook, *English for the Rejected* (Cambridge University Press, 1964).

37 John Newsom, *Half Our Future* (HMSO, 1963).

38 For example, Centre for Contemporary Cultural Studies, University of Birmingham, in *Unpopular Education* (Hutchinson, 1981).

39 Which is where Stephen Lukes confines it in *Power: A Radical View* (Macmillan, 1974). But see Anthony Giddens, *Profiles and Critiques in Social Theory* (Macmillan, 1982).

CHAPTER 8   WORK AND MEANING

1 The two criticisms appear in Claude Lévi-Strauss, *Structural Anthropology* (Allen Lane/Penguin, 1964), pp. 279 ff. E. E. Evans-Pritchard, *Social Anthropology* (Cohen & West, 1951).

2 It is horribly relevant to recall at this stage that the dreadful gate to the Nazi extermination camp at Auschwitz bore the slogan 'Arbeit ist Freiheit'.

3 *Capital*, vol. I (Foreign Languages Publishing House, Moscow, 1887) (1st English edition), p. 72.

4 Most notably, Paul Sraffa in *Production of Commodities by Means of Commodities* (Cambridge University Press, 1960).

5 It is a story well told by David Meakin in *Man and Work: Literature and Culture in Industrial Society* (Methuen, 1976). A different history, in which 'capitalism' is substituted for 'industrialism' is famously told by Raymond Williams in his classic *Culture and Society: 1780–1950* (Chatto & Windus, 1957), Penguin, 1958).

6 Hannah Arendt, *The Human Condition* (Anchor Doubleday, 1959).

7 Max Weber, *The Protestant Ethic and the Spirit of Capitalism*, translated by Talcott Parsons (Allen & Unwin, 1948). R. H. Tawney, alone in England in taking up Weber in the 1920s, went on to document in detail the displacement of older Christian views of usury by capitalists: see *Religion and the Rise of Capitalism* (John Murray, 1926). Latterly, Albert Hirschmann has advanced the crucial ideological victory of the political economy as doctrine to the eighteenth century, in *The Passions and the Interests: Political Arguments for Capitalism before its Triumph*, (Princeton University Press, 1977).

8 The particular consequences of Calvinism for the pioneers who founded New England and were the intellectual originators of American capitalism are boldly drawn by Henry Bamford Parkes in *The American Experience* (Knopf, 1947).

9 This is to repeat Michel Foucault's radically determinist thesis in all his work, from *Madness and Civilisation* (1967) to his most recent essay available in English, *The History of Sexuality*, vol. I (Allen Lane/Penguin, 1979).

10 For a short history, see F. L. Carsten, *Revolution in Central Europe 1918–1919* (Oxford University Press, 1972).

11 In what follows I rely on Peter and Brigitte Berger's schematic structures for the analysis of the contemporary self. See *The Homeless Mind: Modernization and Consciousness* (Penguin, 1973).

12 It is called, in translation, *Economy and Society* (Routledge & Kegan Paul, 1962). Anyone inclined to take Weber lightly must also read 'Politics as a vocation', in *From Max Weber*, edited by H.H. Gerth and C.W. Mills (Routledge & Kegan Paul, 1948).

13 This is a well-known reversal much discussed in the anthropology of pre-industrial peoples, amongst whom the time is told by what they are doing, both for the days and seasons. See the discussion of time in John Beattie, *Other Cultures* (Cohen & West, 1964), and Clifford Geertz on 'Person, time, and conduct in Bali', in *The Interpretation of Cultures* (Hutchinson, 1975).

14 Particularly as written by Noam Chomsky in *American Power and the New Mandarins* (Chatto & Windus/Penguin, 1969).

15 E.P. Thompson 'Time, work-discipline, and industrial capitalism', *Past and Present*, no. 38 (1968).

16 For example, James Britton et al., *Schools Council Examination Bulletin: Multiple Marking* (Schools Council, 1966), and also *The Development of Writing Abilities* (Macmillan, 1975)

17 The statistical axiom of regression to the mean has never been part of their education.

18 See Harry Braverman, *Labour and Monopoly Capital* (Monthly Review Press, 1974).

19 As Peter Herbst would have it, in *Theoreticism and Critical Inquiry*, forthcoming.

20 I recognize that my politics at this point have a distinctly Oakeshottian timbre, but in my view these anti-technicist, humanly specific and experiential learnings can find as perfectly good a home on my Left as his Right. See Michael Oakeshott, *On Human Conduct* (Oxford University Press, 1975).

21 Andrew Harrison's useful phrase, from *Making and Thinking* (Harvester Press, 1978).

CHAPTER 9   VALUES AND THE FUTURE

1 See especially his last, lapidary work, *The New Leviathan*, (Clarendon Press, 1942).

2 Michael Rutter et al. *15,000 Hours: Secondary Schools and Their Effects on Children* (Open Books, 1979).

3 Taken from Krishan Humar, 'Holding the middle ground', in James Curran, Michael Gurevitch, and Janet Wollacott. (eds), *Mass Communication and Society* (Edward Arnold for the Open University, 1977).

4 The meaning of the word is most subtly entertained by Harold Bloom, in *A Map of Misreading* (Oxford University Press, New York, 1975).

5 I take the categories, for my very different purpose, from Charles Taylor's now canonical paper 'Interpretation and the sciences of man', first published in *Journal of Metaphysics* (January 1971); but see Roger Beehler and Alan Drengson, *The Philosophy of Society* (Methuen, 1979). This paper and all those by him on the same subject are now collected by Charles Taylor, in his *Philosophy and the Human Sciences*, (vols. 2, Cambridge University Press, 1985).

6 There is an important contemporary inclination to proceed in planning to the remorseless spatialization of time itself, thus subjecting it to the utilitarian calculus by which all values are numerically convertible. See Joel Whitebrook, 'Saving the subject: modernity and the problem of the autonomous individual', *Telos* (USA), vol. 50 (1981), pp. 79–102.

7 And see controversially definitive account in Derek Parfit, *Reasons and Persons* (Clarendon Press, 1984).

8 For a useful summary, see R. W. Connell et al. *Making the Difference: Schools, Families, and Social Division* (Allen & Unwin, 1982).

9 An anti-utilitarian point expounded by Stuart Hampshire in the title essay to his *Morality and Pessimism* (Oxford University Press, 1976).

10 Starting with the famous Club of Rome report, *The Limits to Growth* (Rome, 1972), and going on via the special issue of *The Ecologist, Blueprint for Survival* (January 1972), to Amartya Sen, *On Economic Inequality* (Clarendon Press, 1973), to Geoffrey Barraclough's famous trio of papers in the *New York Review* 'The End of an Era', 27 June 1974; 'The Great World Crisis', 23 January 1975; 'Wealth and Power: the Politics of Food and Oil', 7 August 1975.

11 The same sort of point is made on behalf of the English working class by Anthony Crosland, in *Socialism Now* (Jonathan Cape, 1974), part I.

CHAPTER 10   THE LANGUAGE OF POLITICS IN THE CONVERSATION OF CLASSROOMS

1 In, for example, Anthony Arblaster and Steven Lukes (eds), *The Good Society* (Macmillan, 1969); Bernard Williams, *Ethics and the Limits of Philosophy* (Fontana, 1985);Alasdair MacIntyre, *After Virtue: A Study in Moral Theory* (Duckworth, 1981). See also the summary of these tendencies in Richard Bernstein, *The Restructuring of Social and Political Theory* (Hutchinson, 1979), and *Beyond Objectivism and Relativism* (Basil Blackwell, 1983).

2 Fred Hirsch, *The Social Limits to Growth* (Allen & Unwin, 1976).

3 If for instance the European Community were to put even so modest a proposal as the Brandt Report into effect.

4 Two such honourable mentions are called for: Michael Banton, *The Coloured Quarter*, (Jonathan Cape, 1955) and *Racial Minorities* (Fontana, 1973); and John Rex, especially in *Race Relations in Sociological Theory* (Weidenfeld & Nicolson, 1970). See also the excellent collection of essays published by the collective authorship of the Centre for Contemporary Cultural Studies, University of Birmingham, as *The Empire Strikes Back* (Hutchinson, 1982).

5 It is very fully tested and criticized by Bernard Williams in 'The truth of relativism', *Moral Luck* (Cambridge University Press, 1981).

6 See Thomas S. Kuhn. *The Structure of Scientific Revolutions* (Chicago University Press, 1972); and John Ziman, *Public Knowledge* (Cambridge University Press, 1976). See also Marcel Detienne, *L'Invention de la Mythologie* (Gallimard, 1981).

7 I am entirely unimpressed by Martin Wiener's argument, in *British Culture and the Decline of the Industrial Spirit* (Cambridge University Press, 1981) that technology was defeated by the genteel culturalists of the Ruskin commando.

8 In, respectively, Carl Hempel, *Aspects of Scientific Explanation* (Free Press, 1965); and Ernest Nagel, *The Structure of Science* (Harcourt Brace, 1961).

9 As summarized and contested by J.J.C. Smart and Bernard Williams, in *Utilitarianism: For and Against* (Cambridge University Press, 1973).

10 That is to say I acknowledge the justice of criticism in such television studies as *Bad New* and *Really Bad News*, Glasgow Media Group (Routledge & Kegan Paul, 1976 and 1979); Philip Schlesinger, *Putting 'Reality' Together* (Constable, 1978); John Fiske and John Hartley, *Reading Tevevision* (Methuen, 1978); Len Masterman, *Teaching About Television* (Macmillan, 1980).

11 I look for support in this statement to Nicholas Garnham, 'Contribution to a political economy of mass communication', *Media, Culture and Society*, vol. 1. (1979). Garnham, emphasizing the play of both liberalism and control in the cultural industries, vigorously repudiates the arguments from Marxism particularly found in *Screen* that everything on television is a form of ideological control: this latter is the Dave Spart view of history.

12 For a devastatingly comical account of which, see David Stove, *Popper and After: Four Modern Irrationalists* (Pergamon Press, 1982).

13 Jurgen Habermas, *Legitimation Crisis* (Heinemann Educational Books, 1975), part III.

14 See John Dunn, *Political Obligation in its Historical Context*

(Cambridge University Press, 1980), pp. 243–300.

15 These are what Raymond Williams calls the agents of 'Plan X' in the concluding chapter, 'Resources for a journey of hope', in his *Towards 2000* (Chatto & Windus, 1983).

16 Bernard Williams's introduction to Isaiah Berlin, *Concepts and Categories: Philosophical Essays* (Hogarth Press, 1978), p. xviii.

17 This, I take it, is what Gramsci meant when he identified the forms of education as the perfectly proper site of political work for the revolutionary. See Antonio Gramsci, *The Modern Prince* (Lawrence & Wishart, 1957). His, of course, is hardly a Marxist, much more a latter-day Fabian's position, communicated with a proper urgency.

18 Taken from Stuart Hall, 'Encoding/decoding', in Stuart Hall et al. (eds), *Culture, Media, Language* (Hutchinson, 1978).

19 I am not trying to privilege ideas over materials, only to claim that the two are mutually embedded. The philosophic issues are a good deal knottier than this allows, of course; see J. L. Austin, 'Are there a priori concepts?', in J. O. Urmson and G. J. Warnock (eds), *Philosophical Papers* (Oxford University Press, 1961).

20 Or as Charles Taylor puts it, in 'Interpretation and the sciences of man', *Journal of Metaphysics* (January 1971), p. 179: collected in his *Philosophy and the Human Sciences*, 2 vols. (Cambridge University Press 1985), 'We have to admit that intersubjective social reality has to be partly defined in terms of meanings; that meanings as subjective are not just in causal interaction with a social reality made up of brute data, but that as intersubjective they are constitutive of this reality.'

21 Paul Hirst, *Knowledge and the Curriculum* (Routledge & Kegan Paul, 1975); and F. Phenix, *Realms of Meanings* (McGraw-Hill, 1964); also HM Inspectorate in *Framework for the Curriculum* (HMSO, 1981), criticized by John White *et al; No, Minister: a Critique* (University of London Institute of Education, 1981).

22 For an exculpation of Plato, see Iris Murdoch, *The Fire and the Sun: Why Plato Banished the Artists* (Clarendon Press, 1977).

23 John Fowles, *The French Lieutenant's Woman* (Jonathan Cape, 1969), p. 387.

24 As classically propounded by J. S. Mill, and revised for the cold war by Isaiah Berlin, in *Four Essays on Liberty* (Clarendon Press, 1961).

25 I owe this suggestion to Peter Herbst.

26 I owe much in these remarks to Basil Bernstein's habitual generosity with his ideas, and his gift of some during conversation.

27 I have in mind Pierre Bourdieu's well-known use of the phrase in his *Outline of a Theory of Practice* (Cambridge University Press, 1978).

28 David Hargreaves, 'What teaching does to teachers', *New Society* (9 March 1978), subsequently elaborated in his *The Challenge of the Comprehensive School* (Routledge & Kegan Paul, 1982).

29 For a history of that discourse, see John Passmore, *The Perfectibility of Man* (Duckworth, 1970).

30 Perhaps with this short list of recent books to hand: Alex Nove, *The Economics of Feasible Socialism* (Allen & Unwin, 1983); Gavin Kitching, *Rethinking Socialism* (Methuen, 1983), John Dunn, *The Politics of Socialism* (Cambridge University Press, 1984). See particularly, however, Charles Taylor's essay-sketch of the benign future, 'The politics of the steady state, in Colin Crouch and Fred Inglis (eds). *Morality and the Left*, a special issue of *New Universities Quarterly* (April 1978).

31 2 Timothy 3:1–2.

32 In a sadly unique example, he might look for help in Mike Cooley, *Architect or Bee: The Human Technology Relationship*, edited by S. Cooley (Langley Technical Services, 1980).

33 The phrase was first T.H. Green's, in his *Prolegomena to Ethics*, subsequently published in R.L. Nettleship's edition of his *Works* (Longmans Green, 1911). See also Inglis, *Radical Earnestness* (Martin Robertson, 1982).

Bibliography

Althusser, Louis. *Lenin and Philosophy*. New Left Books, 1971

Anderson, Perry. 'Components of the national culture'. *New Left Review,* vol. 50, 1968; reprinted in *Student Power*, edited by Alexander Cockburn and Robin Blackburn, Penguin, 1969.

—— 'The antinomies of Antonio Gramsci', *New Left Review*, vol 100–1, 1977.

—— *Arguments within English Marxism*. New Left Books/Verso Books, 1980.

Apple, Michael. *Ideology and Curriculum*. Routledge & Kegan Paul, 1979.

—— *Education and Power*. Routledge & Kegan Paul, 1981.

Arblaster, Anthony and Lukes, Steven (*eds*). *The Good Society*. Macmillan, 1969.

Arendt, Hannah. *The Human Condition*. Anchor Doubleday, 1959.

Austin, J.L. 'Are there a priori concepts?' *Philosophical Papers*, edited by J.O. Urinson and G.J. Warnock. Oxford University Press, 1961.

Bahro, Rudolf. *The Alternative in Eastern Europe*. New Left Books, 1978.

Banton, Michael. *The Coloured Quarter*. Jonathan Cape, 1955.

—— *Racial Minorities*. Fontana/Collins, 1973.

Barraclough, Geoffrey. 'The end of an era', *New York Review*, 27 June 1974.

—— 'The great world crisis', *New York Review*, 23 January 1975.

—— 'Wealth and power: the politics of food and oil', *New York Review*, 7 August 1975.

—— *From Agadir to Armageddon: Anatomy of a Crisis*. Weidenfeld & Nicolson, 1982.

Beattie, John. *Other Cultures*. Cohen & West, 1964.

Beehler, Roger and Drengson, Alan. *The Philosophy of Society*. Methuen, 1979.

Berger, John. *A Painter of Our Time*. Secker & Warburg, 1962; Penguin, 1965.

Berger, Peter and Brigitte. *The Homeless Mind: Modernization and Consciousness*. Penguin, 1973.

Berlin, Isaiah. *Four Essays on Liberty*. Clarendon Press, 1961.

—— *Concepts and Categories: Philosophical Essays*, with an introduction by Bernard Williams. Hogarth Press, 1978.

Bernstein, Basil. *Class, Codes, Control*, vol. I and (rev. edn) vol. III, Routledge & Kegan Paul, 1971 and 1977. CORE 1984 (Microfiche)

Bernstein, Richard. *The Restructuring of Social and Political Theory*. Hutchinson, 1979.

—— *Beyond Objectivism and Relativism: Science, Hermeneutics, and Praxis*. Basil Blackwell, 1983.

Bhaskar, Roy. *The Possibility of Naturalism*. Harvester Press, 1979.

Black, Max. *Models and Metaphors*. Cornell University Press, 1962.

Bloom, Harold. *A Map of Misreading*. Oxford University Press, New York, 1975.

Bolgar, R. R. *The Classical Heritage and its Beneficiaries*. Cambridge University Press, 1954.

Bowles, Samuel and Gintis, Herbert. *Schooling in Capitalist America*. Routledge & Kegan Paul, 1976.

Bourdieu, Pierre. *Outline of a Theory of Practice*, translated by Richard Nice. Cambridge University Press, 1978.

—— with Passeron, J.G. *Reproduction in Education, Society and Culture*, translated by R. Nice. Sage Books, 1977.

Braudel, Fernand. *The Mediterranean in the Age of Philip II*. Harper & Row/Collins, 1973.

Braverman, Harry. *Labour and Monopoly Capital: the Degradation of Work in the Twentieth Century*. Monthly Review Press, 1974.

Brittain, Vera. *The Testament of Youth*. Gollancz, 1942; Pan, 1980; Virago, 1984.

Britton, James et al. *Schools Council Examinations Bulletin: Multiple Marking*. Schools Council, 1966.

—— *The Development of Writing Abilities*. Macmillan, 1975.

Bruner, Jerome. *The Relevance of Education*. Allen & Unwin, 1972.

Burn, James Dawson. *Autobiography of a Beggar Boy*. London, 1855.

Carr, E. H. *What is History?* Macmillan/Penguin, 1961.

Carsten, F. L. *Revolution in Central Europe 1918–1919*. Oxford University Press, 1972.

Centre for Contemporary Cultural Studies, University of Birmingham. *Unpopular Education*. Hutchinson, 1981.

—— *The Empire Strikes Back*. Hutchinson, 1982.

Chomsky, Noam. *American Power and the New Mandarins*. Chatto & Windus with Penguin, 1969.

Club of Rome. *The Limits to Growth*. Rome, 1972.

Collingwood, R. G. *Speculum Mentis, or The Map of Knowledge*. Clarendon Press, 1924.

202 *Bibliography*

—— *An Autobiography*, Clarendon Press, 1939; reissued, with an introduction by Stephen Toulmin. Oxford University Press, 1981.
—— *The New Leviathan*. Clarendon Press, 1942.
—— *The Idea of History*, edited by T.M. Knox. Clarendon Press, 1946.
Collini, Stefan, Winch, Donald and Burrow, John. *That Noble Science of Politics: A Study in Nineteenth Century Intellectual History*. Cambridge University Press, 1983.
Connell, R.W. et al. *Making the Difference: Schools, Families, and Social Division*. Allen & Unwin, 1982.
Cooley, Mike. *Architect or Bee: the Human/Technology Relationship*, edited by Sue Cooley. Langley Technical Services, 1980.
Coulthard, R. M. and Sinclair, J. M. *Towards an Analysis of Discourse: the English Used by Teachers and Pupils*. Oxford University Press, 1975.
Crosland, Anthony. *Socialism Now*. Jonathan Cape, 1974.
Crouch, Colin and Inglis, Fred (eds). *Morality and the Left*, a special edition of *New Universities Quarterly*, vol 32, no. 2, April 1978.
Dale, Roger, Esland, Geoff and Macdonald, Madeleine. *Schooling and Capitalism*. Open University with Routledge & Kegan Paul, 1976.
Darnton, Robert. *The Business of Enlightenment: A Publishing History of the Encyclopédie 1775–1800*. Harvard University Press, 1980.
Delamont, Sara. *Interaction in the Classroom*, 2nd edn, Methuen, 1983.
Derrida, Jacques. *Of Grammatology*, translated by J. Spivak. Johns Hopkins University Press, 1976.
Detienne, Marcel. *L'Invention de la Mythologie*. Gallimard, 1981.
Djilas, Miloslav. *The New Class*. Allen & Unwin, 1956.
Douglas, Mary. *Purity and Danger: an Analysis of the Concepts of Pollution and Taboo*, rev. edn, Routledge & Kegan Paul, 1969.
Dunn, John. *Western Political Theory in the Face of the Future*. Cambridge University Press, 1979.
—— *Political Obligation in its Historical Context*. Cambridge University Press, 1980.
—— *The Politics of Socialism*. Cambridge University Press, 1984.
Ecologist, The. Blueprint for Survival. January 1972.
Eliot, T.S. *Collected Poems and Plays*. Faber & Faber, 1976.
Elliott, J.H. *The Revolt of the Catalans: A Study in the Decline of Spain*. Cambridge University Press, 1963.
Evans-Pritchard, E.E. *Social Anthropology*. Cohen & West, 1951.
Fiske, John and Hartley, John. *Reading Television*. Methuen, 1978.
Flew, Antony. *Sociology, Equality, and Education*. Macmillan, 1976.
Floud, Jean and Halsey, A.H. *Social Class and Educational Opportunity*. Heinemann, 1959.
Foucault, Michel. *Madness and Civilisation*. Tavistock Publications, 1967.

—— *The Order of Things.* Tavistock Publications, 1970.

—— *Discipline and Punish: the Birth of the Prison.* Allen Lane/Penguin, 1977.

—— *The History of Sexuality,* vol. 1. Allen Lane Penguin, 1979.

Fowles, John. *The French Lieutenant's Woman.* Jonathan Cape, 1969.

Frost, Thomas. *Forty Years of Recollections.* Tinsley, 1880.

Gardiner, P. *The Philosophy of History.* Oxford University Press, 1974.

Garnham, Nicholas. 'Contribution to a political economy of mass communications'. *Culture, Media, Society.* vol. 1, no. 2, 1979.

Geertz, Clifford. *The Interpretation of Cultures.* Hutchinson, 1975.

Gellner, Ernest. *Words and Things.* Penguin, 1959.

Geuss, Raymond. *The Idea of a Critical Theory: Habermas and the Frankfurt School.* Cambridge University Press, 1981.

Giddens, Anthony. *The Class Structure of the Advanced Societies.* Hutchinson, 1973.

—— *Profiles and Critiques in Social Theory.* Macmillan, 1982.

—— *The Constitution of Society.* Basil Blackwell, 1984.

Giroux, Henry. *Ideology, Culture and the Process of Schooling.* Falmer Press, 1980.

Glasgow Media Group. *Bad News.* Routledge & Kegan Paul, 1976.

—— *Really Bad News,* Routledge & Kegan Paul, 1979.

Goffmann, Erving. *The Presentation of Self in Everyday Life.* Doubleday/Penguin, 1969.

Goldthorpe, John. *Social Mobility and Class Structure in Modern Britain.* Clarendon Press, 1980.

Gordimer, Nadine. *A Guest of Honour.* Jonathan Cape, 1970; Penguin, 1973.

Gramsci, Antonio. *The Modern Prince.* Lawrence & Wishart, 1957.

—— *Selections from The Prison Notebooks,* edited by Quintin Hoare. Lawrence & Wishart, 1977.

Green, T. H. *Works,* edited by R. L. Nettleship. Longmans Green, 1911.

Greer, Germaine. *The Female Eunuch.* Paladin, 1971.

Grene, Marjorie. *The Knower and the Known.* Faber & Faber, 1965.

Habermas, Jurgen. *Knowledge and Human Interests.* Heinemann Educational Books, 1974.

—— *Legitimation Crisis.* Heinemann Educational Books, 1975.

Hall, Stuart, et al. *Resistance through Ritual.* Hutchinson, 1976.

Hall, Stuart. 'Encoding/decoding', in Stuart Hall et al. (eds) *Culture, Media, Language.* Hutchinson, 1978.

—— with Jacques, Martin (eds) *The Politics of Thatcherism.* Pluto Press, 1981.

Hampshire, Stuart. *Morality and Pessimism.* Oxford University Press, 1976.

204 *Bibliography*

—— and Kolakowski, Leszek (eds) *The Socialist Idea*. Weidenfeld & Nicolson, 1974.

Hargreaves, David. 'What teaching does to teachers', *New Society*, 9 March 1978.

—— *The Challenge of the Comprehensive School*. Routledge & Kegan Paul, 1982.

Harrison, Andrew. *Making and Thinking*. Harvester Press, 1978.

Hegel, J.W.F. *The Philosophy of History*.

Heidegger, Martin. *Basic Writings: from 'Being and Time' to the 'Task of Thinking'*, edited by David Krell. Harper & Row, 1977.

H.M. Inspectorate. *Framework for the Curriculum*. HMSO, 1981.

Hempel, Carl. *Aspects of Scientific Explanation*. Free Press, 1965.

Herbst, Peter. *Theoreticism and Critical Inquiry*. Forthcoming.

Hill, Christopher. *Puritanism and Revolution*. Secker & Warburg, 1958.

—— *The Century of Revolution*. Nelson, 1961.

Hirsch, Fred. *Social Limits to Growth*. Allen & Unwin, 1976.

Hirschmann, Albert. *The Passions and the Interests: Political Arguments for Capitalism before its Triumph*. Princeton University Press, 1977.

Hirst, Paul. *Knowledge and the Curriculum*. Routledge & Kegan Paul, 1975.

Hobsbawm, Eric. *Labouring Men: Studies in Labour History*. Weidenfeld & Nicolson, 1964.

—— with Rudé, Georges. *Captain Swing*. Lawrence & Wishart, 1969.

—— and Ranger, Terence (eds). *The Invention of Tradition*. Cambridge University Press, 1983.

Hobson, J.A. *Imperialism*, 3rd rev. edn, Allen & Unwin, 1937.

Hofstadter, Douglas. *Gödel, Escher, Bach: an Eternal Golden Braid*. Harvester Press, 1979.

Hoggart, Richard. *The Uses of Literacy*. Chatto & Windus with Penguin, 1957.

Holbrook, David. *English for the Rejected*. Cambridge University Press, 1964.

Hoskins, W.G. *The Making of the English Landscape*. Hodder & Stoughton, 1955.

—— *The Midland Peasant*. Macmillan, 1957.

Humphries, S. *Hooligans or Rebels?* Basil Blackwell, 1981.

Hunt, A. (ed.) *Class and Class Structure*. Lawrence & Wishart, 1977.

Inglis, Fred. *Ideology and the Imagination*. Cambridge University Press, 1975.

—— *The Promise of Happiness: Value and Meaning in Children's Fiction*. Cambridge University Press, 1981.

—— *Radical Earnestness: English Social Theory 1880–1980*. Martin Robertson, 1982.

Jackson, Brian. *Streaming: an Education System in Miniature*. Routledge & Kegan Paul, 1964.
—— *Working-Class Community*. Routledge & Kegan Paul, 1966.
—— and Marsden, Dennis. *Education and the Working Class*, Routledge & Kegan Paul, 1962.
Jacobson, Dan. *The Story of the Stories*. Secker & Warburg, 1982.
Jameson, Storm. *Journey from the North*, 2 vols. Collins/Harvill, 1969; Virago, 1983.
Jennings, Paul. *The Jenguin Pennings*. Penguin, 1962.
Joll, James. *Gramsci*. Fontana, 1980.
Keating, Peter (ed.) *The Victorian Prophets*. Fontana, 1978.
Kitchen, Fred. *Brother to the Ox*. Heinemann Educational Books, 1959.
Kitching, Gavin. *Rethinking Socialism: a Theory for a Better Practice*. Methuen, 1983.
Körner, Stefan. *Experience and Theory: An Essay in the Philosophy of Science*. Routledge & Kegan Paul, 1966.
—— *Categorial Frameworks*. Basil Blackwell, 1970.
Kuhn, Thomas S. *The Structure of Scientific Revolutions*. Chicago University Press, 1962.
Kumar, Krishan. 'Holding the middle ground', in James Curran (ed.) *Mass Communication and Society*. Edward Arnold for Open University, 1977.
Larrain, Jorge. *The Concept of Ideology*. Hutchinson, 1979.
Laslett, Peter. *The World We Have Lost*. Methuen, 1965.
Leavis, F.R. *The Great Tradition*. Chatto & Windus, 1948.
Lévi-Strauss, Claude. *Structural Anthropology*. Allen Lane, Penguin, 1964.
Levitas, Mark. *Marxist Perspectives in the Sociology of Education*. Routledge & Kegan Paul, 1974.
Lovett, William. *William Lovett: His Life and Struggles* (1860). MacGibbon and Kee, 1967.
Lukes, Steven. *Power: a Radical View*. Macmillan, 1974.
MacIntyre, Alasdair. *Secularization and Moral Change*. Oxford, 1967.
—— *Against the Self-Images of the Age*. Duckworth, 1971.
—— *After Virtue: A Study in Moral Theory*. Duckworth, 1981.
Maclure, Stuart. *Educational Documents: England and Wales 1816–1968*. rev. edn, Methuen, 1969.
Mannheim, Karl. *Essays in the Sociology of Knowledge*. Routledge & Kegan Paul, 1952.
Marx, Karl. *Capital*, vol. I. Foreign Languages Publishing House, Moscow, 1887 and 1958.
—— *The German Ideology* (with Friedrich Engels, 1848), edited by T.J. Arthur. Lawrence & Wishart, 1970.

—— *Selected Works*. Foreign Languages Publishing House, Moscow, 1972.

—— *Selected Writings*, edited by D. McLellan. Oxford University Press, 1977.

Masterman, Len. *Teaching about Television*. Macmillan, 1980.

Meakin, David. *Man and Work: Literature and Culture in Industrial Society*. Methuen, 1976.

Mitchell, Juliet. *Woman's Estate*. Penguin, 1971.

Mitchison, Naomi. *You May Well Ask: A Memoir 1920–1940*. Gollancz, 1979.

Morris, James. *Pax Britannica*, 3 vols, rev. edn. Penguin, 1978.

Morris, William. *Political Writings*, edited by A. L. Morton. Lawrence & Wishart, 1973.

Morrison, D. and McIntyre, D. *Teachers and Teaching*. Penguin, 1969.

Mphahlele, Ezekiel. *Down Second Avenue*. Faber & Faber, 1956.

Muir, Edwin. *Autobiography*. Hogarth Press, 1954; Methuen, 1968.

—— *Collected Poems*. Faber & Faber, 1960.

Murdoch, Iris. *The Fire and the Sun: Why Plato Banished the Artists*. Clarendon Press, 1977.

Musgrove, Frank. *Patterns of Power and Authority in English Education*. Routledge & Kegan Paul, 1969.

Nagel, Ernest. *The Structure of Science*. Harcourt Brace, 1961.

Nagel, Thomas. *The Possibility of Altruism*. Oxford University Press, 1970.

Nairn, Tom. *The Break-up of Britain*. New Left Books, 1978.

Needham, Joseph and Ronan, Colin. *Science and Civilization in China*. Abridged edn, Cambridge University Press, 1978.

Newsom, John. *Half our Future*. HMSO 1963.

Nietzsche, Friedrich. *Beyond Good and Evil* (1886). Penguin, 1973.

Norman, Edward. *Christianity and the World Order*. Oxford University Press, 1979.

Nove, Alec. *The Economics of Feasible Socialism*. Allen & Unwin, 1983.

Oakeshott, Michael. *On Human Conduct*. Oxford University Press, 1975.

Oakley, Ann. *Sex, Gender, and Society*. Temple Smith, 1972.

Ortony, Andrew (ed.) *Metaphor and Thought*. Cambridge University Press, 1979.

Parfit, Derek. 'Lewis, Perry and what matters', in Amelie Rorty, *Identities of Persons*. University of California Press, 1976.

—— *Reasons and Persons*. Clarendon Press, 1984.

Parkes, Henry Bamford. *The American Experience*. Knopf, 1947.

Passmore, John. *The Perfectibility of Man*. Duckworth, 1970.

Phenix, F. *Realms of Meaning: a Philosophy of Curriculum*. McGraw-Hill, 1964.

Plamenatz, John. *Ideology*. Macmillan, 1971.

Popper, Karl. *The Logic of Scientific Discovery*. Hutchinson, 1959.

Postgate, Raymond. *The Good Food Guide 1965–66*. Consumers' Association with Cassell, 1965.

Poulantzas, Nicos. *Political Power and Social Classes*. New Left Books, 1973.

—— *Classes in Contemporary Capitalism*. New Left Books, 1975.

Quine, W.V.O. *Ontological Relativism*. Columbia University Press, 1969.

Reid, Ivan. *Social Class Differences in Britian*. 2nd edn. Grant McIntyre, 1981.

Rex, John. *Race Relations in Sociological Theory*. Weidenfeld & Nicolson, 1970.

Richardson, Elizabeth. *The Teacher, the School and the Task of Management*. Heinemann Educational Books, 1973.

Ricoeur, Paul. *The Rule of Metaphor*. Routledge & Kegan Paul, 1979.

Robbins Report. *Higher Education*. HMSO, 1963.

Roberts, M.B.V. *Biology: a Functional Approach*. Nelson, 1971.

Robinson, John. *Honest to God*. SCM Press, 1962.

Rorty, Amelie. *Identities of Persons*. University of California Press, 1976.

Rorty, Richard. *Philosophy and the Mirror of Nature*. Basil Blackwell, 1981.

Rowbotham, Sheila. *Woman's Consciousness, Man's World*. Penguin, 1973.

Rutter, Michael, et al. *15,000 Hours: Secondary Schools and Their Effects on Children*. Open Books, 1979.

Sampson, George. *English for the English* (1922), edited by Denys Thompson. Cambridge University Press, 1970.

Sartre, Jean-Paul. *Critique de la Raison Dialectique*. La Seuil, 1960.

—— *Critique of Dialectical Reason*, translated by Alan Sheridan-Smith. New Left Books, 1976.

Saussure, Fernand. *Course in General Linguistics*. edited by Charles Bally and Albert Sechehaye. McGraw-Hill/Collins, 1974.

Schlesinger, Philip. *Putting 'Reality' Together: the BBC and the Presentation of News*. Constable, 1978.

Scott, Paul. *The Raj Quartet*, 4 vols. Heinemann, 1967–75.

Scruton, Roger. *The Meaning of Conservatism*. Penguin, 1980.

Sen, Amartya. *On Economic Inequality*. Clarendon Press, 1973.

Sharp, Rachel. *Knowledge, Ideology, and the Politics of Schooling*. Routledge & Kegan Paul, 1980.

—— and Green, Anthony. *Education and Social Control*. Routledge & Kegan Paul, 1975.

Sharratt, Bernard. *Reading Relations: the Structures of Literary Production – a Text/Book*. Harvester Press, 1982.

Skinner, Quentin. *Machiavelli*. Oxford University Press, 1981.
—— 'Machiavelli on the maintenance of liberty', *Politics*, no. 18, 1983.
Smart, J. J. C. and Williams, Bernard. *Utilitarianism: For and Against*. Cambridge University Press, 1973.
Smart, Ninian. *The Phenomenon of Religion*. Macmillan, 1973.
Somerville, Alexander. *The Autobiography of a Working Man* (1848). MacGibbon & Kee, 1967.
Sraffa, Paul. *Production of Commodities by Means of Commodities*. Cambridge University Press, 1960.
Stove, David. *Popper and After: Four Modern Irrationalists*. Pergamon Press, 1982.
Strawson, Peter. *Individuals*. Oxford University Press, 1963.
Tawney, R. H. *Religion and the Rise of Capitalism*. John Murray, 1926.
—— *Equality*, edited with an introduction by Richard Titmuss. Allen & Unwin, 1964.
Taylor, Charles, 'Interpretation and the sciences of man'. *Journal of Metaphysics*, January 1971.
—— 'The politics of the steady state', in Colin Crouch and Fred Inglis (eds), *Morality and the Left*, special issue of *New Universities Quarterly*, vol. 32, no. 2, April 1978.
—— *Hegel and Modern Society*. Cambridge University Press, 1979.
—— *Philosophical Papers*, 2 vols. Cambridge University Press, 1985.
Thompson, E.P. *The Making of the English Working Class*. Gollancz, 1963; Penguin, 1968.
—— *The Poverty of Theory*. Merlin Press, 1968.
—— 'Time, work-discipline and industrial capitalism', *Past and Present*, vol. 38, 1968.
—— *Writing by Candlelight*. Merlin Press, 1980.
Townsend, Peter. *Poverty in the United Kingdom*. Penguin, 1979.
Trilling, Lionel. *Sincerity and Authenticity*. Oxford University Press, 1972.
Turner, Denys. *Marxism and Christianity*. Basil Blackwell, 1983.
Universities Central Council on Admissions. *21st Annual Report 1982–3, Statistical Supplement*, UCCA, 1984.
Watson, James. *The Double Helix*. Weidenfeld & Nicolson, 1967.
Weber, Max. *The Theory of Social and Economic Organisations*.
—— *The Protestant Ethic and the Spirit of Capitalism*, translated by Talcott Parsons. Allen & Unwin, 1948.
—— *From Max Weber*, edited with an introduction by H. H. Gerth and C. Wright Mills. Routledge & Kegan Paul, 1948.
—— *Economy and Society*. Routledge & Kegan Paul, 1962.
Westergaard, J.A. and Resler, H. *Class in a Capitalist Society: A Study of Contemporary Britain*. Heinemann, 1975.

White, John et al. *No, Minister: a Critique*. University of London Institute of Education, 1981.

Whitebrook, Joel. 'Saving the subject: modernity and the problem of the autonomous individual'. *Telos*, vol. 50, 1981.

Whitehead, A. N. *Science and the Modern World*. Cambridge University Press, 1938.

Whitty, Geoff and Young, Michael (eds) *Explanations in the Politics of School Knowledge*. Nafferton Press, 1978.

Wiener, Martin. *British Culture and the Decline of the Industrial Spirit*. Cambridge University Press, 1981.

Williams, Bernard. *Moral Luck*. Cambridge University Press, 1981.

—— *Ethics and the Limits of Philosophy*. Fontana, 1985.

Williams, Raymond. *Culture and Society 1780–1950*. Chatto & Windus, 1957; Penguin, 1958.

—— *Drama in a Dramatised Society*. Cambridge University Press, 1975; collected in *Writing in Society*, Verso Books, 1983.

—— *Towards 2000*. Chatto & Windus, 1983.

Willis, Paul. *Learning to Labour: How Working Class Kids get Working Class Jobs*. Saxon House, 1977.

Young, M.F.D. (ed.). *Knowledge and Control*. Routledge & Kegan Paul, 1972.

Young, Michael. *The Rise of the Meritocracy*. Penguin, 1961.

Ziman, John. *Public Knowledge*. Cambridge University Press, 1972.

—— *The Force of Knowledge*. Cambridge University Press, 1976.

Index